A COMMI ... journey with

IT TAKES A COMMUNITY TO gro and that community becomes very large. In fact, it may span an entire country.

Our autism journey has been like that, filled with diverse, passionate and compassionate individuals from coast to coast—and beyond. Our journey mates helped us, shaped us and changed us. Here are some of their voices:

Teresa's heartfelt story about raising her son Erik is filled with loving anecdotes of the challenging and at times lighthearted moments parenting a child with special needs. Through her eyes, we glimpse into the mind of her son with autism and his fascination with the things that many of us don't even notice in our everyday lives. It is pure brilliance.

The Hedley journey portrays the myriad of challenges a military family must embrace on a posting, as well as packing up and moving, at times, to the other side of the country. To do so with a child with autism creates a new level of complexity.

Often funny, yet serious at its root, this book shows how it doesn't just take a village to raise a child: in Erik's case, it takes a small town. Supporters of Erik help Teresa see her child in a different light, for as a parent, one is perhaps too close to the forest to see the beautiful flowers in the trees.

Through the trials of high school, hormones and transition to adulthood, this story is a portrayal of how love and compassion overcome percentiles and projection. Teresa's strength to advocate for Erik helps ensure that the world can embrace his potential and help make him the extraordinary person he is. It is, at its core, a great story of hope, compassion and resilience.

–TELAH MORRISON
Colonel, OMM, CD, Director Military Family Service,
Canadian Armed Forces; Ottawa, ON

I highly recommend this book. Teresa is a gifted storyteller, and Erik provides the inspiration for her stories, overall a masterful blend of humour and authenticity. Erik and others like him (my own son, Jaden, for one) have so much to contribute to the great benefit of all of us, if given a chance. We just need to pay as much attention to their unique skills and abilities as we do their challenges. This book is an entertaining and important step in the right direction.

–MIKE LAKE
Canadian Parliamentarian and international autism advocate;
Edmonton, AB

I met the Hedleys in 2014 in Ottawa on Remembrance Day, and while that is always an emotional day, it was even more so that day because it had come just a few weeks after the shootings on Parliament Hill. It was clear very quickly from our conversation about the events we had just witnessed that they were a very focussed family. And it's equally clear from this book that they are focussed on the challenges that exist for them as a family, just as they do for so many other families in Canada. There are a lot of lessons on these pages for all of us, and we can benefit from considering them and acting upon them.

–PETER MANSBRIDGE
former anchor and chief correspondent, CBC's *The National;*
Stratford, ON

Thank you to the Hedley family for inviting us to see the world through the complex and intriguing lens of autism.

–MARC GARNEAU
Canadian Parliamentarian and astronaut; Montreal, QC

This book will be important for any family that is experiencing life with a child on the autism spectrum. What an incredible journey Erik and his family have been on! It has been a true privilege to be a part of their journey, and I know it will help other families to see how profound, and also beautiful, it can be. Erik inspires me with his perspective and approach to life, and I am in awe of the person he is becoming. He is lucky to have the family he has, but they are equally as fortunate to have him in their lives.

–YOLANDA KORNELUK
PhD, CPsych, Clinical Director, Emerging Minds; Ottawa, ON

Meeting Erik, his sister and his parents was truly a joy in my process of learning from the Canadian autism community. Through their creative videos, Erik and his family powerfully advocate for autism appreciation— that different does not mean wrong and is in fact an important part of the joy that comes from being able to learn from one another. Their optimism, enthusiasm, acceptance and unity is a message for wellness and demonstrates the importance of growing as individuals and as a family.

–JONATHAN A. WEISS
PhD, CPsych, York Research Chair in Autism and
Neurodevelopmental Disability Mental Health; Toronto, ON

Relatable, honest and eloquently shared, What's Not Allowed? *is a journey of joy, of moving forward, a testament to the value of staying curious, positive and patient. Teresa's writing paints a thousand pictures. It is handed to us as an experience: the reader feels the moments, each born of reflecting, braving to revisit difficult times, taking time to recall the bright spots, the humor, the happiness. This creates an understanding we can hold, like a memorable painting or film. The Hedley family story is one for us all: it is a celebration to which we can all relate, evolving into whom we choose to be . . . the journey from what's not allowed to knowing what is right—feeling esteemed. This memoir offers comfort, insight, hope, joy and perspective for the family, therapist, educator and physician. What a gift!*

–SARAH FORD HOLLIDAY
MS, CCC/SLP; Lewisburg, West Virginia

Written with such clarity and honesty, Teresa pens captivating short stories in a down-to-earth, accessible manner. She captures her journey with Erik, slowing down time as it were, to allow the reader to linger in those moments. The reader has the opportunity to peer into the joys and challenges of parenting and family life as they "grow up" together. Her passion is apparent to all who meet her and all who will read this! Here, you will find insights that challenge some of the predominant social attitudes around difference—how it can be strange and therefore feared, or remedied by an openness and curiosity to moving towards what was unknown.

–JONATHAN LAI
PhD, Neuroscience, Director of Strategy and Operations, Canadian Autism Spectrum Disorder Alliance (CASDA); Toronto, ON

What's Not Allowed? reaches out and touches the reader—tears and laughter, equal parts—which is the human condition. This book offers a bird's-eye view into the nest where three unique and beautiful children hatched, grew strong and learned to fly. Teresa shares what her children taught her about embracing neurodiversity and how to create environ-ments where kids are "allowed" to shine!

–KATELYN LOWE
PhD, RPsych; Calgary, AB

Teresa has a gift for transforming her world with autism into one of adventure, co-learning, shared struggles but most of all, one of opportunity. Teresa's narrative is a reminder that the perspective of autism can be insightful and joyful. Share the Hedley family journey, and you will see autism with new appreciative eyes.

–NANCI BURNS
MSW, RSW; Ottawa, ON

This insightful dive into the whirlwind of the gifts and challenges of neurodiversity offers wisdom both to other families and to the profes-sionals who support families. Teresa Hedley's honest sharing reaches in and alters the hearts and minds of the reader to look beyond a label into the possibilities that emerge from the willingness to align with what is. What's Not Allowed? *is a shining testament to people with autism being —as Temple Grandin accurately says—"different, not less," and it will inspire readers to feel society is capable of changing for the better.*

–KIM BARTHEL
OT, international speaker, consultant, author; Victoria, BC

What an adventure to be brought into the life of the Hedley family! Teresa is skilled at bringing the reader into the experiences of her family. The imagery, emotion and connection conveyed through honesty, humour, reflection and resilience will have the reader excited to read each story. This book is more than a compilation of stories: it is a testament to a family's perseverance, growth, commitment to each other and to spreading a message of love and learning. The support you have provided each other and now extended to the entire community is invaluable. Thank you for these stories!

–ESTHER RHEE CARNAT
MSW, National Program Director, Autism Speaks Canada; Toronto, ON

Teresa Hedley is a "one of a kind" in the world of autism spectrum disorders: advocate, writer, teacher and parent. She has navigated through the tumultuous expedition armed with a steadfast attitude and a wonderful sense of humour. Not only is she an autism warrior mom extraordinaire, but she is an incredible storyteller who clearly articulates a memorable journey throughout the lifespan of her son Erik.

–PATRICIA O'CONNOR
educator and speaker, Integrated Autism Consulting; Barrie, ON

I highly recommend What's Not Allowed? A Family Journey With Autism *to anyone who has been touched by autism. I had the privilege of working with Teresa and Erik, joining in, for a short while, their search for tools and activities to support Erik's gifts and challenges. I refer, in my mind, to Teresa and Erik, as the "Dynamic Duo." They present as a united front, and they present with great energy. That energy is directed toward seeing autism clearly: what is good, what is hard, what needs to be changed, enlarged, adapted or removed, to support not only Erik, but the entire Hedley family. Autism is absolutely a family affair and this labor of love by Teresa to share their journey brings, with clear-sighted unremitting honesty, the triumphs and trials that come with a diagnosis of autism. This book not only educates, it inspires.*

–ROBIN HARWELL
MA,CCC/SLP, Build The Brain; Dallas, Texas

Teresa and her family are making a difference in the world and are doing what makes them feel joyful. Their products are so insightful, positive, and overall, works of art!

–KATHLEEN ROONEY
trainer and consultant, Crisis & Trauma Resource Institute; Ottawa, ON

Working with Teresa has opened my eyes to many of the challenges that children with autism face, but more importantly, to the opportunities for children and parents to learn and grow together. I am so impressed with the dignity and respect with which Teresa has raised her family. Her excerpts and memories bring you into the world of parenting a child with autism, and her expressive writing style creates a magical space in which we all can learn, grow and explore.

–LYNN HAND
Executive Director, Peel Family Education Centre; Brampton, ON

This is a rich collection of stories that reflect a family's journey with autism. Their courage and commitment resonate, as does the importance of love, perseverance and hope.

–DAVID NICHOLAS
PhD, Faculty of Social Work, University of Calgary; Calgary, AB

I had the pleasure of meeting Teresa and her son Erik at an autism conference and was immediately impressed with her ease in sharing her experiences and the important insights that she offered. What's Not Allowed? A Family Journey with Autism *is reflective of those insights, along with humorous vignettes, raw emotion and guidelines for advocacy. Teresa's memoir invites the reader to join the Hedley family on their journey and is a must-read for parents of children with autism, professionals and the general community who want to understand and support others who are on this journey.*

–ELLEN YACK
MEd, BSc, OT, consultant, author and speaker; Toronto, ON

How do we come to know, across species and as well, across cultures . . . how do we come to know someone else . . . without projections? *I've seen your son out there, along the shore . . . The ocean tells him who he is, and he is vast."*

–SANDRA SEMCHUK
Canadian photographic artist and author; Vancouver, BC

Note: The testimonials reflect the views of the individual, independent of the organization to which they belong and/or represent.

WHAT'S NOT ALLOWED ?

WHAT'S NOT ALLOWED ?

A Family Journey
with Autism

TERESA HEDLEY

echo
BOOKS

Wintertickle PRESS

Library and Archives Canada Cataloguing in Publication

Title: What's not allowed? : a family journey with autism / Teresa Hedley.
Other titles: What is not allowed?
Names: Hedley, Teresa, 1963- author.
Identifiers: Canadiana 20200321242 | ISBN 9781989664018 (softcover)
Subjects: LCSH: Hedley, Teresa, 1963-—Family. | LCSH: Hedley, Erik. |
LCSH: Mothers of autistic
   children—Canada—Biography. | LCSH: Autistic people—Canada—
Biography. | LCSH: Autistic people—Family relationships—Canada. |
LCSH: Military spouses—Canada—Biography. | LCSH: Families of military
personnel—Canada—Biography. | LCGFT: Autobiographies.
Classification: LCC RC553.A88 H434 2020 | DDC 616.85/8820092—
dc23

Wintertickle Press
132 Commerce Park Drive
Unit K, Ste. 155
Barrie ON, L4N 0Z7

wintricklepress.com
@wintericklepress

ISBN9781989664018

~ *To family and friends. Our sculptors.*

"If you believe in me, I believe in me.
If you think I can do it, I think I can do it."
–Erik Hedley

A NOTE ABOUT THE TITLE

"WHAT'S NOT ALLOWED?" IS THE first question Erik asked. Pointing to a sign full of red circles with slashes—the rules—he was puzzling out his young world, figuring out what was okay to do and what was not okay. Fast forward twenty years, and we find ourselves immersed in a worldwide pandemic, very much a "What's not allowed?" world, shaped by uncertainty and governed by arrows and circles. We are living Erik's question. In this sense, we have all stepped into his shoes. And this may be the closest we get to understanding what it feels like to have autism, to slip into the skin and walk around in it for a while.

TO DANGLE THE QUESTION MARK or not? That became the secondary question. "Can we see it the regular way?" So the question mark was tucked behind "allowed," as you would expect. Our reaction was immediate: "*Way* too dull! Predictable. And this journey is neither. Let's let it hang, because, as my sister Lori says, "The dangle *is* autism." There are more questions than answers, more unknowns than knowns and more life lived outside the box than inside. A life with autism is a life in suspension. Thus, *the dangle*.

TABLE OF CONTENTS

Part Two: From Frustration to Fascination 117

Part Three: From Boy to Man 219

FOREWORD
A Conscious Evolution

I have a firm belief that we can consciously evolve in this lifetime, so I continually ask: How can we do this best? How would I like to be? For myself? For others? For the planet? For the things that I care about—that are bigger than myself?

Faith that conscious evolution can be happening everywhere is what guides me—and encourages me to try my best to be a compassionate seed planter. What brings me great joy is being present with people in their journeys in life as they evolve to become the best selves they want to be.

–Kim Barthel

~

I FIRST MET OCCUPATIONAL THERAPIST and international speaker Kim Barthel in 2005, shortly after Erik was diagnosed with autism. Kim visited our home, colourful carpetbag in hand, and she interacted with my son as no one had.

That spring afternoon when Erik is six, he and I learn what belief feels like. Belief is transformative. We become Kim's projection: enabled child and inspired mother.

And on that spring afternoon, mesmerized by Kim's bag of tricks and unwavering conviction, I tell Kim that she is an intoxicating blend of Mary Poppins and Oprah, a mix of magic and wisdom and hope such as I have never before experienced. Kim tells me that there is brilliance in there . . . and that yes, I had better dare to believe. If I do not, who will? She challenges me to tune in. I do. What if I had not?

It is to Kim that we express gratitude for setting us on a path of conscious evolution, a journey dedicated to tuning in rather than buying in, of continuously updating and becoming our best selves. It is from Kim we learn that when nothing is certain, anything is possible.

–Teresa Hedley

~

This moving and elegant memoir is a source of inspiration for me as an occupational therapist and as a personal friend of Erik and his family. As a witness to their autism journey, the Hedleys actively engaged in the process of consciously evolving themselves throughout their connection to all the ups and downs a life with autism delivers.

This insightful dive into the whirlwind of the gifts and challenges of neurodiversity offers wisdom both to other families and to the professionals who support families. Teresa Hedley's honest sharing reaches in and alters the hearts and minds of the reader to look beyond a label into the possibilities that emerge from the willingness to align with what is.

This book exemplifies the power of community. With the desire to support others through their experiences, a form of healing boomerangs right back to Erik and his family, demonstrating the concepts that helping is healing and healing is possible.

Erik Hedley is a truly special being. His dedication to becoming and being his best self is powerful and contagious. *What's Not Allowed?* is a shining testament to people with autism being—as Temple Grandin accurately says: "different, not less," and it will inspire readers to feel society is capable of changing for the better.

–Kim Barthel, occupational therapist, speaker, consultant, instructor, author and friend of the Hedley family

INTRODUCTION

A Diagnosis Is Not a Prognosis

HE IS THE QUIET SPEAKER on Parliament Hill who makes you laugh and makes you cry. He is the young man on the TEDx stage in Toronto who makes you smile. He touches the crowd.

He is the blond boy with autism.

He is the sort of person who draws you in and quietly captivates. He chooses you; you do not choose him, and for that, you feel special, selected. He sweeps you up and along with open authenticity and a raw, unexpected vulnerability. A lopsided smile and a boyish shyness beckon and intrigue. He has presence without effort. You pull for him because he cheers for all of us. He exists without ego and jealousy. He is pure and selfless, and we are not.

He is Erik.

In June 2017, Erik graduated from high school. His teachers presented him with an award that salutes and celebrates positivity and perseverance. He was surprised; he didn't see it coming.

In congratulating him, one of his teachers said, "Erik, we chose you because we appreciate your calm and modest ways. It's not always the loud or funny or athletic or academic students who stand out and get noticed . . . It's the quiet, genuine people like you, too."

Erik thought about this all afternoon with a silent smile.

In hearing this story, my sister Lori chimed in: "I'm so pleased for Erik and never discount his supremely good karma. Being loved by everyone around you is something most of us don't experience. People are going to root for Erik his whole life. They're going to be comfortable with his success. He's just got that touch. Tell him I said so."

Erik makes us all feel beautiful; he makes us better versions of ourselves. And now to autism. That Erik is softly magnetic in the face of a diagnosis, a label and continuous judgment is all the more pleasing. He rises above and transcends words and connotations. He is light and goodness. We all want and need to be a little more like Erik.

When I ask myself how I ought to react to a given situation, I pause, and then I ask myself a different question: *How would Erik react? What would Erik do?* And then I often do that.

This is a story about that boy, about that life energy. It is a journey through and beyond and alongside autism, and it is a celebration of a young man whose gift to the world is his very presence and his very light.

Enjoy the glow.

PART 1

FROM ERIK TO AUTISM

PROLOGUE
Into the Light

I STEP OUT OF THE building and into the dazzling sunlight. I stop and allow the sun to warm me because I feel cold. No, more than cold. Numb. Stunned. But I should not feel this way, because I knew going in this morning what the exit would look like. I knew I was going to meet autism. But I didn't know that the meeting would feel like this. It is not temporary, and it is not light. This is a weighty forever.

I look around and register cars, hear children's voices. Little voices without autism. It seems easy and normal, but my life would be neither anymore. This morning has changed everything. These pieces of paper, pulled close to my chest—a huge stack of them, actually—are a game changer. A life changer. I have been delivered trauma, and I'm not sure what to do with it.

My immediate and overwhelming urge is to pitch it all and go back to the way things were, vague but safe. Label-free. I go as far as walking over to the garbage can beside the door. I think about dumping the papers and walking away, clearing the slate and going back to this morning. I have that option. I know it.

I can make the word go away, but the label will stick, because people will see, will notice that something is off with my little blond boy.

I stand beside the garbage can for a long time, breathing, seeing, thinking but not registering. That is what numb feels like, and that is what autism can do. It can stop you in your tracks.

I focus on breath. And then on the papers, brilliantly white in the noon sun. I blink and emotion spills. I watch as a tear smacks the top paper. Bull's eye. Diagnosis. The word bulges and ripples.

I blink and press my lips together. I force a breath—quick uptake, long and slow exhale.

Release the papers. Let them drop. Walk away.

My inner voice cajoles me, tempts me with a simple solution.

Dump the stack and drive home. Why would you not?

Because I was sculpted differently.

I have "stick-to-it-ness" because my aviator father has gifted me this. You don't walk away from a flight plan without good reason. Innovation and resourcefulness flow naturally: my mother is a skilled seamstress and has always maintained, "We can make that." Creativity and curiosity flourish. Big sister has shown me how to take the ordinary, tip it, and make it extraordinary. Middle sister smuggled rats' stomachs home in junior high school; she taught me that the body is a collection of systems, and that what we do to one affects the whole. I know about cause and effect and that solutions are there for those who dare. Nana has shown me the power of positivity through song and letter writing and through connecting with neighbours and creating community. I accept hard work because Poppa was a workhorse and never backed down from a challenge. And from my great aunts—a cackling pair who loved wine and world travel—I discover that attitude trumps all and that helping is healing.

This is the formative package, the early years. There would be more layers; in fact, with every human encounter comes a layer, and like a waxing moon, I am forever adding depth, forever learning, forever receiving and growing. I have been delivered these attributes genetically and through life.

Dump the stack. Drive home. Make it go away.

Autism is different. It arrives and it parks itself, moves in. It consumes. It is life changing. This is a defining moment. I cannot make it go away. And I cannot walk away.

CHAPTER 1

Womb Traveller

IT IS SPRINGTIME IN BARRIE, Ontario. I am caring for our precocious one-and-a-half-year-old son, Scott, and I am pregnant with number two, later to be named Erik. We call the baby many names in utero, but the one that sticks is Kempy after Kempenfest, the annual craft extravaganza on Kempenfelt Bay. Kempy is due smack in the middle of the festivities, mid-July. Another summer baby.

My pregnancy is straightforward, and aside from the usual fatigue, I feel well throughout. In April, we pack up our portable playpen, the stroller and our toddler must-haves, and trek back to Europe. Germany had been a remarkable launch into marriage; we long to revisit it, climb back inside and revive it, if only for seventeen days. We miss our pre-kinder life: the vibrant NATO base—our first posting as a couple—the costume parties, the old-fashioned German wine-tastings, our eclectic European playground. One can never go back, but one can pretend.

Because I am nearing six months pregnant, I need a doctor's note to fly and travel. And oh, God! I love being back, exploring and rediscovering favourites in the Netherlands, Germany and beyond. Gazing at what I knew, I am revisiting me before Fisher-Price and me before marriage. There is something about antiquities that is grounding, timeless, a reminder that a rich life exists beyond board books and tuna casseroles. I need to be reminded.

But travel with an almost-two-year-old and a baby on the way is exhausting, not at all the way it used to be. I am inflated and diminished: my stomach is huge, and my stamina is small. We stop a lot for breath, for diaper changes and for ice cream. We nap at strange times and in odd places. And we do not drink beer. Frank does; I order fruit juice and tip it into a plastic wine glass I stow in the diaper bag. But it is Europe, and it is thrilling to be back.

RHODOS, GREECE. THE AFTERNOON LIGHT is dazzling, and the room is dim, shutters drawn. I can see slivers of hot white between the blue wooden slats. I ease my belly from one side of the bed to the other, like flipping a colossal molten pancake, slow-mo. The shadow-filled room is quiet; an overhead fan whirs, and I feel guilty for snoozing in the middle of a blisteringly bright afternoon. It is an un-Canadian thing to do, but this is Greece, and the afternoons are slated for escaping the heat. It blasts beyond the patio doors, a relentless thirty-seven degrees Celsius.

I squint at the shutters. They are cobalt blue. Like a Greek postcard. My tiny apartment north of Athens was not unlike this room: compact, marble, faded, dusty, sultry. I allow my eyes to close, and hand resting on belly, I recall that life.

~

A MOVE TO THE MEDITERRANEAN was not part of the plan but a reaction to routine. I had been back in Canada four months, and I missed the exotic life I had left in Japan. I missed the not-knowing, the confusion and the frustration of living on foreign soil. I missed being strange.

Oddly, I enjoyed the novelty of being an outsider looking in, and once back home, being part of the well-worn pack seemed dull and predictable. In Canada, I was just me—not exotic, odd or past due, Japanese for beyond twenty-five and unmarried. I was invisible.

So I scanned the Vancouver newspaper. I found a two-liner about teaching English in Greece and I answered it, faxed in my resumé and booked a plane ticket via Seattle, New York, Rome and finally, Athens. My aviator father had not been keen on this routing—a milk run and a string of unknown airlines—but that paled when he heard the name of my travel companion, a woman from California who had also been hired and was to join me in Seattle.

She called our house one morning and my father picked up, at first charmed by her pleasing voice but then caught off guard by her name. "Could you please repeat that?" he had asked, politely, but by the time he walked the length of the house and handed me the phone, all he could say, with a puzzled look on his face, was "It's for you? A Paradise Meadows . . . ?"

I looked at him, eyes narrowed, wondering what was up because Paradise Meadows was also the name of the cross-country ski area up the local mountain; I figured something got lost in translation. It had. After that, he delighted in coming up with different versions of the name that both intrigued and plagued him.

"My daughter is flying off across the world with Mount Sinai!" he told people, but I corrected him. "No, Dad. She got her name on a mountain top . . . but Mount is not her name." And on it went.

My sister Leslie was equally . . . piqued. "You answered that tiny ad and you're flying off across the world where? . . . With who?!"

"Leslie, it's not the size of the ad; it's what you do with it," I cheeked back.

They got used to the plan, and off I flew with Moonlight Vision, hopscotching across two continents, quite liking her once I escaped the name game. Moonlight and I were exhilarated to be in Athens, to be gazing up at the Greek Acropolis from our late-night taxi, the antiquity lit up brightly against the smoggy November night sky.

"Ohh! It's like we're living in a Grade 7 social studies textbook," I enthused. "In an ancient Greek movie set! And tomorrow we'll hike one of the wonders of the ancient world!"

Our lives in Greece were challenging, cramped, dusty, disorganized, poor yet extremely rich. We learned about the importance of good food and good friends; respect for family and the aging; and the significance of laughter and daily contact, face to face, with others. Many years later, I would read that a Greek island in the Aegean Sea is one of the world's so-called Blue Zones, home to a disproportionate number of centenarians, a pocket of longevity. I would not be surprised to discover this, for I had lived it. I would take this life-layer forward. Human connectivity matters. It enables and sustains us. Unbeknownst to me, a weave was taking shape.

Just as I accumulated labels in Japan, in Greece I became something new. Tall and blond is not strange in the Mediterranean. It's sexy. This was new to me, to feel it and to be the object of men's hissing. Yes, hissing. The first time it happened, I thought it was air escaping a bike tire. But there were no bicycles in sight, only men, lining the dusty village square, a number of them hissing. At what? And why?

"At you!" a Greek colleague explained. "Because you're different."

There was that word again, but here different was esteemed. *How interesting*, I thought. Same person, different environment, similar perception but a different connotation. A different *different*.

While in Japan I had been decidedly odd, in Greece I was sexy and desired. But I knew that like an invisible force field, once I returned to North America, that sexy, too, would evaporate. So I wore it for a year, and I liked it. I became the miniature screen I had imagined as a child, reflecting what was shone upon me. I became what I was told.

~

"CAN I GET YOU ANYTHING?" Frank pokes his head in the door, and a second head peeks through his legs. Scottie, two, holds three metal cars in one hand and a fresh diaper in the other. He is trailing Daddy, waiting to be unpackaged and repapered.

"Oh, hi . . . ," I squint at them, foggy. I am not hungry, but I do have a craving. "Yogurt with honey and nuts?" It's a request, not a question, and Frank understands this. Yogurt, Greek style, has become a staple and for me, a pregnancy craving.

I join them later. I savour the velvety yogurt and the scene in front of me: Scottie is flat on the floor, eye level with a line of German toy cars—reds, blues and yellows, as striking in miniature as their life-sized counterparts. He is wheeling two *politzei* cars toward the others, lining them up, delighted and absorbed, examining them, talking to them, and realigning them. He is so focussed, so orderly, so doting, so utterly enraptured by these cars and their precise line. *Or-dah!* we marvel. He is more German than most Germans.

What we do not know is what we are looking at. It is not until six years later that we learn obsession with order and parts of objects are possible autism markers.

A second line of cars is arranged according to the light spectrum: R-O-Y-G-B-V. At two, Scott is put out when people fail to see the light spectrum, and worse, when they botch the sequence. He insists upon it. It becomes a convenient way to sort his cars, his socks, his crayons and our plastic IKEA bowls. Rainbows pop up throughout the house. It isn't until the fuss around Erik that we think back to the German car display, narrow our eyes at the crayons and the cars and go "hmm." When you think you know what you are looking at, you stop thinking.

Back in Greece, the local women waggle their fingers and hiss darkly at Frank for making his pregnant wife hike fortress walls and explore monasteries. I am certain they think I'm more pregnant than I am. We must be a spectacle, me overblown, legs and arms protruding like an exotic spider and Frank assigned to boisterous, twenty-two-month-old Scottie, reined in on a child leash. The restraint brings more waggling and opinion in loud expressive Greek. I sigh. It's the tether or a little hellion kicking over antiquities. I want to tell them that the harness is about historical preservation, but they are too busy hissing and heaping disapproval to see the leather for what it is.

This is not exactly like our German honeymoon days or my single-girl Mediterranean life, but it is a daily ride. The trip topper is stretching across three hard waiting room seats all night in the Athens airport. While Frank snoozes on and off, I keep one eye on Scottie as he breathlessly pops up and greets world travellers from his Pack 'n Play. At regular intervals, I reach out and push his head back down, like resetting a stubborn jack-in-the-box. My other hand rests on my growing belly. Baby Erik is becoming a womb traveller.

I am drained but watchful this night in Athens. What I do not know is that this sleepless vigil hints at what lies ahead as motherhood expands and delivers. In life, it is often best not to know. Foreshadowing is for the observer, not the doer.

CHAPTER 2

What's Not Allowed?

WE GEAR UP FOR BABY Kempy's arrival, stripping a flowery bedroom and painting it soft yellow. I gain less weight with this pregnancy and my belly is hard and compact, a solid beach ball. "A girl," is the prediction. The night I go into labour, I aim to finish my lists. I am a nester before travelling and before birthing. The frenzy to tick off all projects before Kempy's arrival is building to bursting.

It is July 15, 1998. I check over my list. Again. Zucchini bread is midway down. I am bent on striking this one off. Motherhood knows what needs to be done, so I bow to it, measure and stir and then hold on to the kitchen counter, brace and br-e-e-eathe through the throbbing contractions. In, out, in, out. Hold it. Release. I resume stirring and baking. I feel efficient and invincible. Baking zucchini bread during labour will do that.

Once it is cooled and sliced, I wrap the loaf, apply my lipstick, and we head to the hospital. It is three in the morning. I am nearly fully dilated, and Erik is born an hour later. We take a picture of me handing out zucchini bread to the obstetrics team, baby Erik wrapped and moored on my belly, lipstick barely smudged. Erik is an easy delivery.

Erik is an easy baby. Perhaps a little too easy, but after Scott-the-screamer, I don't question the placid bundle. I feel I deserve this. Erik rarely cries, but he is needy in an exposed way. He has a translucent helplessness, and during his first week of life, I sense it. He is a child who needs sheltering.

I OBSERVE BABY ERIK DRAPED over my father's lap one afternoon, tummy down, head to one side, eyes closed. My father's large tanned hand rubs the tiny shoulder blades. Around and around goes the leathery hand. Erik wears a pale yellow pinstripe onesie and looks like a delicate sparrow, skinny neck unable to support the enormity of the head. *He looks like one of those baby birds at the avian rescue centre. Susceptible.*

And he *does* seem like he is in need of rescue. I can't explain how or why. I feel it. A mother's instinct? It's part of our early bond, our sync. It is as though the little bird will break if I do not get this right.

Something else I notice is that Erik loves to be swaddled. Tightly. When he is cocooned, he is calm. When the blankets loosen, something unhinges. As a newborn, Scott was the opposite. He could only relax after he had kicked apart my efforts to contain him. In years to come, I will smile on both counts. Scott is a maverick and cannot be contained. Erik craves deep pressure and looks to be swaddled, sleeping with heavy blankets and preferring the confinement of a sleeping bag. With Erik, the tight blanket becomes a metaphor. He craves and needs structure, support and containment, a manageable, accommodated environment. Scott unzips his sleeping bag; Erik pulls his snugly over his head. Temperaments via newborn flannel receiving blankets. Go figure.

ERIK, AT ONE YEAR, MEETS all of his milestones: he smiles, he rolls, he crawls, he squeals, he hugs and kisses. He draws our attention, and he softens our hearts. At around a year, cautiously, he walks. "Oh look!" we cry. "The little A-frame moves!" He is our pet chickadee: pale, delicate and with a trademark tuft of white-blond hair, which seems to sway in the breeze like seagrass. He is beyond sweet, and although he does not say very much beyond "dats!"—his version of "that's!"—he is expressive, pointing, gesturing, inviting. His big blue eyes speak for his lips as if to say, "You smile; we'll do the talking." And he has an adorable smile, joyful and ready. A mischievous sense of humour is brewing as well; deep dimples and a crooked grin are part of the precious package. Times are good, light and busy. Beyond delicacy, there are no concerns.

Erik at a year and a half is developing a distinct and highly methodical personality. *Look! How remarkable! He's so organized!* He is particular and meticulous, but so, too, are his parents. *Just like us!* we remark, unaware that in a child so young, his preference for tidiness, devotion to the vacuum cleaner, systems and traditions is way over the top. If I knew what autism looked like, I would see a line of fluttering red flags, but I do not know, and as a toddler, Erik is easy. We are grateful to go with the organized flow.

APPROACHING YEAR TWO, OUR LITTLE blond boy starts to develop quirky interests.

We are strolling along at the park behind our house one afternoon, and I hear it before I register it: a coherent question coming from Erik, not Scott. A little stilted voice pipes up and asks, "What's not allowed?"

I whirl around, astonished, and observe Erik pointing to a sign on a nearby post. It is a series of circles with red slashes through them. No littering; no loitering; no skateboarding. Up to this point, we have heard variations in "dats" plus a few murky words. But this! This is an entire question, straight out of nowhere! And I understand what he is saying. He is pointing at this sign; he is animated, and he is asking what it means.

I feel a release, the sort of reaction that takes you by surprise because you don't realize the brakes have been on for a very long time. I have been waiting for this—for what, exactly? For the birdie to try his wings—willing it to fly? Today it has. And I want everyone to know. Erik is unfurling! My almost-two-year-old is observing his world, taking it in and trying to make sense of it.

In my relief to hear this little gush of language, I have no idea that these words may be telling me something more, deeper and significant. Obsession with symbols and signs is an autism marker.

There are more oddities.

Erik becomes fixated on fire hydrants. We begin to greet the neighbourhood assortment as though they are Erik's playmates. It is clear that he adores each one, and we pause as he circles, chatters and then offers a lingering hug before departure. I am never sure whether to watch or to turn away. The ritual becomes normal, and I know that it is not.

He is also drawn to the toy hydrants that we collect and he takes to bed. I am amazed that these plastic versions exist. *Are there other families like ours?* Uh, no . . . those ones are for the future firefighters. We have a hydrant hugger. There is a difference. It is somewhat odd, this fixation; however, our little boy is beyond happy. But what's with this loving connection to fire hydrants, of all things? And what parent would not indulge a simple pleasure? There are also ceiling fans, washing machine oscillators, cords of any type, chains, dryer hoses and bits and pieces of larger toys— the handles, the cranks and the pull cords. Erik is mesmerized by moving parts. We are puzzled but pleased that he finds joy in his collections, albeit peculiar ones.

I record it all on our clunky pre-millennial video camera. I click, and the red dot captures what I do not see: a chair pulled up to the washing machine and Erik wiggling, squealing, watching the wash; basement toys with wheels plus the vacuum cleaner recorded, lined up according to size, and Erik standing in front of the display, wearing a mannish little red sweater vest, arms spread wide, beaming like a used car salesman; angelic Erik sleeping with his motley bedfellows arranged around his head in the same position, night after night. I have early autism vignettes, but in 1999, I do not know this. I look at quirk and I see cute. I observe a different trajectory, but I see joy and contentment. So I do nothing but record, endlessly record. It is not until five years later that I press replay, endless replay, searching for what I had missed, how I had missed it and what had been right in front of me all along.

QUIETLY, STEALTHILY, AND UNBEKNOWNST TO us, all of the autism markers begin to emerge. They take their time, and with no particular scheme or sequence, they appear. *Pop! Pop! Pop!* The quirkiness compounds. There are cracks in the foundation. I should be alarmed, but I am not. Erik is easy, content, absorbed and very much interacting with the family, inviting us to love his eccentric bedfellows. He hauls his collections to bed each night, arranging them and bidding them goodnight, tenderly, one by one.

Okay, fair enough. To each his own. I leave it at that. But something is poking at pedagogical me, and it will not go away. I am moving from aware to wary. I feel like we are on the edge of something, but I have no idea what it could be. As for the niggling nagging, I push it away. I sit on it and move on.

CHAPTER 3

Dr. Wuuu-ah!

ALL THE WHILE, ERIK SHOWS a keen interest in my expanding belly. The year is 2000, and I am pregnant with baby Heather, dubbed Seppy, as she is due around my thirty-seventh birthday in September. Big brother Scott has started junior kindergarten, so it is Erik and Mommy at home, tending to the house, to volunteer commitments, to Erik's playgroup, and devoted to growing a spectacular Seppy.

Scott is a force, an articulate ball of frenetic energy. He has taught himself to read and spell at three. At four, he has committed his junior kindergarten classmates' names to memory by staring at the masking tape labels above their coat hooks. He comes home and downloads, producing endless class lists on little white squares of paper. He teaches his classmates how to spell their own names. Bored with first names, he moves on to surnames, staring at the coat hooks once again, burning in the part twos, and mastering a class set of these, as well. But his classmates are not ready to learn part two. So he takes on the names of his Thomas Trains, and he spits out their spelling with rapid-fire accuracy. Thomas and James are simple; Rhineas and Skarloey are a challenge, but he conquers these, too. I move between impressed and perplexed.

He's only four, I remind myself, and although awestruck, I wonder at this extraordinary ability. *Is this a good thing? Is this normal?* It is a question I will repeat with both boys.

ONE NIGHT WE HAVE A friend over for dinner, a military chaplain we knew in Germany. He is visiting from his native province, Nova Scotia, and we are having a good time reliving our European posting. Scott lies at our feet, lining up his latest must-have Theodore Tug Boats. The series is based in Halifax, and our maritime friend, Sid, perks up when he hears Scottie shouting roll call: *"Theodore?* Here! *Pugwash?* Here! *Stewiacke?* Present! *Bedford?* Ya, here!"

The animated play continues. Sid is comforted by the Nova Scotian names, and he is stunned when this small child in pale blue snap-up onesie pajamas starts to scribble the words on a square of paper.

"He knows how to *spell* those?" Sid asks, eyebrows raised.

"Mostly."

To this, Scott perks up and looks up. "I'm having a little trouble with Stewiacke," he muses in his high-pitched staccato, erasing what he has written. "How do you spell that, Mr. Jackson?" He has been listening, and he knows Sid is from the east coast.

Uh-oh. I know this is a tricky one with silent letters, a local anomaly. But Sid gives it a go, and instead of thanking him for his efforts, Scott starts to giggle. "NOPE! *Incorrect!*" he shouts. I think it's like this!" And he scratches it out and pushes the paper "S-T-E-W-I-A-C-K-E" at Sid who is a mixture of awe, embarrassment and puzzlement. He is quite red, and I think this is how former US vice-president Dan Quayle must have felt when he bungled the spelling of *potato* in front of a televised visit to a Grade 1 class—a mix of dumbfounded and dumb.

Sid looks at us and cocks his head. "A little prodigy in the making?"

Though brainy, Scottie is too boisterous to be nerdy. He is social and fun and mischievous. When Scottie is in the room, you know it. Erik adores his older brother "Sotty" and shadows him. He references his big brother, which I am later told is a good thing. Erik certainly does not exist in his own bubble. Although he is not interacting as much as I would like, he is aware of the broader context, and he is inviting us to share his interests. All seems passably fine.

I thank Sid for playing along. Somewhere out of the corner of my eye, I spy Erik, running tight circles in the kitchen. He is smiling and is enunciating something over and over, joyfully, in his own space. I watch, proud of my cuties—one for his spelling prowess and the other for his ability to entertain himself, something my parents also cultivated and lauded in their daughters. But I do not register the direction of Erik's smile. Inward. In this moment, I see only a speller and a runner. Oh yes, and the keeper of unusual bedfellows. There is that, too.

ERIK IS INTRIGUED BY MOMMY's changing shape. There is room for one more fixation, so alongside wheels and oscillators, fans, fire hydrants and signage, we park my belly. He accompanies me to my gynecology appointments, dutifully pushing a tiny umbrella stroller with his doll baby on board. He and his doll wear matching red, pink and yellow knit sweaters, a nice Gramma touch, although Frank makes a face at the pink part. "Really?" he says. Erik looks decidedly like my daughter, but he loves this sweater set, and he refuses to not match baby.

Big blue eyes observe as Dr. Wu prods my belly. Once back in the van, Erik surprises me and explodes with suppressed laughter and repeats the doctor's name again and again and again. "Dr. WUUU-AH!" he whoops and then laughs until his face is wet with tears. He loves the sound of "Wu" and tacks on the "ah" for dramatic effect. He makes the doctor's name sound like something a rodeo cowboy would holler to corral a horse, "WU-ah! WU-ah!" I picture spurs, dust, a roundup. The image strikes me as funny, and I laugh along with Erik.

Back at home, Erik hauls out his pencil case doctor kit with the words "Dr. Wu-ah" stencilled on the side (okay, perhaps I fanned the flame). Transfixed, he examines my stretched belly, his little fingers feeling for a miniature foot or a hand. He is taken by a book called *Hello Baby!* that traces baby's development in the womb. He touches the visuals, absorbing the changes, month by month. He is keen to know.

Meanwhile, the relentless "WU-ah!" goes on for a long time. It becomes Erik's default. He cannot stop himself, nor the laughter. Endless repetition. A fluttering flag.

In his bedroom, he develops strict routines with his doll baby. Baby goes to bed on schedule in a tiny white crib that mimics his own. Baby is fed and cuddled at the same time each morning. And then on go the matching sweaters. Frank sighs. The sweaters.

"What a great father he will be one day!" we decide. Erik is awash with optimism and openness.

Outside his fetal fascination, the love of fire hydrants, cords, fans and signs intensifies. I am so busy with junior kindergarten and my due date that I don't stop to ponder what this could mean beyond originality.

ONE THING WE DO NOTICE is that Erik loves to run in circles on the large Turkish carpet in our bedroom. We are in there one night after bath time, and everyone four and under is naked. On this evening, the entire gang runs in crazed circles around the periphery of the large, mostly peacock blue, wool carpet. There is a lot of laughter, the odd "Wuuu-ah!" and another sound, coming from Erik.

As Erik performs his laps, he sings and hums, smiling. When he passes one particular spot, he shouts out the same word each time. "Eye!" Soon enough, Scott imitates and screams, "Eye!" His words are designed to escalate the frenzy, hike it up a notch. Scott thrives on chaos. Baby Heather, meanwhile, crawls as fast as she can, crab-like, giggling. It's one of those moments that is video-worthy, but we sit and watch, enjoying this parenting vignette, wanting to make it linger, without intervention, interruption or interpretation.

We are watching Erik because he is running with intensity and resolve. He is singular within the group, and his headspace is removed from ours. There is something about "Eye!" that beckons us and makes us track his laps. It happens nightly, this commando workout. Naked laps is the current craze. "Eye" persists and normalizes.

And then, one day, Frank puts it together. Erik is not saying *eye*, he is saying *I*.

On the spot where the word is spoken, Erik has spotted what looks like a capital I woven in the decorative Turkish carpet. This carpet was handmade in shifts in Turkey, and it is not perfect. It is, in fact, non-symmetrical, and the only person in our household to notice this anomaly is two-year-old Erik. He has spotted the flaw, or perhaps the beauty, the originality in what looks like perfect proportion. Attention to detail? Oh, yes!

IT IS AROUND THIS TIME, and in this very place, at the edge of the Turkish carpet, that big brother Scott stops me in my tracks. This time, it has nothing to do with spelling, more with language, both foul and funny. Mostly the former.

He is up to something—his usual, curious self—one morning, and I admonish him because whatever he has done jeopardizes the safety of Erik. I am angry and reactive.

"Scott! STOP!" I shout, startling him and making Erik cry. I seem to be shouting "Stop!" a lot, having to freeze time and then redirect. Scott's terrible explorative twos have persisted right through three and four, and I am exhausted. We have glued everything that could possibly be broken. We joke that we have adhesive for all seasons and all reasons, but I am weary of putting together the pieces.

Scott is not taking this, today or in general. He is certain he is right, and on this morning, he approaches the edge of the Turkish carpet and stands in the bedroom doorway, remarkably like a miniature cop, arms crossed over his heaving chest, legs braced and head down, menacing. I am not sure whether he is going to charge or simply scowl. He looks like a bull, explosive, and he is red, fuming. Instead, he does what we have asked him to do all along. He uses his words.

"And YOU!" he says, jabbing a grubby finger toward me, "YOU DON'T *FUCKLE* WITH ME! . . . *EVAH!*"

He is four, and I am flabbergasted. I wonder whether I have heard what I think I have heard; I wonder if he knows what he has said; I wonder where he heard that word; I wonder whether Scott has registered the effect it has had on me, but mostly, I wonder whether Erik has absorbed it and will start chirping it back to us, for days, weeks even. Infinite Fuckle. *Fuckle! Fuckle! Fuckle!* at the local library. So I go into damage control mode and try to muddle Scott's four-year-old brain, both little brains. "Wuckle! Muckle!" I say, and I sound foolish trying to scramble the signal.

"No, I said *FUCKLE!*" Scottie hollers, emphatic and impatient. He runs past me, punching my leg before he slams his bedroom door.

Erik and I sit dazed in the hallway. I would be happy—very happy—to hear a "Wu-ah" at this moment, but what we do instead is what Erik likes to do best. We sit, cross-legged, quietly, and we read. The story Erik chooses, *It Could Have Been Worse*, is his favourite, and the irony is not lost on me.

Down the line, Scott will be graphic and liberal with language; Erik will be conservative and vow to never knowingly swear or offend. I have two little boys sitting on my shoulders: one angelic and one devilish. One is full of vinegar and the other, pure sugar. The parenting puzzle progresses from basic to advanced. The 1000-piece puzzle, autism, is not far off.

CHAPTER 4

The Little Manservant

ERIK AT TWO IS A blend of precious and peculiar. He is original and he is orderly . . . and yes, empathetic.

We work side by side most mornings scrambling to set up breakfast; he is intent upon making the first meal of the day an exceptional experience for big brother Sotty.

I glance over at Erik as I slice strawberries. He is eye level with the kitchen table. He reaches over the edge and realigns plastic breakfast dishes for Scott, making sure the Pooh and Tigger place setting is parallel to the edge of the table. The whole while he is humming, and with each adjustment, he punctuates his decision with "Dats!" as in, "*That's* where this goes . . ." I hear a flurry of "Dats" and then, at last, everything is suitable. Next he runs to the bottom of the front hall stairs, and he camps there like mini-paparazzi anticipating royalty. He is patient and vigilant.

I hear it again, this time shrill, like a herald announcing something grand: "DATS!"

When he spies Scott's foot on the top step, Erik dashes back to the kitchen, his clammy feet pounding on the linoleum and coming to a sweaty halt beside Sotty's chair. And like a miniature manservant, he drags out the chair and booster seat and holds out a bib, waiting. The Prince obliges by sauntering into the kitchen and climbing aboard. Erik strains to push his big brother and the cumbersome chair into position. Scott sits and allows Erik to heave and puff. I watch, fascinated, biting back laughter and completely enamoured by this display of love and devotion—or something. What is it? It's all so precise and there is that word again—orderly. Is this right? But I don't have much time to contemplate it because

I am brought back into sharp focus by big brother's hand, waving Erik off. The manservant has been dismissed.

Erik is a toddler on a mission, and he is anything but aloof and detached. He is involved and compassionate. But he is also exacting, speaking up when something disagrees with his sense of order, something like a meal that is too late or laughter that is too loud or roughhousing that is too boisterous and goes on too long. Too many *toos* cause something to short-circuit in Erik, and he goes into emergency response mode: "Ik don't yike dat! . . . Ik don't yike dat! . . . IK DON'T *YIKE* DAT!"

He covers his ears and shouts, then runs and disappears. All is quiet and we wait. "*Ik don't yike dat!*" One distant volley for good measure.

We smile, but we understand the boundaries. Erik is no pushover, and we respect his voice. He is a study in contradictions: although difficult to wean off the breast, slow to speak, vulnerable and attracted to the non-typical, he is affectionate, loyal, deliberate, ready-to-serve and exceedingly reliable.

"I'm twooo!" he declares, unfurling two fingers, big blue eyes sparkly.

BUT AS TWO SLIDES TOWARD three, there is a shift, a hint that something is possibly up with our sweet middle child. Three is looking like a different story.

As other children migrate from me to we, Erik is stuck in parallel play. It is as though he lives with the sound icon muted. His life is a silent movie clip. He does what others do, but there is very little coming from him. There is scarce interaction.

At home, he likes to squeeze into kitchen cupboards, so we empty one for him and hammer up a mirror. He spends hours compacted in this cupboard, alone with the other Erik.

At preschool, he is obliging and obedient but happily solitary. He has routines, and he is painstaking in everything he does. "He loves to tidy up," his teacher reports. Her eyes do not meet mine. "He *really* loves to tidy up. That's what he does. Other children play; Erik tidies up."

When you are immersed in emotion, invested in something, you don't see it for what it is. Perhaps Erik's teachers do; perhaps if I was someone else's mom, I might, but I am not, and I do not. The screen is greyed out for me. I do not see the picture clearly, and I do not connect the dots. If I could strip that emotion, make Erik not mine, perhaps I would be able to see a little boy cleaning up because creating order is comforting and comfort is soothing and soothing is coping. At school, Erik is coping. Just. But I don't see this.

I am flooded with protective emotion. It is my deflective armour. Or perhaps it is my blinder. Am I blind?

Nothing is too out of the ordinary, but there is irony at play. In creating endless order, Erik is detaching. He adores plastic; he does not adore people. Plastic fire hydrants, plastic hoses and cords—like my hair dryer and the articulated dryer hose—those are reasons to rejoice. Flesh makes my son flinch.

Okay, different, yes, but doable. It could be worse. Frank and I had been shy children, and we attribute Erik's quiet ways to a family history of cautious, reserved, orderly children. A late bloomer is what we decide to call Erik, as we both had been. Give Erik time. He will emerge. Of course he will. Just like us.

I PULL BACK AND TAKE stock, view my life as though at a distance, as though it is not my own. I have a new baby, Heather; a two-almost-three-year-old, Erik, who is helpful and attentive but also the collector of signs, rotary fans and fire hydrants. I have Scott, a boisterous four-year-old prodigy who, on occasion, poops on the playground and can rattle off the kindergarten class list from memory, calling out and spelling first and last names joyously and with absolute accuracy. I am wowed by Scott, perplexed by Erik and mesmerized with my new baby girl. I am too busy and too tired to think much beyond that.

Deep in my motherhood maelstrom, I am aware of my emerging roles, my hats, as they apply to all three of my babies, but particularly to Erik.

Like a Dr. Seuss board book, my rotating head pieces reveal themselves, page after page, almost amusingly so in their diversity:

nurturer, observer, decipherer, detective, partner, puzzler, blender, buffer, explainer, transitioner, translator (of language and life), collector (of fascinations), paver of paths. In my head the hats take form, and they are decorative, like an outlandish costume party. Is this what I look like? Is there room for more?

Though comically eclectic, each hat has purpose, and each is a puzzle piece, delivered through necessity and often without warning or instructions. I see these puzzle pieces jiggling at first—like cellphone apps—before they find their new positions in my daily routine, and then they settle slowly and deliberately into place. *Click*. Another role.

I stand amid diapers and a row of plastic cars and trucks, plus one vacuum cleaner and one shop vac, all arranged according to a deliberate Erik-schematic. I try on hats and wonder why my boys seem to set one another off and why it is that Scott's skill sets are so shockingly out of sync. But mostly I wonder about Erik and why he runs in endless circles, joyfully shouting out gibberish; why he drags a chair to the washing machine on laundry days and delights in gazing at the oscillator. What is this all about? Why is he so drawn to those "What's not allowed?" signs, and why does he hug public fire hydrants? Why the endless lining up and roll call of all things with wheels? And why is my little boy so much happier with a row of cheap Dollar Store hazard signs than he is with eager peer playmates?

Most days I think I should know the answers, but they elude me. I don't have time to ponder them too deeply, anyway. I am treading water, keeping up each day to the whirlwind of awe, hesitation, celebration, joy, confusion and exhaustion. Frank and I press on with the hope that time will diffuse and sort out these mysteries.

Soon enough, the inevitable unimaginable happens: an armed forces transfer. We are posted to Halifax, and in one stroke, Erik's organized world—the only home he has ever known—is dismantled. This proves to be the beginning of Erik's undoing. It is a mighty and confusing switch up, and it is one that accelerates the inward journey.

As our house is emptied of furniture and belongings, and as we make our way east, Erik copes as best he can. He flips through his mini photo books filled with "What's not allowed?" signs, and he clutches his doll baby and his beloved board books. He is self-regulating, trying to make sense of the biggest transition of his young life.

CHAPTER 5

Seeds for the Island

"THERE'S NO LIFE LIKE IT!" Or, as I have also heard it worded, "There's no life. Like it." However you punctuate it, the armed forces offers a distinct lifestyle. You must grow with the flow.

As a young girl, seven, I had walked in Erik's shoes. I had been uprooted, transplanted, and I had been expected to cope. More than cope. Reinvent. Thrive. *Seeds for the island!* That had been my game plan. I would harvest seeds in Nova Scotia and beautify our new home on Vancouver Island. Just as Erik retreated into his "What's not allowed?" signs, I had clutched a little pouch of hollyhock seeds and hung on for dear life. Seeds. Renewal. Growth.

Glancing in the rear-view mirror, I spy Erik, tucked in the middle row of the van. He reads "What's not allowed?" to doll baby. I am reminded of little me, homeless and on the move.

~

MY LIFE KICKED OFF IN Winnipeg but soon shifted to Nova Scotia. My father was an air force navigator, so relocating and redefining became the early rhythm. Transition and change was our background thrum. For me, it was an auspicious beat.

Nearly a year into our Nova Scotia posting, when I was three turning four, my parents took off for Montreal, to Expo '67. My sister Lori recalls them hauling their Samsonites toward the old Dodge, exhilarated. We three girls stood on the front step, waving, left behind in the care of an ancient stranger. Our parents were only gone four days, but it felt amplified.

"It feels like we have a substitute teacher," Lori whispered, and she didn't seem too pleased.

As a preschooler, this was my first exposure to (a) an alternative mother and (b) nature versus nurture and how vastly different three siblings can be.

I surprised myself by adapting well. This was because our elderly caregiver, a meld of Mrs. Doubtfire and Mary Poppins, concocted chocolate and vanilla cookie dough and rolled and shaped the contrasting strands into tiny stovetop cooking elements. At least that's what the cookies looked like to me. I had never seen anything like this. I stood to the side and watched, absorbed, and then eventually pulled up a stool and camped beside her, charmed by her capable hands. They were spotty, crinkly and sure as they braided and coiled the dough. I was captivated.

I also liked her singing. She annotated her movements, and her singsong narrative was joyous, comforting, uplifting. "Rolling the dough, rolling the dough, here we go, we're rolling the dough!" I quietly mouthed the words, and the house was filled with calming, domestic melody as she worked through her chores. I followed her. My sisters scoffed from upstairs. They were not so easily won over. But what struck me then, and often after, is how soothing and reassuring a life narration can be. It is life's closed caption, and years later, I would burst into song with my own children as I guided them through daily routines.

As for the part B, nature-nurture, we were all given the same instruction sheet by our parents, and yet . . . we all interpreted the house rules differently. In carrying out the expectations, we became the three bears of behaviour: the boat rocker, the rocket scientist and the rock, the pleaser—me.

"Oh! Sugar-dee-dee!"

We heard this from the kitchen when something went wrong. This was Mrs. Woodbury's version of swearing. I was impressed that she could funnel her anger in such a pleasing way. I liked the expression, and soon I was "sugar-dee-deeing" around the house, purposefully stubbing my toe on the way up the stairs, just so I could say it.

"Oh! Sugar-dee-dee!"

Leslie was ten turning eleven and was learning a few choice expletives of her own. Sugar-dee-dee irked her, and hearing it in stereo put her over the top. She was quite good at making her bedroom door slam, and even better at cranking up her music. It was surprising how loud a tiny, tinny transistor radio could go.

Leslie didn't know the eff-word (had it been invented?) but instead used blasphemous and creative substitutes and, in that, blasted the sugar right out of the dee-dee. Mrs. Woodbury was rattled, and that only upped the "dee-dee" output, which triggered upstairs retaliation. I was frightened of the escalation and thrilled by it. Leslie was not a pushover, but neither was Mrs. Woodbury. My heart thumped as I crouched on the stairs and spied on them both. I hadn't counted on adrenaline to eclipse the Expo blues.

And there was Lori, eight and scientific, too busy for cookie production but content to consume the product. She wasn't rude to Mrs. Woodbury, but she was not attentive either. She was neutral, preoccupied and hunched over a jumble of hand-painted plastic body parts in her bedroom, which would eventually become The Invisible Man. In her busyness, she became its human counterpart, The Invisible Girl.

As for me, I became Gopher and Go-to, a steadfast sidekick for our melodious maid. My loyalty pleased Mrs. W., and the more she smiled at me, the sweeter I became. I was beyond good. I was the sugar in the dee-dee. For pre-school me, this was foundation fodder. Mrs. Woodbury's reaction revealed something new and astonishing: we become what we are told. We are what we feel. And "sugar" seemed pretty sweet to me.

MY FIRST SCHOOL MEMORY IS of me, frightened, mousy and quiet. And that my Grade 1 teacher's hair mesmerized me. It was a classic 1960s bouffant, aka "beehive": a tangled, back-combed, teased mess that somehow looked untidy and neat at the same time. She was young and pretty, but she scared me because she would yell a lot and praise little. I could hardly believe that pretty could be mean and scary and that pretty could wear a disguise.

Sometimes we spied her, The Nest, after school, kissing her handsome pilot husband in the classroom. This was an air force base, and the school was on base. Hubby was near. Maybe it wasn't all-out kissing, but from our perspective in the cloak room, their lips met. We stood, open-mouthed, but never long. Her hair seemed to house an early warning system, and she would go from kissing to cussing, glaring and yelling some more. I wondered if the pilot was scared, too.

But what she did do right was challenge us. And that is my second school memory: jumping on the bed. Not at school, but because of school. From The Nest came the challenge to learn the alphabet backwards. At the front of the classroom sat the prize, a coveted box of sticker stars, the kind that tasted like spearmint toothpaste when you licked them. A whole box for the person who could recite the alphabet backward—the fastest.

More than anything, I wanted those stars.

Determined to win, I recruited my mother as soon as I got home. It erupted from me in a breathless jumble: "We can win a box of sticker stars if we can say the alphabet backwards faster than anyone . . . and I want to win . . . I want the prize . . . How do I win, Mommy?"

Unbelievably, my mother had been delivered the same challenge early on, and she dazzled me—there on the spot—with a lightening, singsong "Z-Y-X . . . W-V . . . U-T-S . . . R-Q-P . . ." right to the very end. The performance was astonishing. Who knew? So, I listened as she told me how she had learned it, and I took her battle plan upstairs and began jumping on my bed, just as she had done thirty-one years earlier.

I jumped, long and hard. Not tentative jumps, but big thumping kinesthetic leaps until I learned that reverse flow. Cold. And until I broke the bed. *Cra-ack!*

Back at school, I, too, dazzled, won, accepted the sticker stars with dignity and humility and sat quietly, cradling the tiny flat box. And as I sat, I wondered why nearly no one had bothered to memorize the alphabet backwards. It had been easy to win because the second runner-up got halfway and bailed, in tears. I sat, flabbergasted, that much of the room had stopped before they had started. They had not accepted the challenge. I would look back and reflect on this in later years, but in the moment, I was looking to escape this unpredictable woman and head to calmer waters: Grade 2.

CHAPTER 6

The Secret

WHILE I DON'T REMEMBER WHAT my Grade 2 teacher looked like, I do remember what she felt like. She felt like an enabler. She felt very good.

What I also liked about Grade 2 was that it was steeped in order, predictability, respect and gratitude that looked something like this: a number line, an alphabet frieze, a framed portrait of the Queen and the Canadian flag, tilted on a staff in the corner. The flag was our big picture reminder and overseer, as was the Queen. I looked at them both a lot. Context was important to me.

Each morning, we stood beside our wooden desks, saluted and pledged allegiance to the flag, the Queen and the country. And then we sang "Oh Canada." I have a vague feeling that the flag fluttered (was there a fan blowing it?), but this may be my own embellishment. It felt like it was fluttering, and with it, my heart. Patriotism will do that. It causes a stir, and that is a good precursor to learning. We were becoming better Canadians.

Aside from the rituals and the traditions, the belief and the order, what I remember most about Grade 2 is the secret. One day, the teacher told us that she had a secret that was really a secret power. We sat forward, baited. She said that when she was a child, her mother had told her a secret, and that she had kept that secret up until today, until this very moment. And now, she was ready to tell it, to share it with us. I wondered whether her mother would mind, and then I looked at the teacher's pleated skin and decided there was a good chance that her mother was dead. I thought it was likely okay to tell.

We were invited forward, one at a time, to peek at the secret. It was hidden behind a cardboard triptych that sat on a spare desk at the front of the class. As each of us tiptoed up, circled around and peered, all eyes watched, and after the secret was revealed, that person had to walk back to their desk with their index finger pressed to their lips, making a "shh." More than one of us wiggled in our seats. I was so piqued, I thought I might pee.

When it was finally my turn, I felt faint with curiosity. I did the tiptoe, circled the cardboard . . . and . . . there it was. The secret power. I felt immediate confusion, and in that moment, I imagined what Dorothy must have felt when she circled the curtain and discovered that Oz was just an ordinary man. I felt disappointment, but I also felt like I was not as clever as everyone else. All I saw was a small round mirror. Looking out at my classmates, I beamed, faking astonishment. Inside I felt bewilderment.

"Go ahead," my teacher urged. "Look more closely."

I stepped in, and I saw me, big-eyed and wondrous. And in that moment I got it: my secret power was me. I was in control of me, and it was up to me to create great: great moments, great details, great descriptors—and in so doing, to define myself. It was my job to take this superpower forward into the world.

I didn't figure out any of that in the moment. The aha came much later. At that time, I saw big blue eyes, and I felt happy to be me and in this classroom where superpowers were shared. And that was enough. The rest would come later, in ripples of realization. Life is like that. Lessons are time-released. Small round mirrors remind me of that day, of the secret and of my secret power.

SHORTLY AFTER GRADE 2, IT was announced that we would be pulling up roots and moving across the country to Vancouver Island. Another air force posting was underway. Back then, there was no car carrier to ferry the family vehicle across the country. We had to figure that out ourselves. The plan was for Lori and Dad to drive coast to coast; Mom, Leslie and I would fly standby on the military flights.

As the school year wound down, I would lie in bed and whisper to Lori. "I think the Island is going to have all sizes of palm trees. There will be beaches . . . with red-and-white umbrellas! We'll jump in the waves . . ." Anticipation made sleep impossible. Stopping short of treasure, I swished my legs in bed, swimming in my rumpled sheets. I stuck to probabilities: "There will be campfires . . . and singing. Oh! And sunsets!"

Lori snickered and outlined the facts. I nodded but remained optimistic, holding out for tropical and romantic. I collected seeds for the Island—hollyhock, mostly, but also dandelion and rosehips. I thought we could grow gardens. I decided I would become a pioneer.

It took us one week to fly across the country. At seven, that is romance. We three travelled on a military flight: priority five—or Pri-5 for short. We kept getting bumped off flights designated for service personnel. Trenton. Winnipeg. Moose Jaw. This is when our resourceful mother kicked into gear, arranging quick accommodation and booking us on alternative flights. One leg was on an immense, heavy transport aircraft, the Hercules. I found the Herc a thrill because we sat sideways, clicked into jump seats alongside huge, netted cargo boxes. We wore massive military headgear to block out the roar and ate boxed lunches with cheese wedges and sweet pickles.

IN THE END, DAD AND Lori beat us across Canada, setting some kind of driving record, crossing the country in four days. In Sudbury, my dad bought Lori a radio, and when we finally reunited in Vancouver, Lori held up her well-polished wireless like a coveted trophy. We were a family again, and life was about to get underway, west coast style.

~

CHAPTER 7

Different

PLUNK! A STONE HITS THE water. Another. *Plink!*

A small pale hand reaches into the cookie tin and draws out some seeds, pauses and hurls the grains into the water. The tinkling is soothing, like a rainstick. Ducks honk and glide, honk and glide, homing in on dinner. Erik claps his hands and jumps on the spot, jubilant. He repeats. He and the ducks are connected in this hurl-and-honk circuitry. Everyone is content.

We are a family transplanted, and life is underway, east coast style.

Our maritime home is peaceful and cottage-like. Erik is wrapped in nature. We live on the shore of a small lake outside Halifax, Nova Scotia, and we spend hours down at the water, feeding ducks and floating boats. Erik loves water.

As for our house, there is comfort in familiar objects, and there is relief and joy that our furniture has made it across four provinces. Although our treasures are set up differently, our home has a recognizable vibe, like seeing one's teacher outside of school—surprising and unusual but comfortable and right.

To Erik's delight, we create a jungle bedroom for him, complete with a raised bed, lush leafy wallpaper, large plush animals and secret areas to lounge and play. It is an outdoor oasis indoors. I catch Erik exiting and entering—again and again—repeating his initial reaction each time. "Ahhh!" It is fifty shades of green, and where there is green, there is calm. He is our nature boy, and when he is not at the lake with us, he hangs out in his jungle bedroom. Sometimes he invites Scott and Heather to join him.

One morning, I hear giggles from the wild, and I peek in the room. I pause and scan. There is movement under the raised bed, and it's coming from a twist of furry monkeys and blankets. I walk over and pretend to stumble over the tangle. The lump titters. Little voices are in there. Hiding from Mommy is fun!

I sigh. "Oh well, no sign of my children in *this* jungle . . . maybe I'll look downstairs . . ." and I head toward the door and part the wooden beads hanging in the doorway. I will let my little critters win today, but the victory is in the mingling of siblings. If a decorated bedroom is what it takes to attract and unite the masses, we will do that. Erik does not initiate play or keep it alive, so if he needs help from his surroundings, so be it. I am learning, by feel, what I will later learn in textbooks: autism is environment dependent. Erik is at his best outdoors, so we bring the outdoors to Erik.

LIFE CHUGS ALONG. SCOTT EXCELS in Grade 1 and exuberantly declares, "Sign me up for everything!" Baby Heather learns to walk and talk and appears to be a version of her brothers: she looks like Erik, and she is precocious like Scott. Erik, on the other hand, shies away from anything new and prefers that I sign him up for nothing. He is a homebody, and he is content pedal boating around the lake with Mommy and Daddy and hanging out in his jungle bedroom. I respect this, and besides, it's easier to coast and comply than it is to force a social life on a reluctant three-turning-four-year-old.

We try playgroups. Erik does not mingle. "He's shy," I suggest to the other mothers, but I wonder. We try inviting potential play-mates home, but Erik ignores them, hides in his bedroom and is miffed that they are invading our private space, our home. I have to make sure that Scott and Heather are around to pick up the slack. I make excuses for Erik's withdrawal, but it is keenly apparent that something is off-kilter.

It is around this time that Heather and Erik merge develop-mentally. Heather takes charge. She is two and is sharp and feisty, clearly a girl with a plan. But she is not bossy nor is she demanding. She is tuned into Erik, seeming to sense and anticipate his needs and inclinations, drawing him out of himself, inviting him to play and blending him into neighbourhood kid groups. She is a poster child for inclusion. But mostly, she celebrates Erik. She delights in his unusual play choices, and she makes him feel brilliant and appreciated. In Heather we have an on-board social worker and a miracle worker. It occurs to me as I watch them in action that Heather is one of the best things that has happened to Erik. This early bonding becomes a unit we refer to as *the blondies*.

One of the blondies' unconventional play choices is a game they call *Dog and Owner*. Somewhere in the basement, the blondies discover a child harness, the very restraint that prevented toddler Scott from toppling Greek antiquities. Heather buckles herself in and joyfully morphs into the family pet, scampering on all fours, straight blond hair whisked out and damp, as she laps water from a bowl on the floor.

"Woof! Woof! Woof!"

I glance up from what I am doing in the kitchen one morning, stop and watch. It is a sweet spectacle.

Erik, the dutiful owner, holds the leather leash and parades his preschool pet around the main floor. He stops every once in a while to brush her and insists she rest and exercise and eat at regular intervals.

I sigh, reaching for the video camera. While other four-year-old boys talk Transformers and Tonka trucks, mine is topping up water bowls and gently grooming the blond dog.

Thank goodness for Heather. Her presence, spirit and open-mindedness feed Erik so effortlessly. She validates his offbeat preferences, and she validates Erik, period. Heather is a lesson in acceptance: she recognizes neurodiversity long before the term is coined.

ERIK IS FOUR AND ATTENDS a community preschool. I want to warm him up for the real deal—public school. Now that we are solidly out in the community, my son's solitary preferences are drawing attention.

"He's . . . um . . . a little different . . . a loner . . ."

Erik's young preschool assistant seems uncomfortable telling me this. She is not sure what she is looking at, but her expression tells me that she is perplexed. I assure her that he is just shy and that my husband and I had also been shy.

"No, not shy . . . ," she says. "Different. There's a difference."

Inside I am annoyed at her for trespassing, for stepping inside my head and for validating my late-night worst-case-scenario brain; for feeding it, for seeing the truth and for coolly spilling it out. She doesn't know that her casual words create heat in me. I feel the warmth travelling to my face, running down my arms, pooling in my hands. I cannot stop it. The physiological effect startles me, and I fear that she can see it, can hear it when I speak, and that she knows what her words have done. I feel the prickle of tears. I blink and snuff the betrayal.

Outwardly I smile, nod lightly and thank her for her input. It would seem I have a grip on this, that I will investigate and do the right thing. That I will tick this off like some obscure grocery item. In truth, the knot tightens and cannot be undone.

My smile is a mask. Wearing it, I pull on my buffer hat and try to blend Erik in with the other kids. We bring in birthday cupcakes, but Erik glowers as the other children sing to him. It is a strange sight: a joyous chorus and a raging recipient. We invite children to our home, but Erik hides. Back at preschool, I stand on the periphery, on the outside looking in. All of the children blend so effortlessly, except for one little fluffy-haired boy intent on cleaning up. I am certain that in time, Erik will be able to mix and make friends. *Give it time*, I tell myself, but something inside is not convinced. Erik is not connecting. I begin to feel paranoid, as though parents are averting their eyes, fearing their child will be next on my playdate hit list. After a while, I stop inviting. I imagine a collective sigh of relief.

CHAPTER 8

Henna Gaijin

I AM IN THE LIVING room, sitting, sipping tea. Heather is napping, and the boys are in school. The house is silent, as though I have reached out and pressed PAUSE. My gaze falls on the scarlet silk kimono that hangs in the hallway, a remnant from a former life.

~

I FLEW TO TOKYO ONE week before Christmas and three months after I turned twenty-five. I had not lived in Japan long when I learned two things about myself: I was Christmas cake, and I was strange. I wore new words. I was learning about myself through foreign eyes.

We were sitting in class one day early on, ten Japanese adults and me around a conference table. This was a business school, and we were warming up to English conversation by sharing fun facts about ourselves. I told them I was twenty-five and had come to Japan to seek adventure. They looked at one another and giggled, nudged and pushed the best English speaker forward. Toji was nominated to break the news to me, to explain me to me.

"Ah so," he began, "in Nippon—Japan, as you say—we call a woman like you . . . . uh . . . Ca-list-must cake-u."

I was confused, but I smiled, thinly. "Ca-list-must? Pardon . . . ?"

"Christmas cake-u!" someone shouted, reddening, laughing and clearly enjoying the confusion.

Toji continued. "You see, Christmas cake is only good . . . only has meaning. . . until the twenty-fifth of December. After that? No good. Overdue. Just like a woman . . . after twenty-five, she is too old to marry. No good. Telesa-san, you are Christmas cake! Perhaps you should . . . to . . . return to Canada . . . before it is . . . too late for you?"

I was stunned. "You're . . . kidding me . . . right?" I sputtered.

"No, no joke. You are . . ."—he consulted his translator device—"past due!"

They roared, rosy and pleased with themselves for warning me, maybe even saving me from a solitary life. I was incredulous, but I smiled. A Canadian woman meets Japanese men. This would be an interesting year.

I walked home that night past outdoor fruit stands and pottery displays covered with just a trusting tarp. I pondered Christmas cake and how I was made to feel. If I believed it, defeated and defined; if I did not, angry but aware. Labels and stereotypes were rampant and indelible here. But only if I allowed it.

I HAD BEEN WEARING "CHRISTMAS Cake" a short time when I heard a second opinion, and I heard it often. *"Henna gaijin!"* trailed me around town. At least it was unanimous. Everyone seemed to have the same opinion of me, but I hadn't the slightest clue what that was.

I walked to school wearing my Walkman, singing.

"Henna gaijin!"

I rode my bike wearing a skirt.

"Ah!! Henna gaijin!" Ramped up.

I gave direct eye contact.

Big time "Henna gaijin!"

I could not escape it, and I could not imagine what it meant. I was doing my Canadian thing, and the word would appear. I assumed that they were fascinated by my long blond hair and my aqua contact lenses. Maybe they were intrigued. Maybe that was it. So I asked a teaching colleague, a Japanese woman. She blushed. Again, the red face. I waited. "Do they like my hair?" I mused.

"No . . . Telesa-san . . . They call you strange. You STRANGE!" And she covered her mouth, both giddy and slightly ashamed at herself for having been the messenger.

"Strange?" I pondered aloud. "How? Why?"

"Because you behave . . . in a . . . ," she paused to consult her translator device, "in an odd way . . . ," she said, smiling sweetly as she tried on the new vocabulary word, enunciating "odd" in a remarkably odd way. She continued, her gaze somewhere around the tip of my nose. *Higher*, I wanted to say, but I listened instead.

"In a way that is different from the rest. In Japan, different is . . . not so good. You no want to be different, Telesa-san."

I learned that different is feared, mistrusted, labelled and judged all because it is not understood. I tried to explain to my students that different can also be good because it offers new ideas, fresh ways of thinking and of knowing and of doing. And that this is called diversity. But as I looked out onto a sea of navy blue uniforms, I realized that my words were bouncing back to me, undelivered. I pushed on; my lesson was not quite done.

"You have to know that I never set out to be weird or strange or annoying. I'm just being me, a Canadian in Japan. You have your way of doing things, your Japanese operating system, and I have mine, my Canadian rule book. You see, that's what's happening, you're seeing me and trying to interpret me through your lens. What you see is different, yes, but not wrong, just different."

The room became softly unsettled. There were nods and possibly shards of understanding, but not all-out acceptance. I had planted seeds—food for thought—and that was a start.

So long as I acted and spoke according to my Canadian operating system in Japan, I would never be one of them; I would be foreign and strange, an enigma to be puzzled out and straightened out. This was a feeling I never grew used to, never shook and never forgot.

BUT THERE WERE MANY THINGS I loved about Japan, and one of them was this: Buddha's hands. I visited many shrines, and I stared up at the benevolent giant, typically carved in stone. He sat, larger-than-life, cross-legged, and wore an enigmatic Mona Lisa smile. It was calming. But what I noticed most were the hands, because they were always different. The pose I liked best was one hand up and one hand out. I was told that these were the purest teaching hands, for one was the transmitter of information—the hand held up, palm facing out—and one was the receiver of information, the one held out, palm facing up. To teach is to send and to receive; it is circular, a circuit. I never forgot this, and I regarded it as a perfect partnership. The best teachers are learners, and the best learners are teachers.

SIX MONTHS IN, HOWEVER, THERE was a complaint about my teaching.

"Telesa-san looks us in the eye. Please tell her no."

This was what I was told, to stop what is intuitive, natural, like telling me to breathe differently. I was told that I gazed too long, too hugely, and that I was mucking with souls, distracting the speakers. I had no idea I had committed so many crimes. I would rein it in, I promised, but secretly I wondered, *how?*

To my students I was direct, and this made them uneasy, embarrassed for me for not knowing the rules. Nothing is explicitly spelled out in Japan; it is all implied. This drove me crazy, this veiled, layered, honourable communication.

"The manager told me that some of you find my eye contact uncomfortable," I began. "I'll do my best to look somewhere else." *There are worse targets*, I thought.

My students appeared more anxious than ever. Eyes were everywhere, scattered, lowered, even closed.

I went on. "I'm willing to meet you partway; of course I am. But you have to know that when you travel to North America—and for some of you, this is the reason you study English—people will give you lots of direct eye contact. It signals engagement, attunement. Anything else is seen as sneaky, evasive, lacking confidence. You need to know that. So I can avert my eyes, but it's not going to help you. It depends what you want: easy or helpful?"

Language is communication, I explained, and language is also culture. There were so many rules to learn. They felt overwhelmed by the amount of knowing. So did I.

My words spun and settled. Buddha's hands redirected us: we were all learning. It was a process. Breathe.

Years later I would buy a copy of John Elder Robison's *Look Me in the Eye*, and on autism websites, I would read what I could do to make my son give me eye contact, because he did not. "Try a sticker between your eyes." But the cyclops didn't do much aside from make him whoop with laughter. All of this—this insistence that he look directly at me—would take me back to Nippon. Oh, how Erik would love the Japanese, and they him: tall, gentle, considerate Erik. How beautifully he would fit in in Japan where averting eyes is polite and respectful and where less is more. Less is expected. Requested. Perhaps in Japan Erik would be esteemed; in North America he is relentlessly therapied. Who makes the rules and sets the bar, anyway? I would ask this a lot. And why does my son need to look into my eyes? To please whom?

BUT THE BIGGEST TAKE-AWAY MESSAGE there outside of Tokyo was delivered to me in the form of a square of cardboard—about fifteen centimetres by fifteen centimetres—at the height of rainy season, April 1989. It was a lesson and a guiding light that would remain with me for life, and it would change the way I responded to adversity—and diversity.

One wet evening, in walked Keiko Ishii, a junior high school teacher. She often came to her private lesson with samples of her teaching, and I welcomed this. "If you want to learn English conversation," I told her, "speak about what you know and love." So she did. For this lesson, she brought a prop that was also a gift. I knew this because it was wrapped in bright red and white speckled origami paper. "Geeft-to"—gift—she indicated and she pushed it toward me, wearing pride and a mischievous grin. It would be a challenge; she liked to engage in riddles.

"Go on, open it," she urged, and then as an afterthought, "I made it for you." This she indicated by lightly tapping the tip of her nose. It is a Japanese-ism that I liked, the nose-tapping. "*Watashi*," she whispered as she tapped. *Watashi*, I learned, meant *I*.

I nodded and opened it. It was lovely, a Japanese calligraphy—an art form—but I had no idea which way was up or what it said. I turned it in my hands, smiling up at her and murmured a gracious "thank you so much" and "could you please explain . . . ?"

"No! You guess!" she challenged and then more quietly, "Hint! It's what it means to be Japanese."

So I teased back: "Oh . . . playful, devilish, a leg-puller . . ." We had been learning body idioms the last session.

But she didn't fall for it. "No, we are seriously today, Telesa-san . . . what do you think?" she urged, animated, gesturing to the art. She held her breath.

"Hardworking? Honest? Authentic? . . . Honourable?" my voice trailed, hopeful.

"Yes, yes! All of that . . . but more. In Japan, it is very, very important to keep going, to never stop . . . to never let life stop you. In Japan we say . . ." And she stopped to think and reference her notes. "Continue is the power."

I was delivered a defining moment, a snapshot in time that would illuminate the way forward—the way I approached hardship, challenge, adversity and life's darkest times. *Continue is the power* would become my autism backbone. I would become like the Japanese, and I would never give up.

I left Nippon a year and a half later, never fully integrated but fully inspired.

~

CHAPTER 9

Deny, Deny, Deny

ERIK'S FASCINATIONS CONTINUE TO BE unorthodox. He is intrigued by and terrified of the lake behind our house—specifically, two large floating platforms to the right and to the left of our shoreline. These wooden swimming docks belong to our neighbours, Gerhardt, a gregarious German, and Jim, a man we seldom see. We like to pedal-boat around these platforms, but the closer we get, the more alarmed Erik becomes. As we retreat, he grins and calls out to them, "See ya, Gerhardt . . . Bye, Jim!" smiling at the floating docks as though they are preschool buddies. Except that he has none. We smile, wave and echo Erik. *Now we are talking to wood.* There is an uncomfortable sensation that we have become swept up in a dream that we cannot shake. We are encouraging the absurd.

Back in the kitchen, Erik pulls out felt markers and draws the platforms endlessly and lovingly. And then he runs in tight circles, waving his drawings and shouting, "Gerhardt and Jim! Gerhardt and Jim!" with such elation that we begin to cheer. "Gerhardt and Jim" is life's current sound bite.

I look on, and I feel this fixation climb on board just as fire hydrants and signs and oscillators have done. Erik's interests and behaviours are normalizing, both for him and for us. "Oh . . . that's just Erik!" we say but we are beginning to think something more.

I have a disconcerting feeling that will not go away: while open-mindedness is good, maybe we need to steer Erik closer to other four-year-olds. I am happy that he is happy, but his brand of contentedness is also a source of concern—and isolation. While others his age are bonding over shared interests, my son is drifting ever further from whatever normal is. Erik at four has specialized exceedingly early. *What does it mean? And what should I be doing about it?*

ERIK'S START IN PUBLIC EDUCATION is lurching.

Erik does not yearn for school. He shies away and hides, hoping I might leave him in peace in his jungle bedroom. We talk about kindergarten and taking the bus and wow, how exciting this will be! He's a big boy now! But the problem is, he doesn't want to be a big boy. He wants to stay small and four and alone and in his themed bedroom with his favourite books and the oversized fuzzy centipede that Gramma has sewn for him. "Just let me be four," his enormous blue eyes plead. Let me be me.

But I don't do that. I sign him up to start school before he is ready because it's what everyone else is doing. He is four turning five. He is ready. But honestly, he is not, and somewhere inside, I know it. But I push ahead, register him and cajole him into thinking he is ready. We walk down the street to the bus on day one, talking brave thoughts but both thinking, *Really?*

Scott is raring to go. He is in Grade 2, finally having squirted out of two unnecessary years of kindergarten and a nurturing Grade 1. He is ready to burst out of the gate. Truly, Grade 3 would be a better fit, but we play along with the script and rein him in. And as I think about it, I laugh, almost, at the contrast. One son is cajoled; the other is curtailed. In one I dredge for conversation, and from the other flows a steady and exhausting stream of words. They could not be more opposite, my boys. Years later I will be surprised, startled, to discover that my sons are different sides of a very similar coin. But right now, I see only the individual faces, and to me, they are in no way connected.

As for Heather, after the boys board the school bus, she turns to me and glares, "Now I wee wee maaad!" She scuffs at the dirt and takes off up the road, leaving me in the dust to ponder what it all means.

So much for our mother-daughter time. She wants more than anything to be on that school bus. I turn from her stormy little figure to Erik's small white beseeching face, fuzzy in the bus window.

Where are you sending me and why? it seems to say. My stomach feels taut, and running to catch up with Heather, I hold her little hand in mine. We walk up the hill toward home as the school bus puffs diesel and disappears around the corner, carrying with it my little boy.

IT IS AROUND THIS TIME that a conversation I had with my mother-in-law a few years back dislodges and surfaces. I remember that it had started with an honest question. Knee-deep in diapers and baby food, I could not begin to imagine an answer. In all honesty, I did not have an answer.

"What are you doing for *yourself* these days?"

The only reply I could think of was pert, defiant, *In my copious spare time?* So I kept that in my head. But what I said was this, "Sleep, if I'm lucky." I knew I could do better. This prod lay dormant somewhere deep inside, ready to respond when the time was right. In Halifax, the right time comes.

I sign up for a weekly learn-to-run program, and I do just that. I learn to run, fast, long and hard, away from gut feelings and diapers and dinners at six. I run and I run and I run, up and down historic Citadel Hill in the centre of the city, until my breath becomes ragged and my heart pounds. It feels good to break free, to get away and to reclaim a tiny bit of me.

But escape is not easy. Everyone in the family is supportive of my new hobby except Erik. When he spies me gearing up to run, he also runs—down the basement stairs to blockade the garage door. He stages sit-ins, plunking himself on the stairs, crying and clutching my leg, begging me not to go out. As I look down at him, I think, *He's like a little human ball and chain.*

This would not be the last time I would entertain such a thought, and each time, I would feel a flood of guilt. After all, Erik was just being Erik.

I learn to love running and begin meeting a friend, Anne, another runner-mom. We do a ten-kilometre run three times a week while our youngest children are in preschool. I am feeling fit and, finally, balanced. So what is it about running that I like?

The tone? The time out of time? Or the sensation of running away from all that matters?

ONE MORNING, I GET A call from school. It is Erik's kindergarten teacher, and the voice message has a tight edge to it.

"Can you come in? I think we need to talk . . ."

Something inside me also tightens. It's like hearing one's licence plate announced over a store intercom and being asked to report to Customer Service. *For what?* You begin to imagine the worst. But something inside has been expecting this phone call, and I am strangely apprehensive, curious and relieved. How can I be all three?

I am in Erik's classroom. His teacher and I sit in tiny plastic chairs. I feel off-balance, but it has less to do with the miniature seats and more to do with the strained look on her face. Something is wrong.

"You're getting a lot more from him at home than I am here at school."

Erik has homework in kindergarten, and he dutifully works on it in the familiarity of our kitchen. At school, he produces dribbles, almost nothing. His teacher describes his behaviour to me, and I am both surprised and not.

"Um . . . ," she begins. She does not make eye contact. This cannot be good. "He spends his days quietly coping, taking everything in through those big, serious blue eyes of his, but he seems utterly . . . *incapacitated* here at school. Petrified." She looks away again, pauses and then continues. I am sitting on the edge of my very tiny seat.

"Teresa, he whines, he covers his ears when things get overwhelming, and he really doesn't produce any work at all. When we need to switch gears, things get worse. To me, he looks frozen, like a deer on the centre line." She looks directly at me now.

"He copes by endlessly clicking a pen cap. He is more interested in his pen than his peers. He loves the clicking . . . ," she says and her voice trails off. We are both on the edge of our seats.

The room is expectant. I can hear the fluorescent lights. They hum. I swallow.

As we talk about this endless clicking and Erik walking the periphery of the playground, I feel my body react. I am heating up again, becoming agitated and sweaty. I have lost my voice, and I am holding back tears . . . and yet, I want to know more. *I want to know what I already know.* It's just that my intuition doesn't have a name for it yet. But the teacher and her doctor-colleague do.

"I think your son has Asperger syndrome," she says quietly, looking down at her hands.

I have no idea what she has just said, but all the same, I understand. She tells me that she has described Erik's behaviour to a developmental pediatrician friend of hers and that everything adds up. Autism. She had also taught Scott and has described his emerging brilliance to her colleague. The Hedley family fits the mould.

Although I ought to be appreciative, I am shocked. I deny. I come home and google autism and that word, Asperger. There is no denying: we are a good fit.

I talk to Frank, and we decide that while the overlap is evident, perhaps Erik has some traits, but that's it. Autism is a spectrum, after all, and we all possess the traits to some degree. We know we ought to do something, but life becomes frenzied again. We are posted to British Columbia, and we are gearing up to drive across Canada. A follow-up and diagnosis will have to wait.

But the door has opened a crack, and I begin to see Erik in a new light. Knowledge is power, and knowing that he might be wired differently changes the way I see him. I begin to understand my son.

CHAPTER 10

Do the Right Thing

SPRING HAS COME TO HALIFAX, Nova Scotia. The ice has melted, the bulbs are up and so is our FOR SALE sign. It is official: we are on the move again, this time 6,343 kilometres west to Vancouver Island.

We have three children under seven, and keeping things afloat and real estate ready while planning for a major move is tricky. No, not tricky. Herculean. Nearly impossible. But it has to be done. Where there's a will, there's a way. And now, we have the added dimension of a possible diagnosis.

I am busy. But I am also curious, and although I resist the notion that sweet Erik might have autism, I am drawn to reading more about it. Everything about it. I am compelled and repelled. I want to fill myself up with knowledge because then at least I might know for sure one way or another. I want to know; I don't want to know. Autism is not part of the plan.

Knowledge *is* power—to see the right thing; to deny the right thing; to understand the right thing; and to do the right thing. As I read, I silently rebel—angry, incredulous and lost, trying in one moment to brace for impact, and in the next, to beat back the likelihood of a diagnosis. I see myself from above, the computer screen bright with new words, me, drawn close, motionless, my face illuminated and dull. But oddly, the words are a relief because there is kinship and comfort in shared trauma. My breathing slows, and I am learning what I might need to know. What I read *does* fit; Erik is close, and if I can make things easier for him in the meantime, I will.

School seems to be getting worse. Erik comes home from kindergarten and retreats to his bedroom. He tells me nothing about his day. Zero. He is icy, stunned. We are both stunned, and I imagine us as dazed bookends to all that is happening between us. He is just coping. And so am I.

SENDING ERIK TO ALL-DAY KINDERGARTEN seems extreme to me. He is young and attending from 8 a.m. to 3 p.m. is taxing mentally and physically. So instead of adhering to the rules, I call on heart and instinct, and it tells me what makes sense for a little boy so clearly out of his comfort zone. Not this.

Take him to the water and feed his soul.

I hear my inner voice speak, and what it says makes sense: to tap into Erik, immerse him in what he loves. Water.

I start pulling him out of school two afternoons a week, and those hours are idyllic for us both. We dress in our comfy clothes and become marine biologists on the lake behind our house. Pedalling the little blue and white Mother's Day boat, we visit beaver lodges and hover on the glassy surface adjacent to the muddy entrances, still, patient, holding out for incoming traffic. We imagine a cross-section of the twiggy accommodation and marvel at the exterior: conical and symmetrical. How do they build these so perfectly? What is their language? The engineering is exquisite.

Sometimes we say nothing. We sit and watch and gesture. We are communicating, and it is rich. In our stillness, we are telling each other that silence is rare and it is sacred. Our days are bursting with sounds. And now the only sound we hear is a distant lawnmower and the wind as it sweeps down the lake and tugs at a nearby dock. Ropes groan and then go slack. Closer to me, I can hear Erik breathing through his nose, deliberately and loudly. This style of breath is also visual: Erik's face is peaceful, focussed, and his tongue pulses up and slightly out, forcing air into his nasal cavity. There is a rhythm to it, this breathing, and it sounds yogic, tranquil. In years to come, we will call this Erik's *happy sound*; the only thing that compares is the contented purr of a cat. Erik purrs on the lake. He does not purr at school.

We pedal over to the bobbing bleach bottles and decorate them, adding one glittery whale or dolphin sticker to each bleach bottle marker. I suggest plastering the markers, going wild with the stickers and creating a masterpiece, but Erik is disciplined—more so than his mother—and insists on frugality. "One sticker each time," he says. *That's the rule. We don't waste stickers.*"

To an observer, it would seem he is parroting me, but in reality, he is reminding me and parroting himself. We count the stickers, one per visit, and we imagine that we are scientists on a vital mission. Tipping back our heads, we contemplate the clouds, and we conjure up distorted faces and warped, cottony characters. Now *this* is bliss.

Best of all, we create two labels. On one of the bleach bottles, which flags a cluster of large, protruding boulders in the lake, I write in bold black letters, "ERIK HEDLEY MARKER." Erik beams.

"I am the bottle's *owner*?" he asks shyly.

"No, you are the bottle's *protector*," I say. "The bottle is for everyone who uses the lake. It shows boaters where the rocks are . . . you know . . . close to the surface. But your job is to make sure the bottle stays safe—and beautiful," I add, handing him a sticker.

"Erik Hedley Marker" becomes covered with sparkly foil stickers of whales and dolphins and sea turtles, not quite lake material, but this is the age of Nemo, and Erik adores the ocean. We pretend.

The other label is for Erik, and it is inspired by the first, the marker. On a piece of masking tape, I write the words "Lake Protector," and I stick that on his orange life jacket. He glances down at the tape, strokes it, and like a novice employee handed a box of new business cards, Erik revels in his title. In this role as warden of our community lake, Erik is focussed and responsible. Give a dedicated person a title and watch them grow. Erik is thrilled. He is talking, and he is fully present, fully engaged. I like this word *fully*, and it is one I aim to cultivate in Erik.

Our pedal boat expeditions are mindfulness at its best: there is nowhere else we would rather be. Water delivers us to higher ground; it is as though we have escaped something that doesn't fit. We are freed. Maybe this is how my father feels when he is flying. I smile as I pedal around the lake, silently thanking him for helping me know what to do.

I think of my grandmother, Mary, and to hot dogs skewered and roasted over beach fires and served in driftwood beach forts. I feel the enchantment here on the lake I felt as a child, roaming freely on the beach.

~

EARLY ON, MY GRANDPARENTS WERE vague faces in black and white photos. With us in Nova Scotia and them in Vancouver, we were Canadian counterparts, living separate lives, east and west. Things improved when we moved to Vancouver Island and trekked across the Strait of Georgia to visit their Surrey home. Nana and Poppa were a remarkable duo, and like my mother and father, one created beauty, the other function.

Oh, how Mary's gardens grew, attracting busloads to tour their backyard retreat; pausing at the desert-like rock garden to admire the chunky purple agate and the smooth pink granite, the billowy lava and the puffs of coral tucked among cacti and emerald succulents; stepping inside the earthy greenhouse to inhale horticulture in its fundamental form; strolling along the narrow Asian corridor where decades-old bonsai trees grew to no more than a gnarly twenty-five centimetres in chipped ceramic vessels. There were rows of tumbling sun plants; fragrant shade plants; trellises bright with sweet peas that smelled like honeyed perfume when you stuck your face in them. Little arched bridges ferried you to quiet destinations. How I loved to run and gesture and make up imaginary garden tours, spilling out facts that were most often wrong.

What I remember most was the subtle fragrances and the feeling of being immersed in a hushed land far removed from the ordinary gravel road and rural landscape out front. Here, I could pretend I was Mary Lennox in *The Secret Garden*, a botanical explorer and recorder of all things Latin. Nana taught me the proper words for plants, and I carefully jotted them down with my hot pink Flair marker. I was Nature Girl, soothed and recalibrated. That's how I always felt afterward: renewed.

When I was eleven, Mary and Jack moved to a windswept beachfront property. This time they were closer, at Miracle Beach on Vancouver Island. Mary liked the spirited name, and there was something miraculous about nibbling grilled cheese in a driftwood lean-to. In this, Mary was an intuitive early educator: meet children where they love to be, and you will tap into their soul.

~

IN PULLING ERIK OUT OF school and taking him to the lake, I aim to do the same. In discovering these soulful places, Erik shifts from overwhelmed and withdrawn to animated, engaged and expressive. Sometimes he is quiet and contemplative, but that's all right. We need to be both.

Years later, Erik will tell me that our pedal boat afternoons are the only memories he has of kindergarten. The rest has very likely been scrubbed from his timeline.

Sometimes rules need to be bent. I am told by the school that we should be adhering to attendance guidelines, and I politely reply that we will make the attendance quota. And besides, I know where my son is. He is with me, and he is peaceful. He is talking, and he is engaged, enamoured with life. I am doing my best to ease his anxiety, I tell the school. I need to keep my son in our world. And that is all that matters.

CHAPTER 11

Anticipation

As for autism and Erik, I read, I ponder and then I scrutinize Erik with new discerning eyes. I find myself staring at him and then quickly looking away, not wanting him to feel inspected and dissected. It seems strange to be doing this, to be regarding little Erik through this diagnostic lens. To me, it feels like betrayal, as though I am being dutiful but disloyal. I am not convinced Erik has both feet solidly on the spectrum. He is close but not fully—there is that word again—on. We have a neighbour across the street whose daughter has autism, and Kaitlyn is non-verbal, breathtakingly beautiful and solidly locked into her own space. She and Erik are close in age, but to me, that is the only overlap.

Later that year when Erik is diagnosed with autism on Vancouver Island, Kaitlyn's mom will write to me and offer support. She will say, respectfully, that she has always wondered whether Erik is on the spectrum. Knowledge truly is power because she has seen what I have not. And she has been correct.

But for now, we need to make a smooth passage across the country. Transitions and change are excruciating for Erik. I don't need a diagnosis to tell me this. So I set out to make sure that our twelve-day summer trek across Canada will be as pleasant and predictable as possible.

The days will be long, and attention will be short—that much I know. The online autism literature tells me that children on the spectrum do not have a solid grasp of time, time passing and how best to fill their time. I learn that children with autism are visual and that they need to be taught this way. Perfect. It is also the way I process, learn and teach. This ought to be a reasonable fit.

Autism or not, I remember how untethered Erik was when we left Barrie three years ago. This floating sensation translated into whining, withdrawal and a lot of self-chatter—comfort chat—in his own space. He was the unravelling child: the farther we drove from home, the tinier he became. I want to avoid unravel and withdrawal.

This time we will strike out proactively and take all three kids on our spring house-hunting trip as we have done in the past, but this time we will make them an active part of the decision-making. Instead of depositing them at a sitter, we will have them come along from house to house, tiny clipboards in hand. We will immerse our children in this move.

"Look, you guys!" I say, pulling out markers and notepads from a shopping bag a month before departure. "We'll make a house-hunting trip travel kit! You three will be like mini real estate helpers . . . We'll be a team!"

I try to infuse them with excitement and responsibility. They appear crow-like, drawn to the vibrant markers and the glittery stickers. But what they *really* love is the compact camera we have purchased for this trip and beyond. It is a small device we call the *kids' camera*, and they are thrilled to have something that is exclusively theirs—their eye on the world that did not belong first to us. *This* could be fun! My hope is that they will become what they are told, what they hold *and* behold. That is the plan.

In April, we fly to Comox on Vancouver Island and prepare to dig in. We have one week to purchase a house. In life, there is a gap between paper and practice, between life imagined and life lived. But we do manage a version of the paper plan because the choices are slim, and the real estate trekking is minimal. Having three ducklings in tow with checklists and spaces to draw what they see turns out to be stabilizing. There is a sense that we are in this together—an attuned army unit, a team. By the time the house is purchased, the kids have seen it several times: bedrooms are staked out, the backyard is scoped out, and the neighbourhood is mapped out. We are processing our new life.

Curiously, the experience illuminates each of our children with uncanny precision: Heather has made a few fast friends; Scott has noticed that the house addresses increase, inexplicably, by increments of fourteen, and Erik has photographed our new home with the attentiveness of a claims adjuster. Light switches, heat vents, light fixtures, doorways and vistas through windows and doors beckon; captivated, he captures them all. Erik is partway west in his mind's eye. He has created a set of transition visuals.

BACK IN HALIFAX, WE ARE a family without mess, odour or clutter. That is the real estate façade. We dash out whenever there is a house showing, and we plan for the July trek across Canada. Thinking visually, I make Erik a travel binder, the first of many graphic diaries throughout the years to follow.

"Look, Erik!" I say one afternoon after a pedal around the lake. "I've made you a cross-Canada travel book! Your very own!"

I flash the cover, and he stops running happy circles in front of the television and meanders over. Erik loves comparisons and contrasts; the binder cover lures him. It's a split screen, with our current Nova Scotia house for sale on the top half of the page and our soon-to-be BC house sold on the bottom. You cannot judge a book by its cover, but this one is promising. It is also bait.

"For sale . . . and sold!" Erik chirps, resuming his happy circles. And as the laps build, "Old and new! Here and there! Near and far!" Like a clown producing infinite coloured hankies, the word pairs keep coming, and Erik giggles, hopping on the spot now, sounding Seuss-like as he inventories the contrasts.

His eyes are bright. He is beyond baited, and he runs a few more joyful circles, processing and repeating what he has just said. I let him do what he needs to do. He reminds me of an aircraft spooling up. Eventually, he parks himself next to me, wiggly, and we open the binder together.

Page one, a map of Canada tucked into a clear folio sleeve, details our route. Numbered stickers on the plastic overlay show the overnight stops. Erik has an overview, and like a Braille corridor, he closes his eyes and traces our route across the country, bump by bump, with his index finger. He does it again, eyes open this time. The happy sound kicks in.

As for how the days will play out, I have diagrammed a typical day with the help of Google Clip Art on page two of his travel book.

"What are these pages?" he asks, jabbing a finger at a section of plastic folders filled with paper. Some are blank, some printed. "Well," I say, "these blank ones are for drawing what you see as you look out the window . . . or maybe you want to do this in our hotel room at night. But only if you want to."

Big brother Scott translates his world through Lego and action figure play, re-enacting what he observes around him. Erik draws his perceptions, sketches it out until he figures it out, making sense of the swirl that is his life.

"And these ones," I say, indicating the printed pages, "these are Spot the Difference."

As he registers this, I hear an intake of breath; I feel a little squirm beside me, followed by a ramping up of the happy sound. Erik is purring. "Can I do one now?"

"Sure!" I say, and I set him up at the kitchen table with his new book. He and the binder are fast friends.

There is one more thing. With about a month to go before our summer departure, we make a countdown chain. As we cut construction paper strips for our chain, I am again age seven.

~

I AM STANDING BESIDE MY wooden desk, at attention, saluting the Canadian flag. Our wise teacher has taught us to manage time by making it concrete, something we can see and comprehend. She has us cut strips of construction paper, all shades or a themed colour, depending upon the season or event, bend the strips into loops, staple these together into a chain and write numbers on the links, one for each day. We hang up the chain and count down to the special event by ripping off one link per day. As the chain becomes shorter, the target day draws closer. If there is something that needs to be done, we have a visual for how much time we have to do it. As a big-eyed child, these chains ground me, organize me, prepare me and excite me. I love these chains!

~

THIRTY YEARS LATER, MY CHILDREN, Erik especially, adore these chains. Seeing is soothing. Predictable. Reassuring. Erik craves all three.

There is something else. I am told that in our buy-it-now-have-it-immediately world, the joy of anticipation has become obsolete. There is pleasure and gratification in waiting, wondering and imagining. I want my children to celebrate the wait.

We cut and we staple and we dangle our masterpiece from the kitchen curtain rod: thirty links, multicoloured, cascading to the floor like a storybook serpent. Each day, we rip off one construction paper loop, and like a Christmas advent, we count down. We anticipate.

Once on the road, the cross-country books take over. I make three because what's good for Erik is good for all. The books get us to BC. Time out of time on the road without any social commitments or expectations is an ideal life. But it's not a real life. No matter, aside from a van malfunction in Sudbury, Ontario, and putting in way too much time hanging out at an oversized roadside attraction, the Big Nickel, while the van is repaired, we make it to the Pacific coast. We are overjoyed to be on Vancouver Island. Our new life has begun.

CHAPTER 12

Rose-Coloured Glasses

As EXCITING AS IT IS to be back on the west coast and immersed in glorious peaks and salt water vistas, it is a strange summer in many ways. My grandmother Mary's health is failing; my father's cancer has stepped up and spread out, and my son is dangling somewhere between speculation and diagnosis. It is our limbo summer, waiting for things to get better or to get worse. We are three for three: worse, on all counts.

But this is the story of Erik and autism, and our focus will remain there. As with anything in life, though, there is context, and that backdrop plays into my capacity to absorb, to cope and to function. Autism is never stand-alone. I am juggling on many fronts. This is nothing new, but sometimes the context is beyond the ordinary, as it is in the summer of 2004. We are bathed in death and disease, and in that context, we tackle diagnosis. We live in 3-D.

WE SETTLE INTO OUR NEW life, our new house and our new neighbourhood. Everything is new, and I like this because it is both exhilarating and forgiving. We are not expected to be good at anything: we are new. With time, there are expectations, but right now, we are the newbies on the block, and much is excused. But at the same time, first impressions matter. They count and they cement. This occurs to me as I peek out the living room window one afternoon.

From behind a window shade, I spy our three children playing basketball in the driveway, now four and five children. The neighbour's kids have drifted over. Our young ones are starting to connect and to seamlessly integrate, just as children do. Most children.

I sigh as I note the fluffy-haired outlier. Erik is not playing basketball. He is running, but not with the group and not for the ball. He is running precise, animated circles in our driveway. I use the word animated because of the way his legs flick up behind him, elf-like as he runs, and because on his face is a kaleidoscope of lightning expressions, appearing and evaporating rapidly, like clouds in a brisk wind. Pressed to his right eye is a red snow reflector, and as he runs, he frames his path with this reflector. He is clearly happy, very happy, performing his version of seeing the world through rose-coloured glasses, and by all accounts, he is having an incredible time on his own, outside the group.

And then I hear it, a shrill question from one of the little boy neighbours.

"Hey! *What's with your brother?* Why does he *do* that, run with that red thingy?"

Time stops. They all turn to stare at Erik, and like the Grinch, stuck, but not for long, Scott steps up and explains, "Oh, that. Well, Erik is very energetic and he likes to run . . . and his eyes are light, see? Pale blue. The red plastic thing is to shield his eyes."

Scott is matter of fact. He does not apologize; he simply explains and carries on. I am proud of him. I could not have done better. And because he is cool about it, the others shrug and turn away. Basketball is back on, and Erik is out of the spotlight . . . for now.

I observe a quick flash between Heather and Scott. They can both exhale. This will become the new norm, this explaining. I imagine Scott and Heather trying to comprehend and describe what they do not understand. Now *that* is a neat trick. Our brother's behaviour is odd, but how to make it seem regular? Normal? Acceptable? Understood? And what *is* it, this cloak that Erik wears? It's hard to explain what you don't know.

As I turn from the scene and step away from the window, something else strikes me. Whatever this is we are looking at, it has not been abrupt and in no way foisted upon us. It has been subtle, stealthy and steady: a slow, low drumroll toward different.

ANOTHER FORM OF SELF-REGULATION THIS limbo summer is the ongoing search for, identification and collection of "What's not allowed?" signs. They are abundant, and Erik is keen to collect them all, as the challenge goes.

We visit a beach, and there are rules: no dogs off leashes; no doggie-do on the beach; no removing driftwood; no allowing dogs to chase birds; no swimming alone; no littering; no loitering; no campfires outside the designated rings. The signs, when you are open to noticing, are ubiquitous. Erik has woken us up to rules, signs and symbols. Have I spent a lifetime looking but not seeing?

We compile seven mini photo books of these picture signs, all before the age of digital photography. We are diligent, and Erik is delighted. He is coping, and we are obliging, doing our best to accommodate and understand his perspective. It seems like a small concession. The signs and the books make him happy. And a happy Erik is a happy family. I would later be told and quite agree, "When one member of the family has autism, the whole family has autism." At this point, we are not officially there, but unofficially, we understand that we are sliding in two directions: on and all in.

Another bit of self-regulation is the emergence of Jungle Boy. I read that children with autism often attach to a character, real or fictitious, and become that persona. The theory is that it is easier to take on the traits and sound bites of a beloved book or movie hero than it is to make sense of who you are, especially if you are struggling each day to figure that out.

Late mornings throughout this 3-D summer, true to the literature, Erik pulls on a silky Peter Pan costume, and he hangs out in his jungle bedroom, pointy green felt hat bobbing from stuffed tiger to leafy wallpaper to mini spotted sofa.

"Welcome to my jungle home!" a joyful falsetto squeaks, clicking on a sound effects device. Songbirds and a burbling stream float us south of the equator. The effect is soothing, immersive.

"What would you like to do today?" Jungle Boy chirps, stepping aside. "Fish or swim?"

In this, our curious boy blurs to Jungle Boy, calm and content in his leafy lair. Leave him in his emerald oasis and Erik is the best version of himself. Remove the pointy green felt hat and shiny jade costume, take him outside and expect him to integrate with neighbours? Things become tricky, cloudy and turbulent. Autism is looking more and more likely.

What I do not know is that we are not alone. There is autism in the 'hood, but I don't see it, at least not right away.

ONE DAY I AM IN the kitchen, and I notice a great rustling in the cherry tree at the side of the house. A raccoon? Again? No, much larger this time. It's a neighbourhood boy, and he is wedged near the top of the tree, gorging on sun-ripened cherries. My song brain kicks in, switches gears, and as though selecting a Jeopardy category, chooses "Television Commercials from the 1970s": Jell-O.

Hey, you kids, get out of that Jell-O tree! comes to mind, but I do not open the window and shout at him. I meander outside, and there I meet the boy's mother at the base of the cherry tree, trying to coax her son down and out of our yard. She is embarrassed and is trying to normalize his behaviour. It is familiar, this smoothing over, and something begins to click in.

This is the boy, age twelve, highly articulate and intelligent, a ninety-seventh percentile academia kid, who runs through our house with Scott, strumming on the guitar one moment, feeding CDs through the mail slot the next, and outside, seemingly invincible or oblivious to street hazards as he weaves his bicycle back and forth across the street. There is a pattern, I decide, a link between this boy who picks cherries and Erik who runs: autism.

IN THIS MOMENT, I MARVEL at the chance and frequency of autism in all three of our recent neighbourhoods. Back in Barrie, two doors down, twins with autism; in Halifax, Kaitlyn, adjacent to us, profoundly affected; and directly across from us, Cooper, with a handful of spectrum traits: a tiptoer, curious, social, likeable, highly intelligent, highly active and also highly unpredictable. And now, the brainy, cherry-picking mathematician here in Comox. We have been three for three. Will there be more?

AUGUST RECEDES AND SEPTEMBER BECKONS. We head back to school. All three kids are in a French immersion elementary, which is also my former junior high school, a reassuring relic from the sixties and seventies. It is bizarre to be here again, wandering the hallways and entering Erik's Grade 1 classroom to realize that this was the science wing. I bisected an earthworm in the very spot where Erik sits for morning circle. Except that he does not sit. And here we are, firmly rooted in the present: Grade 1.

I am positioned at the back of Erik's Grade 1 classroom. It is September, and I strike early. I am here ostensibly to help the teacher, but in fact, I am here to spy, to observe my son, to see him in action, or inaction, at school. I am not disappointed. I am, instead, startled.

Quiet, compliant Erik is anything but cooperative during circle time. He is decidedly outside the circle, the outsider. While the class sits cross-legged and gamely recites the days of the week *en francais*, Erik is sprawled a metre to the side, detached. He picks at his shoe. A rubber flap on the side of his runner fascinates him. *Thud, thud, thud.* He does not look up, and he does not recite. He is working the rubber flap, breathing hard, and every once in a while, he shouts something—a peculiar whoop—out loud. Very loudly.

"Ahhhhharrrr-gah!"

While the class laughs, I sit in disbelief. Erik?

I remind myself that autism longs for groundedness, predictability and order; that context is everything and that environment calls the shots. Erik is not back at home in his quiet safe haven. He is wandering in the minefield that is school, and he is reacting. I am beginning to understand. While other children can easily regulate to their surroundings, Erik cannot.

So this is autism? I wonder. I am about to find out.

CHAPTER 13

Cirrus . . . Seriously?

WHEN A PHONE CALL COMES a week later, I am ready. It is not the classroom teacher calling, but the special education teacher assigned to the school. There has been some discussion. Could we please talk?

Here we go again. But this time I am prepared. I have lived this script before; I have rehearsed the lines. I have been digesting a possible autism diagnosis for five months and across many thousand kilometres. I am halfway toward acceptance—or at least, acknowledgment.

I speak with the special education teacher on the phone that afternoon. She talks; I listen. I breathe. I can hardly do either. The conversation becomes indelible, my reactions, etched. I am sitting on the bed in the master bedroom, tracing the quilting on the bedspread, stitch by stitch, over and over and over, with my index finger as she speaks. I am learning new words. I am forcing calm.

She continues to speak, and I continue to trace. The stitches become a tiny track for my finger, and I notice by feel that it is a figure eight. In the years to come I will look back on this loopy pattern, and I will see that it is somehow appropriate, for our path will not be linear. It will loop back on itself many times. I keep tracing.

"He perseverates," she says. It's a new word, and although I have never heard it, I know that it describes Erik: he who repeats. "He also stims." Another word for the word bank. I keep on tracing and retracing the swirly, silky stitching, processing, processing, processing . . . We are circling the rim. I know that, and I just want her to get at it, to say it. So I jump in, free-falling with forced confidence.

"You think he has . . . autism?" I ask, in a voice I do not know.
"Yes. We do." And of course, he does.

THE BALL IS ROLLING, AND I cannot stop it. Everything I read and see points to autism. So I say, "Yes, book the appointments. Let's do this." We are underway.

Are there waits? No, this is Vancouver Island in 2004. We are asked by the school multidisciplinary team whether we want a referral to the popular pediatrician with the long waiting list or to the fellow with no waits. We choose the latter. All we need is a referral to a psychologist.

Erik likes the doctor because he has a big woolly docile sheep-dog that pads down the hall, right into the diagnostic room. The dog is a slow dutiful plodder, and we feel comfort in the canine accompaniment; this is more like an animal shelter than a chil-dren's clinic. In the inappropriateness of the furry escort, there is zero stress. I laugh to myself, *Who is outside the box?*

As for Erik, he perseverates over the drooling dog; lies on the furry floor of the examination room, lining up miniature cars and studies his right hand at close range (for animal fur?). While I speak with the doctor, he then toe-walks precariously out of the examination room, avoiding eye contact and sidestepping scat-tered dog toys. We are an impressive bundle of red flags, and we get our referral.

As Erik lies there rearranging his cars and spinning their wheels, I speak with the doctor or, rather, listen to him. I am not given much time to speak.

"Well, we're looking at *something*," he begins. "There are pills I can prescribe for the inattention, but he may gain weight . . . There are always side effects . . ."

In the middle of processing, I jump in, "No, no pills, please. Skills, I want him to learn . . . what he has . . . and what to do . . . and, what *is* it that he has?" I ask. I feel my brain numbing.

"Well, could be some OCD . . . Tourette's . . . maybe PDD-NOS . . . ," he says.

I recognize the first two but not the last. "What is that one . . . the last one?" I indicate.

"Oh, a non-specified, lesser form of autism," he says, and then, leaning forward, "and that would be the *best*-case scenario. What you do not want," he says, "is for this to be full-blown autism."

I feel light-headed, as though we have been baited and have stepped smack into a trap. Perhaps the dog has a function after all? For better or worse, we are in.

Erik and I sit in the psychologist's office. Because Erik is six, I accompany him into the interview room. We pull up to a little table covered with chunky puzzles and toys designed to gauge how a child like Erik reacts and interacts. He is asked to describe a picture—an animation of children playing in a busy playground. Easy. He does this all the time. But he baulks and gazes, instead, beyond the interviewer to a window that frames something much more interesting—cloud formations. *Cirrus. Seriously? Has the psychologist ordered up wispy, white clouds, Erik's favourite? Does he have to place Erik facing the only window in the room?*

These random thoughts fill my head as I observe my son. I know Erik can describe the picture; he has done so for Frank and me countless times at home as we read bedtime stories. But when it counts, he sells himself short. Or perhaps he is revealing his authenticity. *I would rather talk about clouds than comics, thanks.* Perhaps only that. But the experts have asked for comics, and Erik cannot stop talking about the cirrus clouds beyond the interviewer's head.

"Weather change!" Erik chirps, jumping up from the table, scattering the puzzle and gesturing with his right hand, eyes ablaze. "We might get rain tonight!"

And at that moment, I know what we are also going to get. A diagnosis: classic autism.

I drive home deep in thought, head in the cirrus clouds. It was never that Erik could not talk about the comic. It was that he would rather talk about clouds. He did not perform when a performance was necessary. Either way, my son has a new name. Am I shocked? No. Devastated? Yes. We have been wading in jelly up to this point. Now we are standing in cement.

In one defining moment, my child's name changes. While he has been Erik up until today, in a pen stroke he is now something different. One moment, Erik; the next, Autistic. And this will stick. People like labels and categories, and my son has both.

From this day on, I will devote myself to proving my son's worth. Erik *has* autism; he *is not* autism, but people do not comprehend this. Erik has been neatly classified and categorized. Stamp. I begin to look for ways that this label can possibly work for us, because so far, it feels damning.

According to the *Diagnostic and Statistical Manual of Mental Disorders*, our son has a severe and pervasive disorder. These words strike hard. Severe. Pervasive. Disorder. How could this be? And what now? Pervasive is heavy-duty. It means that whatever Erik has, it has the potential to percolate into every nuance of his being: social, communication, behaviour, speech, sensory, motor skills, and ability to learn, to process, to reason, to function, to connect and to love. Like an oil spill, autism is everywhere.

My question becomes this: *Where do I start and where do I stop?*

What baffles me is there doesn't seem to be a roadmap, a guidebook or a plan in place. Why not? We are not the first to mop up oil, attend to the spill. I crave order and direction, a blueprint—please? I find none.

"WELL, YOU COULD START WITH social skills. He will need to be taught pretty much everything from scratch. And you could always hire an occupational therapist. He will need help with the sensory bit."

There is a lot of *could*, and this strikes me as odd. Autism seems slippery and its treatment arbitrary, as though we have stumbled upon something new when, clearly, we have not.

I am told a lot, and every word is heavy, weighty and gloomy. Song brain tries to cheer me up and calls up Journey's "Don't Stop Believin'." But my head aches, as does my heart; I feel blindsided even though I should not. I have had months and the span of a large country to warm up to this. I had a warning shot. But you never know how you will react and what *devastated* or *trauma* or *shock* feels like until you are wearing each of them. All at once the words grow flesh, and they attach themselves to you. In an instant, you are steeped with feeling and knowing. You are wrapped up, tangled in these words, and nothing else matters.

My second question is mostly to myself, and it is this: *How much do I buy in and how much do I tune in?*

Erik is still Erik, after all, and we have made it this far on our own. *Is it really this bad? Do I need to believe everything? To buy in to what I am told? Surely he is not all of this word, this damning pervasiveness? Is he? Have I been given the whole picture? Both sides? Is this objective or subjective, this report? Autism cannot be all deficit? Can it?* It seems all or not, and I have a hard time believing that we are a slam dunk.

My head is awhirl, awash with plans one moment, hesitation and dread the next, and then denial. I want to throw this fish back. This is not the word I want for my son. We become what we are told, and this is not what I want to be told about Erik. I feel very tired. Defeated.

I come home and sit outside on the deck with Frank. We sip wine and we talk, examining autism as though back in school, dissection tools in hand. I report what I have heard, what I feel, what I know. I feel overwhelmed.

Frank is thoughtful, but more than anything, Frank is frank. He is not as outwardly devastated as I am, but he is attentive, discerning. He does not jump easily, and maybe this is part of his dental training and, beyond, his army persona. He weighs and considers and does not get lost in speculation. This is good because I do; I project and I torment myself with gloomy *what ifs*.

"Erik is still Erik," Frank begins. "Let's carry on, sign him up, treat him the very same way and see where this goes."

CHAPTER 14

Puppet or Puppeteer?

I SIT WITH MY WINE and allow Frank's words to float and to settle. I wish I could be so pragmatic. Logical. But I am not. And this is not black and white. I foresee grey. Lots of grey. Glancing over at him, I think back to a simpler time.

~

BEFORE WE WERE MARRIED, WE were interviewed by the minister who would perform the ceremony, part of the obligatory screening and marriage counselling attached to the church. I figured our romance was none of the church's business, but being a list ticker, I went along with it.

I was asked a simple question, and I tried to keep a straight face. The question was "Why Frank?" and I knew what I was supposed to say, what the right words were, but my brain was forming something else, "Well, he's a handsome army dentist with lots of accumulated leave, a posting to Europe and a bank account that he can't seem to whittle down. I thought I could help." This was my inner dialogue and, entertaining as it was, I did not say this. Instead, sweetly, "His glass is always half full and so is mine." I meant it, and I passed the test. We were halfway there.

Now, his turn. "Why Teresa?"

"Because she potentiates. She makes something good out of anything. And I want to be a part of that."

In telling me this, his reply, I melted. It was thoughtful and authentic and very much frank Frank. It was also the way I wished to be seen, a potentiator. So I accepted and wore that label. This was one I liked.

I married a man much like myself. He is organized, meticulous, a planner, a traveller and a systemizer. Much later, I decided that we are a perfect storm for autism. He, a dentist in the army—very systems-oriented—and I, a teacher with a curriculum development and training background. It is the marriage of two structured, systematic people. Order is in the genes.

In Germany we lived a fairytale. Our home was a section in a medieval castle wall, part of a grand estate situated on the Dutch border. Newly married, we moved into the old castle wash-house, freshly renovated with turrets and keyhole embrasures. Just outside our home and the outbuildings that made up the outer wall, there was a moat. Beyond that, a German *Schloss*, complete with a baron and a baroness and their three beautiful daughters. It was a magnificent setting and an extraordinary life. For three years, we travelled and hosted gala costume parties in the larger of the two castle turrets, and I worked feverishly on my master's degree; Frank, on NATO teeth.

We returned to Canada late summer, 1996, with our Dutch-born baby boy, Scott. Next came Erik and Heather, and as the toy arsenal grew, our life became decidedly less romantic. Germany had been a remarkable chapter and launch into marriage. It was all diapers and Disney for the foreseeable future. But that was okay; we were too busy to lament the loss of exquisite Rhine wine, our trusty BMW and Euro-travels. We had produced three children in four years, and we were a busy Ontario family. We had switched gears.

~

WITH AN AUTISM DIAGNOSIS, WE have again switched gears. To live is to adjust.

Frank's plan sounds so simple—and it is, looking in from the outside. I feel comfort and also vague resentment because I am front line, and I am too close to this battle, wearing the muddy boots. I know that we will regard Erik the same way at home, but I also know that once this label is bared, our son will be forever viewed through it, not alongside it. I know what labels can do because I grew up, thankfully, with mostly very good ones. But as a teacher I have seen the flip side, and it is clingy and damning. The good words enhance and uplift; the bad ones adhere and obscure. It is the sticky ones that people use as lenses. I have seen this, too, and I fear it for Erik.

There are also irrational but valid thoughts. *Make this go away.* What if we accept this word—because it does seem to fit—but what if we choose not to use this information? Autism is, after all, largely an invisible entity. "Thanks so much," we could say to the doctors, "but Erik is our son and we've decided not to travel this path. We've decided that his self-esteem and mental health are too important to be cloaked in what right now is a negative descriptor. We don't want this for our son." And who would? I am certain they would understand. What parent would not?

In these random thoughts, I am chasing my tail. I keep coming back to the fact that Erik, in public, is floundering, and this may only intensify as he gets older and there are increased social expectations. We need help.

There are also selfish thoughts. I have no choice but to be front line. Part of me wants to be a second-line troop and return to teaching and simply observe Erik, once removed, miraculously made better by others. But I cannot. Frank has the primary career; I need to be there for Erik. I am Erik's mother, and as such, I wear his other shoe. I am walking Erik's walk, and I am his first responder, his lifelong teacher. I am Erik's translator and spokesperson. I am his anchor, and ironically, he is also mine. By default, we seem to be inseparable, puppet and puppeteer.

My friend Sarah will later suggest that, big picture, I, too, am a puppet: I work Erik's controls but ultimately, autism controls me. Autism is two way. Buddha's hands speak the truth.

I suppose what I really want is a choice, not a foist. But this is part of the motherhood package, and I have heard that we are given exactly what we can handle. In taking on this diagnosis, I am becoming more of who I am. I heed the call to step up and to step in.

I RETURN TO THE EXPERTS. I am told that my child will always need my scaffolding. I am told that my child will always need an assistant at school. I am told that autism precludes connection and friendships and reciprocity. I am told my son may never learn to read. I am told that my son lacks empathy. I am told that connecting with others will be nearly impossible for him. I am told so much.

I am also told that Erik might be better off going to school in English. He is having a hard time making connections non-verbally, so it is best he communicates in his mother tongue. I get this, but it means pulling him out of his school because it is completely French, no English. This also means separating Erik from his siblings. With a pounding heart, I go school shopping.

But first I sit and think about what it is I want for Erik. What am I looking for in a school? I would not go grocery shopping without a list, so why would I head out school shopping empty-handed? I sit and write my intent. It's hard because I know so little about autism. But I do know my son, and what I decide is this. I want:

1. a school headed by a principal who is open to neurodiversity. Good leadership has a trickle-down effect. I want the right atmosphere, sculpted by the right leader.
2. a school with enough specialized staff and materials to support Erik. If the school is too small, the resources might be insufficient; if it is too large, Erik might become lost in numbers. I am looking for "just right" in the three bears of school size and scope.
3. a school with teachers who look beyond the surface. I want a teacher who is creative and teaches to her students, not at them. I am looking for Miracle-Gro because Erik needs nurturing and an infusion of nourishment.

There is more, but these are the essentials. Leadership. Resources. Nourishers. I am looking for all three, and with my list written, I feel focussed. I am ready.

I call principals and set up interviews. There are two tepid meetings, and like a game of Battleship, I get a few partial hits, but mostly misses. Just when I am feeling that I am being too picky and idealistic, I find a match for Erik, right up the road from our house. I am struck by the kindness of the principal. He wants to get this right for Erik—teach to Erik's original inclinations. He is a glimmer of light.

"We'd love to have Erik join us. All students are welcome here at Valley View Elementary School."

I think I might cry.

I drive home, and I am feeling more hopeful than I have felt in months. I am also feeling realistic. We face another hurdle: transitioning Erik from one school to another. This will be three schools in a matter of months. It will not be easy.

CHAPTER 15

An Astute Individual

WE LURCH. WE LEARN. I begin to have a series of epiphanies. I realize, as each thought crystalizes and settles, that these personal truths are seeded in my past. My reaction to autism existed long before I was handed Erik's diagnosis.

How I see my child is how my child will come to see himself.

In this realization, I am reminded of my father.

How do I see Erik? Original or damaged? Teachable or limited? Astute or average? Disabled or differently abled? The words I choose will dictate outcomes. With words, I sculpt. With words, I was sculpted.

~

IN MY LANKY HEIGHT AND pale blue eyes, I looked like my father. I was Tom's boy, his shadow, hovering, helping, absorbing. I was with him constantly and was in awe of his capabilities. In my eyes he could do anything, and his abilities and attributes were many. He was a navigator, a pilot, a flight instructor, a poet, a pool player, a woodworker, a guitar player, an inventor, a singer, a comedian, a car mechanic, a gardener and a storyteller. But most of all, my father was a teacher. To him, life was an ongoing lesson, and he taught me many, constantly, and I drank in the flow of his words and wisdom.

My father wanted me to be smart, or at any rate, to feel smart. So, he taught to it.

"When something bounces or stretches," he would coax, "it is said to have . . ." And he would smile a dimpled smile and wait.

"Elasticity!" I would shout, blond ponytail animated, and I could see he was beyond pleased. This was our standard fare.

While the rest of the family grew weary of elasticity, he and I never did.

He also taught me about the firmament and basic navigation and flight and how to gap spark plugs. But our greatest mutual love was hockey. We would sit and watch our beloved Montreal Canadiens, and he would teach me about offsides and power plays and three-on-ones and player stats. Eyes twinkly, he would delight me by making up witty, risqué names for fictitious Russian hockey players. "Oh, Tom!" my mother would chastise, but the tears streamed from my eyes, and on he would go, relentless, funny, animated. Naughty.

He and I loved words—plays on words, alliterative word combos—and the way they rolled off the tongue, elevated and coloured life. Together, we discovered that words are our greatest tool. If knowledge is power, words are the power source. This realization awed us. And with my father, I would learn to handle my toolbox with reverence and with care. Words matter.

I also loved flying, and I thought every dad could fly. I never grew tired of soaring across the spine of Vancouver Island to the rugged west coastline, or staying local, picking out familiar landmarks and occasionally gripping the copilot controls for precious seconds, sweaty but honoured by his trust. I was mesmerized by the view from above, but more so, by the way my father became more of himself when he was flying. He was carefree and passionate, and I noticed something different about him: he was liberated. He was honouring his soul.

MY FATHER FED ME BELIEF. He told us that when he was a young boy, he would cut a cord of wood after school, and after dinner his mother, drained but steadfast, would say the same five words each night, "Learn me your lessons, Tommy." By this she meant, "Tell me what you learned at school today." In this, he became the teacher, and the lessons learned would be cemented through repetition. In that simple command, the weary fisherman's wife was pedagogically perfect: she was showing interest in her child's life. Years later, I would read in Erik's school newsletter that the strongest predictor of school success is not what you think it is. It is not socioeconomic status or cram school or technology or connections. It is parental involvement. She delivered and so did my dad, always asking us, in modern language, to "learn me your lessons."

In this context, I was reminded of the sticker stars and of the unorthodox battle plan to learn the alphabet in reverse. Maybe my victory had less to do with the plan and more with my planner. And then I felt bad, wondering whether those kids who had scoffed the challenge had done so because there was no home team. No one was invested. Perhaps no one took the time to ask.

"Teresa, you are an astute individual." My father told me this often and emphatically. Not "smart" or "intelligent" but "astute." I nodded sagely the first time and then ran upstairs to my bedroom to look it up. Beaming, I decided that if he thought so, it must be true.

"I am an astute individual," I would recite to my mirror, even when I did not particularly feel it. But I hoped that it would sink in, take seed, and that I would become it. I didn't stop at astute. "I am sweet. I am happy . . . like a flower," I announced to my reflection, and sure enough, my looking glass echoed these words back to me.

"Tinkerbell," my father would say, cupping my face and looking directly into my eyes, "words shape and words create." And then he would kiss the top of my head, lightly, for punctuation. Those tiny kisses reminded me of wax stamps, fleeting, but physical seals of approval.

So, if I believed it, if I acted out those words like a pretend game of pantomime, would I become it? And even more incredible, would other people believe it? It seemed easy and unlikely. I was willing to try.

MY FATHER SANG. HE STRUMMED the guitar and serenaded his daughters, tailor-made songs that warmed and pleased us. To Lori and me, he colour-matched and softly delivered, "Beautiful, beautiful blue eyes." To Leslie he switched back to the song's original title, "Beautiful, Beautiful Brown Eyes" as he sang directly into her glossy hazel eyes. He made us feel very, very special. Prized, in fact.

He ramped things up with his storytelling, and he didn't need books. His craft was improvisation, and he was animated, comical, and quick with voices and elastic facial contortions. Like flight, storytelling unleashed him: the somewhat shy persona lifted, and like a glittery performer on stage, he delivered. We sat rapt, eager, wanting more.

He told us about growing up as a boy in Nova Scotia and how he and his buddies—Mars, Wallis and Douglas—would go into fits of laughter over a certain line in their Grade 1 reader: "The baby lay mewling and puking in his mother's arms." "Mewling" and "puking" tickled them, and in recalling the words, his face flashed delight, dimples. We would lean in, elated, transfixed by his story-telling. Daddy was funny!

Years later, he would say to us, "If you can inject a little levity into a situation, do that!" Later still, during autism's darkest days, we will draw on my father's sparkly wit: "Make Erik laugh!" will become our go-to catchphrase.

My father would also tell us about us, about our baby and tod-dler years, feeding us our fledgling life history through stories. In the absence of an external hard drive filled with imagery, we were served up our lives, some true-to-life tales and others a stretch. The embellished ones were our favourites because in these he would let loose. It was a practise round for life, a make-believe slide show, and a sample of what was possible for each of us, should we choose to choreograph in colour.

"We are stories," our father-storyteller would remind us in later years. "It's up to each of us to make them good, to write our own scripts."

Daddy-the-singer-storyteller was also full of guiding light. One of his favourites was this: "Just do your best." As a child, that was something I could do. Sometimes he ramped it up with "Always do your best." In this I became a little more of him—a person of integrity. If you say it, you must do it. My big blue eyes widened and took this in. The one I loved most was his default, often punctuation for a help session, dimples and blue eyes alive, "If you can't come to your ol' faaatha, who can you come to?"

BUT DADDY THE NAVIGATOR WAS gone a lot, and sometimes for weeks and even months at a time. To keep the connection going, I made him a travel mascot. It was my pleasure to create something special because I hated my boyish undershirts. I devised a plan to transform all of them into a collection of family mascots.

I ripped off the shirts, and with the first one, I designed a soft bunny, hand-painted with the '70s fad, Liquid Embroidery. Bunny took shape via cotton balls and hand stitching. I presented my lumpy product before one of my father's long-haul treks to the Azores. "Tinkerbell, thank you," he said, gently tucking the scrawny rabbit into his flight kit. Bunny accompanied the crew on all of their exercises. That's what they called those trips to far-away places like Bermuda and Greenland and Iceland—exercises. Bunny became a fixture on the Argus aircraft, and in time, their plush St. Christopher, escorting the crew safely back into Canadian airspace.

Father and daughter shared a bond through a skinny rabbit, through words, through flight, through hockey, through elasticity, through spark plugs and through life spent in one another's company. It was an ordinary childhood and this is what pleased me— that it was unswerving. As an adult, I would learn that the best thing a parent can give a child is their time. And in time, words. And in words, form.

"You are an astute individual."

~

HOW I SEE ERIK IS how Erik will see himself.

CHAPTER 16

We Can Make That

THIS JOURNEY IS AS MUCH mine as it is Erik's. Erik is only as good as I am, and his progress will mirror my resolve. In this I smile. Pure Audrey and her powerful trio: Where there's a will, there's a way. We can make that. You don't ask, you don't get.

~

WHILE IN OUR FATHER WE girls had a teacher, a mentor, a storyteller and a perfectionist, in our mother we had a strikingly beautiful innovator, an artist, an athlete, a community doer, a tease and a playful, outspoken role model. We had a balance.

I noticed my mother was pretty early on and that she was aptly named. While my father bore a resemblance to Elvis Presley in a blue-eyed, dimpled, slicked-back hair sort of way, my mother looked a little like Audrey Hepburn. She was a dark-haired beauty with a lipsticked smile. She told us that when she was in high school, she wore soft cashmere sweaters in pastel colours and that she had a pet chameleon, which was the rage in the late 1940s. It wasn't technically a pet, more like a brooch, she told us. We were intrigued and repulsed. "You wore a *lizard* to school?" we would shriek, and she would nod and add for effect, "Yes, he had a little glittery collar and a leash, and I used to let him walk on my shoulder. He liked the fluffy cashmere. Eventually, I shortened the leash," she added, thoughtfully, "so he couldn't get at my neck."

MOSTLY, THE MOTHER WE KNEW was not this one, but a reasonable facsimile. She was an officer's wife, and as was the style in the '60s and '70s, she, too, was a renaissance type. She could sew and curl and golf and paint and garden and make paper flowers and cook and play cards and ski. She wasn't so keen on housework, but our house was always "good enough for government work," she would tell us. We didn't know what that meant, but it seemed to strike her as funny. Much later, we would hang a sign in the kitchen that summed up Audrey's creed: "I'd rather be golfing." Tom's was similar, "I'd rather be flying." Both lived their passions and squeezed in the necessities. Or vice versa.

I also noticed that my mother was very good at making conversation. "People usually want to talk about themselves," she told me, "so let them. Let them talk, and with each discovery, you ask more. It's not that hard," she added, "and Teedah, you'll always learn something." We have two ears and one mouth for a reason, I would read as an adult, but as a child I was privy to the real deal. My mom made it look easy, but it is an art form that takes practice.

But mostly, our mother was not a word-mincer. She said it how it was. She asked for what she thought she deserved. She was a self-advocate before the term existed. "You don't ask, you don't get," she'd tell us, matter-of-factly, and she would encourage us to try this on, to speak what we believed. This made me cringe because I was excessively shy. I felt by asking for my money back or by asking for a raise at work or a discount on an item that I was overstepping boundaries, asking too much, being rude. But in shadowing the expert, I learned the technique, and when she would nudge me forward like a bird tipping from the nest, I felt wobbly but ready. It was early advocacy.

MY ELEMENTARY YEARS WERE LARGELY set to a metronome. It was the sewing machine, and it was constant, a purring rhythm-maker that greeted me most days after school. "Mommy, I'm home!" I would hear a muffled "in here" but I already knew where—in the sewing room, which doubled as our rec room. In that space was crammed a wood stove, a pool table turned Ping-Pong table and most often my mother, bent over this improvised cutting table. She would look up with pins in her mouth and motion to what she was making, often a swirly '70s knockoff outfit for one of us or something flowy and elegant for an up-coming officers' mess function. We rarely bought store-rack clothing. We sometimes did, but these were temporary house guests, a means to an innovative end. My mother would haul clothing home, lay it out on the Ping-Pong table, and like a determined Grinch fashioning a "Santy-Claus suit," she would cut a pattern directly from the "borrowed" clothing. That item would then be repackaged, returned to the store— "sorry, wrong size"—and she would whomp up an Audrey version, musing the entire time, "Who would ever pay that kind of money to buy this? We can make that!"

Alongside the clever copies was a robust will. We were taught— it was established—that one never gave up, because if you did, you would know the result, and that was most often not the result you were after. So, you kept on going until you achieved your goals. Giving up, or in, was not an option. And neither was reporting an aborted mission.

MY MOTHER KNEW THE VALUE of fun and leisure and life balance. This was a good thing because by necessity my father was the opposite, working two jobs and rarely taking time, having time, to kick back and just be.

"We'll make this funsy-wunsy!" my mother would say to me, and we would devote afternoons and evenings to candle making, to beading, to sitting, elbow to elbow, late into the night on the sundeck, cocooned beneath blankets, luxuriously wrapped in something we both loved: reading. While my father fed me words and the joy of stringing them together, my mother was never without a stack of library books. Stories pulled us away and delivered us back, renewed. At fourteen, Audrey decided I needed to golf, and later, in university summers, we sat out on the sundeck, arched over a cribbage board with gin and tonics and lots to talk about.

IT WASN'T ALL PERFECTION; LIFE seldom is. When the winter and spring greyness parted way to sunshine, I returned home to silence and an empty house. Rain equalled sewing and sun equalled golfing. My metronome was no more. But I was okay with that. There would be notes, of course, but I didn't need to read them. I knew where my parents were: my dad would be flying and my mom, golfing or somewhere in the community, involved. Or both. I would arrive at the front door, reach in through the mail slot and fish back the dangling key, let myself in, and call for our cat, Irving. Together we crept around the still house, explorers.

While I would discover in a Grade 6 reader that I was a "latch-key kid," to me, home alone was anything but deprivation. Silence signalled glorious self-determination. For me, the house was a banquet of possibility: an opportunity to be, to sightsee, to snoop, to unwrap Christmas presents, to ferret through my sisters' bedrooms, to try on forbidden clothing and to narrate my exploration non-stop, as though the chatty host of a home-alone infomercial. I was grateful for the opportunity to let loose. I felt grown up, in the same moment respected and recklessly irresponsible, a raider, a plunderer, utterly unrestricted. I liked the challenge of making a mess, and then, like Dr. Seuss's Thing One and Thing Two, breathlessly piecing it all back together before I heard the crunch of car tires on the driveway gravel. Oh, the adrenaline! Autonomy and independence grow when they are planted. I was a willing and wily seed.

Back to latchkey. That someone would see the shadowy side surprised me. While the label held an aura of neglect, I saw it as a sign of respect. I recognized the time alone for what it offered, not for what it denied.

~

AND AUTISM? LIKE LATCHKEY, FLIPPING the lens may allow me to see what I would otherwise miss. We are so much more than all we are not. Where there's a will, there's a way. You don't ask, you don't get. We can make that.

I hold the cards. I work the strings. Alongside Erik, this journey is also mine.

CHAPTER 17

Travel Partners

HOW I SPEAK ABOUT ERIK and autism is how others will speak about Erik and autism.

I can complain or I can explain. I can despair or I can repair. I can be one of many autism ambassadors teaching others what it is like to have autism and what it is like to support autism. "It's not what happens to you but what you do about it that matters most," Frank reminds me, reciting a guiding light he learned as a boy.

If you don't like something, change the way you think and speak about it.

This is also pure Emmeline and Harold, Frank's parents. My wise in-laws, both teachers, embodied the power of positive thought and reframing. Surely autism cannot be all bad? I will distill the good and serve it up to Erik and to those around me. There is a side of autism, autism the good, that is shortchanged, unspoken. It is time to balance the equation.

My approach to autism has been here all along, brewing and percolating. *Is the way I sculpt an accumulation of everything to this point?*

I rewind the tape once more. I select a drizzly night outside Tokyo, when Keiko Ishii urges me to unwrap the packet.

~

"OPEN IT!" SHE PRODS.

I take the square and unwrap it. There in my hands I hold the future. It is a Japanese calligraphy, and I have no idea what it says, but I can tell by her expression that it is golden.

"Guess," she says, her eyes twinkling. "It's what it means to be Japanese."

"Hmmm . . . Work hard? Be honourable? . . . Don't stop?" I offer.

"Yes! Yes! 'Continue is the power' we say!" and she beams. "Telesa-san, you must never, ever give up!"

~

CONTINUE IS THE POWER. JUST keep going. Because if I stop, I will stagnate. And so will Erik.

This is a partnership. Walking through the world labelled and alone will be daunting and damning, but together and as a family, we can figure this out. A journey is better with travel partners.

I rewind again. Childhood. I cannot imagine the script rolling out any other way than the way it has.

~

I GREW UP ON VANCOUVER Island, the youngest of three girls. New clothes were not part of the package, but I always had a pretty good selection of the best of both sisters. My wardrobe was soft, frayed and faded; it came with stains and stories. People pay for ripped and retro, but back then, that was the way it was. It was my normal.

I was a carefree child, meandering and exploring with my friend Leah most days after school. The beach was our backdrop, and on the sandy set we would re-enact what we had learned at school: rolling seaweed, stuffing it with high-tide debris and skewering the wads with driftwood spears. Voila! A coastal delight! Where the rain forest met the shore, we would build our fur trader forts, harvesting the towering conifers for trade goods, and in the next moment, squirt back out into the sunlight to gather more beachy props. I was a child of the ocean and of the Pacific coast.

IF I COULD SONG-MATCH MY sister Lori, it would be to Thomas Dolby's "She Blinded Me With Science." Lori saw the world in cause and effect, in words and in perseverance. You experiment, you learn. When I was ten and Lori was fourteen, she would pull on her off-white *judogi*, gi for short, and practise judo flips on me in the backyard, instructing me first how to fall and land, and then applauding my eager elasticity. I felt battered but overjoyed that she wanted to do something with me, even if it meant off-loading her little sister—*thump!* like a weighty backpack.

Early on, Lori and I shared a bedroom and talked and imagined into the night. She taught me girl wisdom and handy words.

One day, I lay sprawled across one of the twin beds, devising ways to strike out at a neighbourhood girl who had disappointed me. To this, Lori encouraged words rather than war, and she tossed a notepad toward me, followed by my pink precision-point Flair marker. I loved that marker, and I was eager to use it to battle back.

"Make a list," she advised. "You'll feel better."

With Lori's help, I devised a title: "Things I Don't Like About Joanne." I began to embellish the heading with storybook swirls, but Lori shook her head. More words were coming. Was I ready to record? Number one on the list pleased me because it contained a choice vocabulary word to park beside "elasticity" and "behooves" and "penultimate" (Tom's Trio).

"She betrays me."

As I printed "b-e-t-r-a-y-s" in careful pink script, I felt relief. And then surprise. And then wonder. There was a *word* to capture my six-year-old torment, to lasso it and to calm it? A word could untangle the knot, stretch it out, sort it out? Other people felt betrayal? They used this word, too? My body loosened. Shared emotion reduced the burden. Or maybe shared burden reduced the emotion. I wasn't sure which, but I felt better, lighter. Normal. Knowing my response was typical lifted the weight. I felt the capacity of words to clarify and to create change. My father's wisdom grew sturdier legs.

A DAY BEFORE OUR FATHER was due to fly home from an exotic and far-flung location, Lori would get to work on a rhyming banner to hang in the entrance of our house. Welcoming Daddy home became a tradition we all loved, and Lori had the presence to make it visual.

"A ho-ho-ho and a hus-hus-hus, you're back from (fill in the blank) Greenland/Iceland/Ireland/England/Azores/Bermuda . . . for a time with us!"

Our father would beam. Who wouldn't? But he knew the drill and what, invariably, would come next, after the hugs.

"Daddy! Daddy! What j'a get us?"

And he would always produce. From his kit bag he pulled tropical pencil cases; hand-stitched aprons embroidered in bright chunky wool; zip pouches; pens with tiny boats that floated back and forth on a viscous turquoise sea, past palms when you tipped them—in triplicate. It was a joyful reunion, and Lori's spirited signs cemented the vibe.

Years later, Erik would remind me, "If I can see it, I can remember it."

LORI WAS SMART. SHE WAS a doer, and she was daring. In Grade 9, she smuggled home the stomach of a rat in the front pocket of her OshKosh B'gosh overalls. She beckoned me into the upstairs bathroom, shut and locked the door and tipped the pocket toward the sink. *Plop!* Out fell an unremarkable sac of grey skin that smelled remarkably like dill pickles.

"The magic," she explained to me, "is this . . ." And she carefully lifted and fitted the stomach up to the faucet and filled it to bursting with warm water. Together, we watched it drain, and that, she explained, was the route to the intestines. I was impressed, excited to be a part of this. And there would be more. Eyeballs and organs large and small would arrive home via that pinstriped denim pocket. While other students dutifully dumped their formaldehyde bits, Lori would wrap them to go and bring them home to share and to explore, to take them beyond.

A research scientist was in the making, and in observing the experimentation, I learned that when you turn something a different way, you often see it in an entirely new way. And that going beyond is a thrill and is always worth the effort.

WHILE LORI WAS MY SCIENTIFIC springboard, Leslie was my arts and entertainment guide. Her theme song was undisputedly Trooper: "We're Here for a Good Time." This was evident back in the tumultuous Mrs. Woodbury days, and it spilled over in animated family dinner conversation. Eyes crinkly with laughter, Leslie would recount her school day, often in high-definition charade and usually with nothing held back. She didn't seem embarrassed to re-enact the salacious, graphically, at the dinner table, demonstrating words like *groping* and *petting* smack in the middle of mashed potatoes and gravy. I would sit, mouth full of carbs, having had no inkling that words like *petting* even existed beyond Irving, and wondering whether petting the family cat was still above board.

Leslie was an early version of Urban Dictionary, and for this I was grateful. Sex and slang weren't topics that my parents were going to bring up at the dinner table, even if they knew about them, and I figured they didn't know as much as Leslie did.

If Lori and Tom were the word masters, Leslie was the artistic renderer of anything we could throw at her. If you wanted "groovy letters" for a project title page, you went to Leslie. If you wanted to transform your ideas from practical to marketable, you consulted Leslie on that, too. Her school projects were gallery worthy—dull stats jazzed up to become splashy marketing brochures. Mundane to marvellous is the way I saw it, and it was a trick I wanted to learn.

The sibling source was platinum. I watched in awe and absorbed what I saw.

~

I HOPE IT WILL OCCUR to Erik to do likewise.

CHAPTER 18

It's a Greeeek Word!

WHAT DO YOU DO WITH a hot potato? Unwrap it? Toss it or let it cool?

I sit with this question for days, weeks, diagnosis in hand. What do I do with it? Do I share it or tuck it? Is it private or public? Who needs to know and why and when? I weigh, dismiss, decide and then un-decide all over again.

The biggest quandary is how much to tell our little blond boy. Is Erik to be introduced to autism? Does he already know, *feel*, that "one of these things is not like the other one?" Or will this news blindside him? Will he understand what I am saying? Or will this information slide down his slender body like raindrops along the spines of an umbrella and settle to drip off the tips? And if some of the words do seep through, if he gets this, what will he do with the information? How will he feel? How will knowing he is wired in a unique way affect him? His sense of self? Self-esteem . . . self-worth?

How will Erik grapple with "different"? Because he is going to keep hearing that word. *Different. Different* and *just.*

"Erik, you're just wired in a . . . *different* way."

"Erik, you see the world differently, that's all. You're not less, just *different.*"

"Oh, with Erik, we just need to do things differently in order for him to succeed. He needs a *different* approach, a *different* path, a *different* understanding . . ."

Different. Different. Different. It's all about that word, and alongside *autism* and *diagnosis*, it's here to stay. How will my son feel about different? About all three words? And do I want to puncture his happy little being with these barbs, these heavy-weights?

I glance over at Erik. He is flipping through a stack of "What's not allowed?" books, making his happy sound, tongue pulsing, breath erupting in soft bursts. His index finger traces the bold red circles. He is learning about the world, one symbol at a time.

Erik is content with Erik. It is how the rest of us perceive and deal with *different* and then project it back onto people like Erik—*that* is the tricky part, the game changer. There is so much projected upon us; it is what we do with these projections that shapes the outcome. It is clear to me that I will need to teach Erik the what-we-do-with part. He will need to be taught to define himself outside the pool of light that is cast upon him.

Do not allow others to define you. Define yourself.

You are the constant. It is the projection and the projectionist that change.

I HOLD THE NEATLY STAPLED pages, the diagnosis, in my hands, and I run my index finger over the grand finale, *autism.* I ponder the human inclination to classify and to label and to judge. Is it because we fear that which is not the same? Perhaps we are hardwired for this, to suss out which of these things does not belong and then to protect ourselves from the outlier. Same is comfortable, predict-able, like us, so we crave it, need it. *Different* is hard to figure out, unpredictable and requires work, tolerance, understanding and possible defence. It must be survival.

I will need to explain all of this to Erik, what I am realizing myself. Autism invites me to peel back layers and think about why we do what we do and then piece it all together and take it for-ward. In this peeling back, I am discovering that so much of what we do, how we act and react, is without thought. It is rote, a pro-grammed response and adherence to what is. Much of it doesn't make sense, but we do it anyway. *Autism wakes me up to "why."* Autism suggests alternative ways of thinking and being. I am not keen on sameness; I enjoy different, which is why I set out over and over seeking it. There is so much to convey.

AS A FAMILY, WHAT TO do? Do we tell Scott and Heather, and for what purpose and how and when? Will they understand what I am trying very hard to comprehend and articulate? What is autism, after all, and how do we want Erik's siblings to take this forward with others? With Erik?

I think of my sisters and of all that I have learned going along for the ride. I think to rats' stomachs wrapped to go and to thrilling vocabulary dispensed over peas and pork chops. Peer and sibling education is juicy; this source, Heather and Scott, is golden. It is the how and the when and how much that baffles me. I don't want Erik-care foisted upon them. This needs to be natural, not some kind of hefty burden. I sigh, my head full.

Beyond the five of us and our immediate family, what about our extended travel mates—neighbours? friends? school parents? How much do they need to know?

From what I observe, the word autism has a profound effect. I say autism, and my conversation mate says, "I'm *so* sorry" or "*Rainman* . . . fascinating!" or "enigma" or "solitary" or "silent." I am not fond of this brand of word association. It is often negative and ill-informed. I am not looking for sympathy or pity; I am looking for understanding and direction, inspiration and strength. I start to question, all over again, my motives for disclosing . . . and again the tail chasing: Whom? Why? When? How?

~

THE WORD *AUTISM* TAKES ME back to a former life, to white-hot Greece and to my cramped, dusty classroom there.

I am standing in front of the class, a mix of teens and business people, trying to explain a new, complex vocabulary word, and I am met with grins, pride and clarification.

"Miss! Miss! It's a Greeeek word!"

Ah, yes, much of English is Greek or Latin, and those words that inform literature and medicine are typically Greek. I am learning.

~

I SIT, TWENTY-FOUR YEARS LATER, and unwrap autism. I discover that it, too, is a word derived from ancient Greece. I hear their voices, "Miss, it's a Greeeek word!" If I had known then that our playful volley would colour my life in such a profound way, I would not have believed it. Sometimes it is best not to know.

I google the word and learn that autism comes from the root *autos* meaning "self." It describes behaviour that is hinged upon self and a solitary state. But what about the *selfless self* I also see? While Erik prefers his own company, he remains sweet, thoughtful Erik, endlessly tidying up, creating order and deferring to others, making certain he doesn't overstep boundaries. He exists without ego. So why isn't this also highlighted? Why the persistent dwelling on the *can't* do nature of Erik's being? What about all that Erik *can* do and *is* in spite of or maybe even because of autism? Somewhere along the line, autism has become shortchanged. If you get the word attached to you, God help you. That is my impression, early on. It is not a good one.

I return to an earlier thought, and it is one that plagues and pokes me: what do I say to Erik? He is six, enamoured by rules and whales and is intrigued that his teeth are loosening and falling. Do I spoil this innocence and sit him down for an *autism talk*? Try to explain something that does not belong in a carefree childhood? Does Erik need to go there—now? As soon as I unleash the word to Erik, and certainly beyond to all, everything will change. One short conversation, and Erik will become autism. A shadow will be cast. And one can never step fully into the sunlight again.

These thoughts taunt and niggle as I work to digest the diagnosis. I decide that this perplexing whirl is part of the process of comprehension and assimilation. I stop and I breathe, deeply, a lot. I need to dissect autism, piece by piece, before I share the outcome.

I HAVE BEEN DELIVERED TRAUMA: the child I thought I had according to age and stage and typical development is not the child I have. I need time to try this on, to mull it over before I share autism with others. I know that my reaction will be mirrored, and like a cookie-cutter imprint, taken forward by those around me. I need time to sort out what I think and create scripts for myself, to journal this and make sense of my emotions and thoughts and intentions. From this, I will have speaking points recorded, rehearsed and ready when I need to illuminate autism and advocate for Erik.

I draw from the past in order to negotiate the future. I dust off the family mantras. Guiding lights keep me afloat and focussed.

This brings my churning mind back to the start. What will be the consequence of unwrapping this hot potato? Unwrap or toss or let cool? When? How?

I will not unwrap it. Not yet. But I will not toss it. I will let it cool and allow time to do its work. Time makes sense of the incomprehensible; time heals, and most of all, time tells. I will know what to do in time. *Doubt means don't.* It is an Oprah gem that has become my default. If you are not completely certain, do nothing. I will allow this hot potato to cool.

CHAPTER 19

Wave After Wave

DIGESTING THE DIAGNOSIS IS COMPLEX. The word *diagnosis* in itself is alarming, and then there is what the word actually is—autism.

I start with diagnosis. I apply word association, and I get this: bleak, heavy, not good, why me? digest, deny, confusion, learning curve, new normal, too young. The words keep coming, and although the term is intended to be neutral, simply a verdict, in this context, the word is an omen. It is a forecast I do not want for my child. For us.

No child deserves this. Childhood is innocence and freedom and running and exploring and giggling and getting messy and going back for more. Childhood is possibility. Light. Childhood is not juggling heaviness and responsibility and worry and scheduled appointments. It is not about darkness, nor is it about being scrutinized and repaired. Childhood is an unfurling. It is our time to be without worry or constraint. Without borders.

Before autism, I remember flipping through a stack of Christmas cards and reading about a handful of friends whose children had been diagnosed with something over the previous year—diabetes, epilepsy, Tourette's and cancer. I thought of the child and of the parent, feeling deeply for each of them but not able to imagine what it might be like to be seriously derailed. I felt sympathy but not empathy. Had I known about Erik and autism, I could have applied empathy. "Could you imagine how hard that would be?" I commented to Frank. "Living with a *diagnosis* for your child?" Unbeknownst to us, we were next up to bat.

The inclination to toss or to bury the potato is strong. But I do not. *Okay, so I have this in front of me. What is it, exactly?* That takes me to the other word. Autism.

Autism is not immediately tainted because it is new, and in that, I offer it possibility, hope and a curious mind. I want to get to know autism, to give it a chance. But this word is tricky. It swirls and twists. It is multilayered. I dismiss it and it retreats for a time, but it always comes back. It is slippery. When I think I have a grip, I do not. I regress. Processing autism, I discover, is a form of grieving. It comes in cycles, and the waves keep hitting the shore.

ONE WAVE IS ALL ABOUT perception and endless questioning: pervasive, severe and disorder are intruders. I still see gentle, kind Erik. Quirky, yes, but severely out of order? No, not at all. He and his original ways are familiar to me.

And then comes self-judgment. Should I have seen more, earlier? Why didn't I? How could I have possibly explained away Erik's toe walking and desire for routine and solitary play and his fascination with examining his fingers; his love of signs and symbols; objects and their shadows; chains, hoses, fans and fire hydrants?

I scrutinize family videos with illuminated eyes, knowing now what I know. I see a sweetie running in circles, drawing the same pictures over and over and holding them up for us, saying the very same thing each time. I see a little guy hunched over a mound of Lego, building the same structures again and again. I hear stilted, mechanical speech, lots of repetition and Erik expertly echoing us.

I rewind and press PLAY and watch it again. And again. With educated eyes, it is evident that something is amiss. I marvel how everything could be reasoned away before.

"He's just shy."

"Frank and I were both shy as children; so is Erik . . ."

"He likes alone time to create . . . Look! He's an inventor!" And maybe he is but in this vignette he is also solitary and encased in a bubble of self-chatter and self-absorption.

I chastise myself. Shouldn't those offbeat inclinations have been neon clues? Why have I been so slow to respond? Why have I not seen what others have seen?

ANOTHER WAVE BEGS FOR MY understanding. I need to know autism inside out. I need to know everything I don't know. Where is Erik on this spectrum of autistic traits? How much of Erik is autism and how much is Erik? What are the causes? The treatments? Where are the service centres? Who pays? Where to start and where to stop? How will Erik respond to treatment? What will his future look like? Mine? Ours? How will I educate myself? What do I do with the evaluations? The diagnosis? Who needs to know? What do I tell Erik? How does autism therapy dovetail with a public school education? I have endless questions. I have so much to learn.

There is also a wave of fear. I fear that autism will rob Erik of who he is, that he will not grow to his potential. I fear that Erik will never be independent, that he will never be able to function without us in the wings, his scaffolding. I fear perception: that others will see him as damaged, as less; as a glass half full or worse, half empty. I fear the autism label will result in immediate judgment, in a serious downgrade. I fear people might sell Erik short and that he may start to believe what he hears and sell himself short. There are so many unknowns. There is a continuous wave of fear.

Following fear are waves of despair. Why Erik? And can I do this? I feel responsible for his development. The mountain face is steep. Daunting. How best to travel? And will I be able to keep going, positively and optimistically day after day? Repeat. Repeat. Repeat. Can I do that?

WITH FEAR AND DESPAIR COMES bigger, deeper, tangled emotion. Lots and lots of emotion. So big that I call this wave *Great Big Emotion*, or GBE for short. I am bombarded by layered and contrasting reactions, fleeting emotions, and when I visualize GBE, it is an amorphous, whirling and tangled mass, changing shape and scope and colour from one day to the next and even within each day and from moment to moment. Within a day I feel sadness, fear, anxiety, elation, hope, frustration, encouragement, pride, hurt, wonder, ignorance, disappointment, fascination, awe, hopelessness, surprise, anger, confusion . . . a daily pummelling of emotions so strong that it leaves me pulled, incapacitated and, most often, plain exhausted. Sometimes I am brought, unexpectedly, to tears when I need to be an articulate advocate.

Great Big Emotion is not convenient and often not welcome. It is unpredictable, and it knocks me off-balance and off-course. In time, I will learn to harness these emotions and channel the energy positively. GBE has the potential to be the force that keeps me moving forward. It creates resilience, and surprisingly, it feeds me resolve. But right now, I do not register this. I feel weighted and annoyed and sometimes embarrassed by it, by how profoundly—pervasively—autism has affected me.

THIS BRINGS ME TO A wave that is closely aligned with all that comes before. I begin to question my new role. What am I now, outside of Erik, Scott and Heather's mother; Frank's wife; and Audrey and Tom's daughter? My hats multiply: scaffolding, researcher, advocate, translator, scheduler, therapist and homeschooler.

To humour myself, I re-create *The Cat in the Hat* vignette, and I imagine myself wearing a ridiculous variety of colourful, stacked hats—all sizes, shapes and styles. I walk around with these teetering hats, balanced, somehow balanced—and with an unreadable expression on my face, uncertain whether I am pleased with my collection or overwhelmed by it. And that is how I feel: a bit of both. I will accumulate more and more hats (twenty-four hats?). But the current collection consumes me. Each hat requires so much of my time and energy.

As shock subsides, a wave of resolve forms: I will work to bring out the best version of Erik. We will approach his struggles through his strengths and interests, and we will use both outside services and an eclectic mix of strategies in the home. We will never give up, never stop trying. If I stop working the puppet strings, Erik will stop moving forward—stop moving, period.

AS THE MONTHS PASS, THE waves slow to a steady ripple. I take the wisdom handed to me by therapist Kim Barthel, and we applaud everything that is going right. We build Erik up before we take him apart.

Teresa, live with more celebration and less expectation. This is what I tell myself.

I resolve to tune in to the boy in front of me, recognizing, even if the literature at times does not, that Erik is and will always be a work in progress. See the good. Celebrate everything he is doing. Limit the great expectations. There is no true failure, just failure to meet expectation.

AROUND THIS TIME, THE ERIK wave begins to crest. As his social space becomes more complex, Erik becomes more complex. Behaviours emerge to calm the commotion: constant running on his toes, humming, finger flapping, whispering, pacing, eyes wide, lips moving, oblivious to all that is around him. Erik is self-regulating. It is perplexing to those who don't know what the rituals represent and the purpose each serves. Do we mask the behaviours, replace them with something socially acceptable? Explain Erik to Erik?

What would I achieve by doing this, disclosing his neurology to him when he still cannot tie his shoes?

In time, Erik needs to know. Erik needs to know because he needs to be self-aware. If he is going to help himself, he needs to understand himself. In this I am taken back, as I often am, to little me, Grade 2. I need to tell Erik the secret, about his secret power, about himself. That will be the easy part—the attributes. But I also need to teach Erik about autism. That will be the hard and challenging part. He needs to know both and in that order. First Erik and then autism. It makes sense, in time; but right now, I'm not there yet. I am processing.

CHAPTER 20

Helicopters and Bouncy Castles

I DON'T LIKE INDECISION. THIS is not me. Why can't I decide? Because this is not about me. Yes it is. What I do and how I do it could be a difference-maker for Erik. I need to do this right. I need to be certain.

I see our family life as a square puzzle, the type with the big picture broken into a series of smaller sliding squares within a plastic frame. Sometimes you can buy the puzzle with the big picture in order, and that is pleasing. The temptation is not to ruin it, not to start sliding squares around, creating mayhem. I remember, as a child, I used to pay close attention to each move I made, so I could backtrack and restore order.

But sometimes the puzzle comes with the little squares out of order, so the overall picture is nonsensical to start. What needs to be done is this: shift the small squares to somehow create a harmonious big-picture square. But it's hard, very hard, because with each slide comes a possible collision. There is a lot of shifting and sliding required before the picture ever becomes what it is supposed to be—normal.

When you have a child diagnosed with autism, no matter how hard you shift and slide and ponder, you can never get to the launch picture because it was never yours to begin with. It does not exist the way you imagine it. Neurotypical is the expectation, but you cannot get there because it is not your reality: it's the child you thought you had; it's life played out in the mind.

Life with autism is a puzzle—a baffling enigma of shifting squares. Normal becomes something new: normal is what you live.

I TAKE ANOTHER SIDESTEP. I think, as I chase my tail, about keeping autism entirely to ourselves. If the label is as damning as I have been told, why spread the word? Beyond the school, the diagnostic staff and close family members who already know about the diagnosis, why disclose beyond the informed?

And then, no surprise, the analytic, systematic side kicks in. Frank, in sync, chimes in because he is also a list-maker, a weigher, a discerner. We divide a page: pros and cons to disclosure.

Pros include funding; access to services, supports and materials; camaraderie; self-awareness; greater understanding for those who take the time to understand autism; and a sense of community. If we disclose, there will be clarity and help; we will not be alone on this journey.

Cons involve the stigma that a label imparts and the reassignment from individuality to a classification in a deficit-based category. There will be judgment and immediate limits. Erik will be on the outside looking in, relegated to a spot just shy of neurotypical. There will be isolation, and life will be about defining oneself outside of the label and proving oneself worthy. If we disclose, there will be stigma and a recast identity.

On the flip side, if we do not disclose, the journey will continue to be murky and muddled; we will meander. I am not a proponent of *murk* and *muddle* and *meander.*

Outside of speculation, reality begs us to tune in: as Grade 1 progresses, Erik is not keeping up—scholastically, socially, physically and emotionally. He is solitary. This Greek word is not going away. Autism is instead growing wild, becoming invasive. I feel as though our little boy is being crowded out and swallowed up. We need to curb the advance, smooth out the edges and allow the best Erik to emerge. If this label is the path toward services, supports and emergence, then perhaps we need to go there.

DISCLOSURE COMES IN CONCENTRIC CIRCLES, small to large, starting with family. Unlike incoming waves, these waves move outward, generated by us. Their effect is seismic.

"There's nothing wrong with Erik!"

That is my father, ever the proud poppa and optimist. He tells me what he sees in Erik, how when he reads with Erik that Erik has the entire storybook memorized. My father knows this because Erik can rattle off the pages without looking at them. Poppa is so impressed. I think, in truth, he sees bits of himself and aspects of me in Erik's makeup. We all adore words and how they sound and what they can do; we all like repetition and structure and orderliness; and we all laugh at oddball things. We get one another. What does all of *this* mean? My father is not so sure that whatever Erik has—or *is*—is not simply a thick or thin slice off the genetic block, and nothing more. Either way, Poppa is undaunted, and he remains, until his death one year later, Erik's number one believer.

"Erik will surprise you!" my father says to me, eyes twinkling, because he sees what I dare not see. He sees brilliant splinters cloaked in something enigmatic, but he sees the good and he appreciates Erik. I love my father for bravely speaking outside of projection and stereotype; for tuning in to his grandson; for speaking with unswerving belief, and for saying those four words: "Erik will surprise you." I hold these words very close to me. They fuel my conviction and stoke my resolve. They also become Erik's go-to guiding light: Erik. Will. Surprise. You. Four simple words that become our default and our source of faith.

My mother is, as always, practical and impervious. She is not one to become easily ruffled, and for that I am grateful. I appreciate her no-nonsense manner. We can do this. We *will* make this. Where there's a will, there's a way. And yes, naturally, if you don't ask, you don't get.

"I'm sure that with your care and direction, Teresa, Erik will do just fine. One step at a time," my mother tells me, holding out a brightly coloured plush object she has stuffed and stitched. It's a plump figure eight made out of purple, green and yellow scraps of felt.

"W-what's this?" I ask, pinching the soft double loop.

"An eight!" Her tone is matter of fact. Can I not see what it is? I am about to ask the next logical question, "Why?" when she jumps in.

"Haven't you noticed that Erik loves the number eight? He says it all the time and he prances. It excites him, so I made him one. It's Erik's eight."

Erik is beside himself that he owns a number eight. Gramma's intuition and straightforward offering expresses to Erik that she values what he values. And right now, this is all I need.

"Don't look too far ahead," she says to me. "Focus on this road. You'll travel the others in time."

"ERIK, WHAT'S NEW IN YOUR jungle bedroom?" My sister Lori admires Jungle Boy's green felt hat. He does a little hop and runs down the hall toward his room. She knows to follow.

"This!" he squeaks, pointing to the jungle window. Taped on the glass are X-rays of a snake, an owl and a small rodent. These transparencies come from a science website, and Erik loves them. Now he knows what's hidden inside each creature. Curiosity is part of the overlap between these two, and together, they imagine.

Auntie Leslie is intrigued by Erik's perception.

"What are those?" she asks, gesturing to the small stack of laminated cards in Erik's hands.

"My objects and their shadow cards!" he announces, thrusting one hand out. And then he closes his hand and snatches it away, skipping impishly with his cards, his comfort companions. When he comes to a semi-stop, Erik and Leslie examine the pairings— the cherry tree out front and its shadow; the basketball hoop and the shadow it casts; the flag and its shadow; our neighbour's granddaughter and her shadow double. In this Leslie is delivered a facet of autism: a fascination with the ordinary, but seeing something extraordinary in each glance.

My sisters don't allow the label to do its dirty work. They see, instead, the mostly cheerful, sweet, fair-haired boy who observes the world a little inversely. Nothing and no one has changed. Reaction to *different* will dictate acceptance or not. Comfort with an alternative perception is what it comes down to. Either you accept it or you do not. You cannot change your neurology, and you should never have to apologize for your wiring. You may be able to soften the circuits and repave pathways, but essentially, you are you.

NOT EVERYONE CONTINUES TO SEE Erik. Some are blinded by the new, bright diagnostic light, and it makes them uncomfortable. I can tell by the way they avert their eyes or take sneak peeks that they have begun to view Erik through the lens of autism.

"So you have Scott, Heather . . . and . . . an autistic child?"

No sign of Erik. It is painful.

Some act as though Erik no longer exists, as though the absence of neurotypical has wiped Erik out. Erased him. They do not speak directly to him, unsure how to be around Erik, as though with a label, he has shrunk, atrophied, become something less than he was last month. But he has not changed. *They* have changed. There are whispers, quiet questions. Some speak openly, as though Erik is not present. He hears both.

And others see Erik, or rather, autism, but no longer see worth. Our autistic child, words I do not use, is a project to be worked on, to be polished, resuscitated . . . to be fixed. Perhaps this is an unfair take on well-meaning friends and family, but it is the impression I get. I wonder, though, how *I* would react to a diagnosis outside the family. Would I be accepting and open-minded? Or would I steal glances and look for signs, ticks, clues? Would I be fascinated and flabbergasted and not know how to be? What to do, to say? In all fairness, how would I be?

I am not sure which reaction is the most difficult to deal with, to smooth out, but there is one that rankles me, and it is this: *autism isn't real.* A few look on, and wishing to be kind or conciliatory, I'm not certain, insist that autism is less a neurological condition and is, in fact, fabricated by our son and enlarged by us. It is an age-related blip. Erik will get over it.

"He'll grow out of that. He's young. He wants attention," the voices muse. Erik paces and perseverates and prances. What these onlookers do not understand is that behaviour is communication and that Erik is reacting to his environment. They think he is making this up.

As for me, I am told to relax, step back and, for God's sake, stop hovering.

There is that label for me. The helicopter parent: one who hovers, fusses, overprotects. It strikes me that those who create these labels are not the ones wearing them. The statements are judgments from the other side. Those who project have not stepped into my life, so they do not know why I do what I do. I do it because I understand what I am looking at, and they, often, do not. I am reacting to what I have learned; they are reacting to what they see.

"It's not about hovering. It's about enabling."

The words percolate.

Think of a bouncy castle at a kids' party. With an infusion of air, the castle has form, shape and function. Without air, the castle is limp, without form and without function. The castle has the same components, but they are dysfunctional. It's the same with Erik. So instead of helicopter, my role is generator, until Erik can work it out on his own. It's not about whirling air. It is about delivering air.

CHAPTER 21

Mary Poppins and Babe Ruth

I GET TO THE POINT where I stop introducing Erik and autism in the same breath. I stop talking about the label and focus, instead, on Erik's abilities and needs.

"Erik has a fabulous memory and an uncanny sense of direction. We call him our EPS . . . our *Erik Positioning System* . . . it's really amazing! What we are trying to do is help Erik read non-verbal body cues, because that's hard for him."

I notice when I do this, people relax and lean in because this is familiar territory. These words mean something. Diagnostic criteria do not. Friends and family understand sensory sensitivities and the need for predictability and the use of visuals to teach. This is concrete and relatable, whereas simply floating autism out there is vague and heavy with misinformation. I am the sculptor.

SCHOOL IS NEXT ON MY to-do list. Erik has to want to go.

Staff at Erik's school need to be told about the diagnosis. Disclosure here is simpler: this is illuminated ground. But I do want staff to recognize what might trigger Erik and, of course, what works. I ask for frequent breaks; visual schedules; instructions written down and in small steps; samples of the end product; cues to transitions; transition objects; support during recess and unstructured time. I request it all. You don't ask, you don't get.

Sometimes I am met with a look that tells me I am asking too much and that the learning accommodations are dispensed, not requested. And that accommodations are a lot of work. I think of my father, the intuitive flight instructor who knew—*felt*—that in order to learn something, you must do it. You must hold it in your hands.

~

I AM TEN, AND I am spying. I open the cupboard close to the kitchen table. It doesn't contain what you would think, but that is its magic. It's full of aircraft instrument panel parts—round, heavy, mostly black plastic orbs, with little airplanes and horizons set in liquid on one, numbers and tick marks on the others—and this is because my father teaches weekly ground school in our kitchen.

While the rest of the family clear out after dinner, keen pilots file in. The door closes and the cupboard opens. Out come the bits and pieces: the tachometer, the altimeter and the air speed indicator. Eager hands touch and examine what they are meant to master. In this, my father is a natural instructor: we grasp by grasping. I register this as I spy through the crack in the kitchen door. These airplane parts are not clunky accommodations; these objects are the best way to teach navigation.

~

So I TELL THE STORY of my father and flight, and when required, I add Mary's story.

"Mary Poppins was the ambassador of accommodation. Her umbrella was only half of her fame; it was her bag of tricks that won us over. It's the tactile and visual and kinesthetic pathways that kids love. This is where connection happens. It's all about the props!"

Who can deny Mary's impact?

So I ask for everything that will make learning easier for Erik. And I keep asking. In this I thank Babe Ruth, for it was he who said, "One can never beat the person who never gives up."

I think about the lone child sitting outside of morning circle in Grade 1, picking at his running shoe. I want to make sure that the environment is set up to reach Erik, to draw him in. How can we invite Erik into morning circle in a way that excites him, calms him, celebrates him and feels right for him? And beyond that, how can we keep Erik in the larger circle, socially, with his classmates? I imagine inclusion at every level, by every means available.

A happy Erik is a happy class. Happy Erik nine to three o'clock is happy Erik at home, after hours. And that means a happy family. Everything is connected. The dominoes are dynamic and predictable—and malleable.

"TERESA, YOU WILL BE TOLD again and again about everything that is wrong with Erik. Never forget about everything that is *right* with Erik."

In these words, I am gifted a nugget of insight and hope. This jewel is offered by a speech and language pathologist. I visualize a small pillow and a sparkling gem. That is the effect. It is another golden message and a reminder that in looking at the half-filled glass, there is always a choice. I hold these right words close and repeat them when navigating bumps and side roads.

A simple and profound truth percolates, dislodges and floats upward. I grasp it. *The way we think and speak about our children becomes their inner voice. And that inner narrative guides our children's thoughts and actions.*

The realization strikes me as I am grocery shopping. Autism is never far away. Insight is invigorating and intimidating. *I am scaffolding and sculptor.*

DISCLOSURE IS SPOTTY. WE TELL teachers but not classmates and parents. We tell immediate family but peter off at the fringes. We tell close friends but we do not sound the trumpets in Christmas letters. We are inconsistent but consistent with our intuition: we tell those we feel can help and those we know will see autism for what it is, a layer but not impenetrable. A part but not a whole.

And then one day, it happens. The word belts out for all to hear.

"Erik is *autistic*!"

The voice is jubilant, triumphant. A little girl has cracked the code.

"Erik has autism!"

The announcer is a sparkly, curly-haired girl in Erik's Grade 2 class, and she is very proud of her forensic prowess. In truth, she has an inside edge. Her mother is an education assistant at Erik's school and has talked about autism freely at home. Precocious

Alison has put two and two together: Aha! Erik plus idiosyncrasy equals autism. It's a perfect fit!

After she makes her announcement, things change. Some kids are sympathetic but are not certain why they are consoling Erik. He has *something*, but the *what* is shadowy, foreign, Greek. Others shut Erik out because *different* has a name now. They are wary, closed and cautious. The classroom teacher and I confer. She intervenes, and with Erik tucked away in the quiet room with his assistant, she talks to the class and does her best to explain autism and Erik. But the problem is, we have not yet told Erik.

Is there a minimum age for disclosure? Should there be?

At this time, I join a moms' autism group, and as a gathering of parents whose young sons and daughters have just been diagnosed, we spend hours discussing the to-disclose-or-not-to-disclose dilemma. Some decide to go for it and tell. I hold back and watch, curious to see how the diagnosis is received in their families.

The reports are mixed. "He gets it!" And the following day, "Okay, maybe not."

There is also the built-in excuse. "Well, I have autism . . . I can't do *that*."

I conclude that these children are too young to process something we moms cannot grasp. Just as there is a minimum age for new drivers, should there not also be a minimum age for the newly diagnosed? The brain needs to be developmentally ready. I don't feel Erik's is, so we hold back.

IN THE SPIRIT OF SELF-AWARENESS and feeding the brain exactly what it *can* handle, we tell Erik everything he needs to know about himself. We applaud his strengths: the attention he pays to details; his uncanny sense of direction; his curiosity; his astonishing memory, and we explain and support his struggles. He is getting to know himself short of *the word*. For an elementary school child, this feels right.

And Erik? Therapy slowly kicks in and something clicks. Self-awareness? Natural maturity? Self-regulation? It's not clear what is causing the nudges, the reshaping, but something is prodding the circuits. Erik is joining our world, our conversations and our space, and always one to please, Erik makes a declaration that floors me and allows me to exhale a little.

"I will do everything eventually, Mommy!" he announces, running frenzied circuits on the Turkish carpet.

Erik has borrowed a line from one of his favorite preschool board books, *Leo the Late Bloomer*, the tale of a slow-to-bud tiger cub. Perhaps Leo's halting development relieves the pressure. Like Leo, Erik will bloom. In Erik time. The word can wait.

As for Scott and Heather, we give them tips and tricks before we get to the autism talk. That can wait, too. "Invite him to join you outside, but give him time to think about it. It helps if you give him a hint about what you're going to do. Like if it's to play Frisbee, leave the Frisbee in the hall by the door. This is like a menu choice. He can see it, so he knows what he's going to be doing. And then tell him when. Show him on his watch."

They nod.

Frank and I also want Scott and Heather to know that teaching is two way, and that as much as we input, we learn by noticing Erik's original take on life.

"Erik's good at seeing details and patterns. We learn just as much from him as he learns from us. You know how he notices light and shadow? And the way he shows us sharp shadows, sneaky shadows and surprising shadows? Like that. He notices what we miss. Sometimes I take pictures of shadows with only a little bit of the object at the edge of the frame. If it weren't for Erik, I'd never think of doing this."

More nods. We are giving them speaking points, inviting them to become autism ambassadors. And then an unexpected thing happens. The more we praise them, showing that we notice what they are doing, the harder and more consistently they try.

Like Buddha's hands, one held up and one extended out, there is a notion that help is reciprocal. We see proof. Erik is enabled, and Scott and Heather become enablers. There are still the usual kid squabbles and pokes and frustrations, but we are also seeing the flip side of sibling interaction.

I keep my eyes open, poised to disclose. In the meantime, I am ready to discover more about my son. Buddha's hands re-emerge. It's the circle of knowledge, and I visualize this when I interact with Erik.

More celebration, Teresa, less expectation.

I have decided not to fret about disclosure. The messenger will come. I can't imagine what it will be, exactly how we will tell Erik about autism, but I'll know when I know. Our journey has words and a partially peeled back title. Everything in due time. And in the meantime, I am learning what to do with the hot potato. The puzzle pieces are beginning to slide and take shape.

CHAPTER 22

Miracle-Gro Mom

WITH SEUSS-LIKE HATS IN HAND, we set out daily, energized and resolute in the morning and exhausted and out of sorts by dinnertime. The autism path is in no way linear. Like the swirly bedspread stitching, it is a track punctuated by sidetracks and repetitive loops, shunting us back to the main line, but forever lengthening the journey.

And that is the new normal: everything taught, everything repeated, and everything retaught. Repeat, repeat, repeat. We go off track a lot. Derailment is a precursor to repetition. Swimming lessons? Level one, three times. School? Remediation. Free time? Life skills learned and hammered out in a fluorescent therapy room. We don't know it, but if we could peek ahead to graduation, we might slump: Grade 12—two versions. Driver's Ed? Six cracks at the written test in Ontario, two in British Columbia. Repeat, repeat, repeat, but eventual, gradual, thorough mastery. Everything in time. Everything in Erik-time.

Erik's journey is my journey. Our journey. A family odyssey.

As glue and paver, I set the pace. Erik's growth parallels Mom's resolve. If I falter, Erik falters. I am Erik's scaffolding. I am his puppeteer, pulling strings and working the mechanisms from the rafters. Perhaps we are shadow puppets: I move and Erik moves; I stop and he wavers.

I sculpt. That possibility heartens me. At the same time, I feel liable. I must get this right. Can I do this? But more to the point, can I sustain this?

What happens when I let go of the strings? Turn off the projector? *That is not an option.*

Like a tiny bubble of air, another realization surfaces and fizzes: *This autism odyssey is powered by unexpected sources.*

The primary energy is my own. A Miracle-Gro mom. That's what I tell the mirror, even if some days it feels forced. It's worth a try. I recognize the source.

~

"SHE MAY LOOK LIKE HER father, but she thinks like her mother and acts like Mary King." Frank raises a glass at our wedding, and we toast to Nana.

Nana sang, often and happily. She was a replica of Mrs. Woodbury, singing herself through the day, narrating everything she did and was about to do—and sometimes even what she was thinking: "And now I am drying the dishes, drying the dishes, and after we will take lunch and maybe eat it outside, eat it outside . . ."

As a child, I loved this exuberant singsong, and maybe it was the start of my own song brain, randomly pulling up lyrics to describe the moment like an on-board juke box. Mary's musical narrative was my organizer, laying out the day before us in song, offering a roadmap through melody. And knowing what to expect, I could relax and not feel hijacked through my day. Colour commentary began early, and it felt good.

It is from Mary I inherit potentiator: one who encourages and vigorously cultivates. It was in Mary's garden that I learned this. I saw the results of fertilizer, and I was hooked. If I could, why would I not enable plants—and people—to grow higher, faster, more beautiful? It is a Miracle-Gro mentality: an invitation to displace "will never" with growth, "larger faster"; to surpass expectation; to never say never; to never give up; and to never allow can't or won't into the equation. It's pure Mary.

~

ENTER AUTISM. I CANNOT CONTROL the outcome, but I can do something about the effort. And I can fertilize. That I *can* do.

I am also powered by others' energy: the negative and the positive and even the neutral, the facts, like, "Teresa, you will need to be Erik's scaffolding in life, in all areas, all the time." I replay it in my head. This one frightened me at first. But there is nothing like fright to generate a fight. Fright arrests me, but it also propels me. This double edge is startling and pleasing.

I could look at the "Erik will nevers . . ." and thank each naysayer for provoking fear and anger and despair. Thank you for powering me. The negatives sting, but the bleak words kindle a reaction, an internal flame.

The positives feed me guiding light. The "Erik will surprise you" and "Never forget all that is good in Erik" are bouquets, sources of strength. In the good and the bad, I am offered the yin and the yang. I need both. I am powered by both.

ERIK-CARE IS AT THE CENTRE of my scope. There are additional details in the target range: a marriage, two more children, parents, extended family, friends, a new town to map and scope, a social life . . . and yes, me. The context, the pulls and pushes, draw from me, and what is left is the energy I devote to autism. No, reverse that. Autism comes first. The rest flows in its wake. I am operating on many fronts; my energy and resolve are divided. How well I cope with autism depends upon the height of the other fires.

I am caught up in the eddy, in the contextual spin, and it shapes and drives my emotions, energy and response. As the autism hats accumulate, other pulls pile up: my husband is settling into a new dental position at the air force base and all that that entails; we are unpacking and arranging our house; all three kids need to be integrated into social activities, and my father's cancer is spreading. Our new normal dissolves. But most immediately and abruptly is my grandmother Mary's death, without warning, on Halloween.

"I'VE NEVER BEEN TAKEN FOR a walk by a *unicorn*!"

The voice is deep and delighted. The words belong to Nana, ninety-eight. Feisty, positive and full of song, Erik calls her a survivor. Tucked into her wheelchair, she hums a tune from the 1940s, "Mairzy Doats," and as she does, she begins to clap. Four-year-old Unicorn Heather pushes her down the hall of the extended care residence.

"Oh . . . mairzy doats and dozy doats and liddle lamzy divey . . . A kiddley divey too, wouldn't you?"

The unicorn stops pushing, clicks on the handbrakes and spontaneously starts to dance, a furry purple spectacle, right in front of Nana. They are a sweet sight: old woman singing and clapping; small unicorn hopping, sharing a pre-Halloween moment. Jungle Boy and I watch from beyond Nana's wheelchair.

"And if the words sound queer, and funny to your ear, a little bit jumbled and jivey . . . Siiiing, mares eat oats . . . and does eat oats . . . and little lambs eat ivy . . . Ohhhhh . . ."

Jungle Boy can't resist. He rushes in, swept up in the kooky lyrics, pointy green hat bobbing alongside the glittery white horn. I marvel at the chemistry and the impulse. Together they are ageless. The old and the young are not tripped up by numbers and stereotypes. Neither is autism.

On this visit, Nana tells us about crossing the Atlantic in 1912 on the *Empress of Ireland*. Mary, Heather and Erik merge: they become bold child explorers. Mary's family had planned to cross on the *Titanic* but changed their plans and delayed their crossing until the fall. Nana pauses. Had the bookings not changed, we may not exist. She resumes. Running around the dazzling *Empress*, Mary is thrilled to be free-range, unattended and age six.

"I had never seen flush toilets before!"

She is that child again, discovering new. "You flushed the toilets by pulling a little chain . . . ," she says, tugging at the air. "So I pulled those chains for all I was worth!" She laughs again, deeply, as she remembers. Unicorn, Jungle Boy and I are captivated.

"Come back on Tuesday," Nana says and smiles as we prepare to leave, "and I'll tell you more stories."

We promise to do this. We are eager to hear the next installment.

But that never happens. Three days later, on Halloween, Nana's life is over. Her ninety-eight-and-a-half-year-old heart stops. And that is the end of a life of stories; of music and of flowers; of friends and of oceans. Nana has scripted her final act.

Mary's passing, three months into our new life, ushers in an ominous tempo. The absence of Nana comes as we are growing roots and smack in the throes of the diagnostic process. I mourn the loss of my grandmother, and I mourn the loss of a neurotypical child. My father's cancer has metastasized. Again. We are looking at unbearable normals on all fronts.

It is an emotional fall. Energy and resolve are moderated by life context. We are all doing our best. I tread water, fully clothed.

"Do you know what it means that Nana died?" I ask Jungle Boy. Erik thinks for a moment. "Yes," he says solemnly. "That she doesn't like Halloween!" After we have established that her last day on earth and Halloween are in no way coordinated, he nods. "Understand?" I ask again.

"Yes!" he whoops with a happy hop. "They made Nana into a *statue*!" And he continues to dance, right out of the room.

I ponder the whoop. It isn't until four years later that Erik is able to explain. We are looking at a cross-Canada photo book and he points to a larger-than-life statue of Terry Fox we visited on the northern shores of Lake Superior. "They made Terry into a statue," he says, "just like Nana."

And then a lightbulb goes off—mine. *Important people become statues after death.* Nana had been important. Sweet Erik has immortalized her in his mind. I also imagine Nana as a statue, a monument to positivity, to a life well lived, to Miracle-Gro and to minor miracles. It has taken Erik to help me see this. And it is not the first nor will it be the last time Erik will invite me outside of my neurology, illuminate life and help me to see. I am growing Erik-vision.

PART II

FROM FRUSTRATION TO FASCINATION

CHAPTER 23

September Twentieth

IN THE MIDST OF DEATH, we are delivered a microscopic gift: life. I am pregnant with number four, and we are thrilled. Excited. Disbelieving. At nearly four months, I cautiously tell others, and I dig out our worn copy of *Hello Baby!* I invite Scott, Erik and Heather to see the first ultrasound. We are beyond elated; I love having a gaggle of pregnancy cheerleaders.

The room is dark and hushed except for the machine, which glows and whirrs and illuminates my belly and its contents. I sit propped up, surrounded by my children and my husband. I flinch as the cold gel is applied to my stomach. We all stare at the screen, waiting for the smudges to make sense, to form a tiny human. With the coming together of spine and profile and rudimentary legs and arms, we hear it, life: a heartbeat.

"It's there! I see the heart, *beating!* . . . right *there!*" squeals Scott. We are hushed and hungry for more—more views, more explanation, more evidence.

But our ultrasound tech does not mirror us. Her mouth and her manner trigger a silent alarm. Is this her normal or is there something more? No matter, the gel is wiped and we are sent home with our first photo, grainy and grey, but beautiful. Life, in spite of death, is good. We need this glimmer. We deserve it.

The phone rings two days later. There is a problem. My smile disappears and a mask slides into place.

"The baby is not developing normally. It has what is called fetal hydrops, which means that it is unable to eliminate the fluid from its body. The tissues are bloated. The baby will not likely live." The voice is factual, flat, as though describing the day's weather.

I am stunned, unable to speak. When I get off the phone, I contact Frank, who is out of town at a conference.

"You need . . . to . . . come home," I whisper. "Our baby is dying."

The baby we have dubbed Sunflower, our ray of sunshine in the dark days of death and diagnosis, wilts and dies. At four and a half months in utero, he stops moving, and I know something is wrong.

In the weeks to follow, I must undo this pregnancy, dismantle it. I need to schedule the removal of baby Sunflower and rid the house of pregnancy clothes. I need to write and tell everyone what happened, days after sharing the very good news. But mostly, I need to undo this with the kids, backpedal and go back to the way we were—five not six. All three are devastated, but none more so than Erik.

Each day he asks me the same question, "Where's the baby who died?"

What did they do with the baby who died? He wants to know. He needs to know, to close this somehow. To stop the unravelling. Each day I repeat the story I told the day before. I am picking at a scab that will not heal. As I process the loss, so does Erik. He sings out his confusion and sadness in a bizarre and taunting ritual.

He runs in tilted, fast circles, laughing wildly, shouting and singing what would have been the baby's due date, September twentieth, two days after my birthday and ten days before Heather's. It was going to be a happy trio of September birthdays. Our wonderful family news has halted, and Erik can't figure out why. So each day, like a dutiful cuckoo announcing the hour, he warbles our woe, reminding us of what was meant to be and what went terribly wrong.

"September tweeeeeeny-eth! September tweeeeeeny-eth!" he shrieks, again and again, exaggerating the word twenty, running and whooping out the date, heightening our loss. I am reminded of "Dr. Wuuu-ah!" but this time there is no humour. "September tweeeeeeny-eth!" lasts for months and it annoys us, but we cannot stop it.

I will later learn that Erik processes by repetition, *perseveration* in autism-speak, and that it is difficult for him to turn his heavy emotional train around. So he sings our torment. He is our little town crier, the proclaimer of pain and misfortune. In hindsight, I realize that he is becoming what he sees: Nana sang; Mommy sings, and so do I.

Do not judge Erik from neurotypical shoes, I am told. Because if you do, you'll be wrong. Change the shoes. Step into his, if you are able, and you will see that *doing is saying*. Behaviour is communication.

This is a lesson I will never completely master because I am me and Erik is Erik. But I will try to remember to change the shoes. Henna gaijin. I never set out to be strange or different.

As for me, I erase the damage and convince myself that this was never meant to be, that it is better like this, easier like this, just us five. But it hurts. My father gets this, and in his fragile state with cancer-riddled bones, he gently wraps his arms around me, and he lets me cry it out. With very little life left in him, he is still Dad, my go-to guy. "If you can't come to your ol' faaatha, who can you come to?"

BACK IN THE CLASSROOM IN Erik's new school, his curious mind is engaged but not in the Grade 1 lesson. He is focussed on quirky delights, on bits of Erik-intrigue. One fascination is the classroom sink. Erik sits at the back corner of the room so that he can survey the class. He dislikes eyes on the back of his neck, so he is the designated classroom eyes in the back right corner. This is where he becomes aware of the stainless steel sink submerged in a counter at the back of the room.

A sink in a classroom?! Erik is mesmerized. He finds it out of place, humorous, ridiculous. *Why is it here?*

One day, he quietly stands up and turns the tap on full force. As the water rises, he cheers the faucet and jeers the drain. To his delight, he is about to achieve a classroom flood! But then it happens. A large hand reaches over and turns off the tap. Another hand jerks him abruptly away. As he stands in his time out, he frowns. He was so close.

Later that day, as I read about the transgression in his agenda, I ask him why on earth he tried to overflow the classroom sink. He says he doesn't know. It takes years for intent to dislodge, to rise and to present itself: it had been a science experiment about efficiency. Which would win? The faucet or the drain? It bothers him that the question remains unresolved.

Does it bother him that he has been misunderstood? Not particularly. Another aha moment: his world exists alongside or perhaps partially submerged in our world. He feels no need to explain one to the other. It doesn't occur to him what others think of him. It does to me, to us, but not to Erik.

TEN YEARS INTO THE FUTURE, I will tell the flood story to a mother of a boy, seven, with autism. By high school, the stories of Erik's youth will be part of our autism lore, our family entertainment. We will have outgrown them, but they will not be forgotten. The mom is relieved to learn that curiosity can fuel the most fabulous misadventures. Through the telling of the flood, I attempt to cast her son's behaviours positively.

"Natalie, they say that adventure begins when something goes wrong. Your life will not be dull."

We laugh and clink our glasses together. We are fused through autism, and in this we feel a kinship. We understand the weight and the sacrifice and the worry, but also the intrigue in off-road tourism. We both live the package. She goes on to describe something that happened the day before at her son's swim meet. It's classically good.

"So I know he can do it. He's an excellent swimmer," she says, "but for some reason, he gets through about half of the lap and he slows down, deliberately, and he comes in second. I mean it's still good, second, but he could have come first. He won two other races that day. So what's with the pause halfway through?" She looks perplexed. Her forehead wears pleats from the previous day. There is something she does not understand, but she continues.

"And then it happens again. He's swimming a great race and he's in the lead, but bizarrely, he looks up and slows down again and lets people pass him. Third. He comes in a solid third." She shakes her head.

"I wondered whether the coach had had a talk to the kids about, you know, sharing the winner's circle. I'm okay with that, of course. So I ask him. 'Matthew,' I say, 'it looked like you were slowing down out there on purpose. I think you probably could have won all of those races, but you let other people win.' And so I told him I was proud of him for thinking of others, for doing that. But the funny thing is, he looked confused."

Now I feel *my* forehead crease. Where is this story going?

"So he tells me something that completely floors me. Teresa, when he tells me what happened there in the pool, I think to myself, So *this* is autism? And I begin to understand my little boy's mind a little more. Here's what he said: 'Mommy, I like red and I like blue. If I won *all* the races, I'd only have blue ribbons. All blue. I don't want all blue. I want some of each. So, after I won two blues, I changed to red. I came in second *three* times because I *love* red. But I don't love white. My least favourite colour is white. So I only came in third once, because white isn't even a colour.' He looked so proud of the reds. He loves red. Go figure. I thought he was being generous, but no, it was all about collecting a complete set of coloured ribbons . . . and minimizing third, white."

We both sit there in silence for a minute, digesting the intent, because that's what we've become: interpreters of intent. It reminds me of when my kids were babies and I would try to translate their crying: it might mean hunger; it might mean heat; it might mean fatigue; it might mean gas; it might mean poop. I was forever scrolling through the *might means*. Now, as a mother of a child with autism, I'm at it again, pondering and interpreting intent. And so, too, is my friend. The ribbon riddle is one teaser neither of us would have solved. This bothers us because we figure we're pretty good at this by now. Point for Matthew. He wins this round. Perhaps it takes autism to deliver a collect-the-whole-set mentality. Winning at all costs is clearly not for everyone. Never think you know for sure.

CHAPTER 24

Finger Pulls and Guitar Strings

GRADE 1, PART TWO, IS going well. Too well, perhaps, but to me no news is good news. Aside from little blips like the flood and notations about solitary playground preferences, I hear nothing. I have been waiting for *nothing* since Erik started school in Nova Scotia. Blissful nothing. A normal day. And he appears to be having them, stringing them together in a promising strand of nearly neurotypical. It's about time.

I exhale, but I do not relax. Like the quiet child squirrelled away in the corner of a house, silent can also mean busy. Into something. I want to know what Erik is into at school, so I ask him about his days. I am met with a pause and then giggles. He looks embarrassed to tell me something, like by telling me, truths will be spilled. I am concerned, but I try to mask it.

"I don't have to work anymore!" he gushes. The words are starting. "I have finger pulls instead!"

"Finger pulls? What's that?"

He grabs my right hand and demonstrates by gently pulling one finger at a time. It's like he is milking my entire hand.

"And there's also the guitar. She plays the guitar for me and she sings. That's what we do. Finger pulls. Singing. The guitar. In the small room. The quiet room. There isn't any work in Grade 1. Only fingers."

I meet with the classroom teacher and the education assistant, the *she* Erik refers to. Turns out Erik is out of the classroom more than he is in it: anxiety reduction trumps academics. He is not following the Grade 1 curriculum. Silence, after all, is not golden.

The classroom teacher senses my discomfort, and she calls for a meeting with the principal and the learning support teacher, the

EA and me. I am about to be back-filled. The meeting day arrives, and I ask why Erik is not learning how to add and spell and subtract and read like everyone else.

"Because Erik isn't ready to learn," I am told. The voice is matter of fact.

It is the learning support professional speaking. She tells me, and those gathered, that Erik is six but socially and emotionally four. He's too young to be fed what others are eating. The school has decided to focus on self-regulation first. I let this sink in. I have not been consulted or advised. This plan was decided for us, for Erik, and in this I feel dazed, uninformed and out of the decision-making loop. While I think the school's strategy with Erik is somewhat correct, I am worried that Erik is slipping behind, losing ground on his peers. His skill sets have stalled. But the voices are not done.

"And what we've decided for now is this: we're going to modify Erik's education plan and focus on learning-readiness. It's the only way forward. Modify. Please sign." A paper slides toward me.

In my head, another word appears: simplify. Make it easier for Erik, but in the process, halt him. Stop him before he starts. Back off the tap and slow the flow. It is then that another voice, clear and resolute, speaks. It utters a single word. "No."

The voice is mine. It surprises me. It speaks unleashed, without rehearsal and without thought. It speaks from the heart. It is pure reaction.

"I'm a teacher and so long as I'm home with Erik, I will teach him. No modification. No signature. Just tell me what to do and I'll do it."

My words are a pistol, announcing the start of something new: twelve years of tutoring Erik at home. He continues to attend school during the day, but he can relax now, knowing we will follow up each day, after hours.

"CAN HE WRITE?"

I am handed Erik's Grade 1 writing journal. It's full of dates and blank pages. Each Monday morning, Erik painstakingly copies the date from the blackboard, and then he sits. He clicks his pen.

I have seen him do this at home: the writing followed by the clicking. Why the writer's block?

I find out from Erik's education assistant that when she asks about his weekend, Erik's response is "Hmm . . ." and more clicking. He can't remember what happened. The weekend vaporizes by Monday morning. If he cannot remember, he cannot write.

I google it. *Make the abstract visual*, I am told. If he can see it, he may be able to do it.

We begin to print out a strip of photographs each Sunday evening. Beside each photo, we jot guide words to describe the weekend, like *bike ride* or *watched a movie* or *played in the yard*. At school, the results are promising: the images unhinge the memories; the words kick-start the flow. If Erik can remember it, he can say it. If he can say it, he can write it.

It was never a writing issue. It was a retrieval block.

"GRAMMAIGOTANEWSQUISHYTOYANDITSREALLYSQUISHYWANNATRYIT?"

"I didn't understand a thing he just said."

My mother says this a lot, because Erik's speech is hard to follow. I'm used to his staccato voice; to his pseudo-Bostonian accent; to his singsong cadence; to his inclination to blur and jam words up against one another like rowdy bumper cars.

"Erik, slow down. Gramma didn't get that."

"Gramma. I got a new squishy toy and it's really squishy. Wanna try it?"

He also repeats himself. "It's a *lake*!" is his current favourite. I'm not sure where he heard it, but it strikes him as funny, or maybe he likes the way the words sound together or the way his tongue must nudge the back of his front teeth to articulate "lake." I'm not certain, but to Erik, it's a goodie, and he hollers "It's a *lake*!" again and again while he runs his happy laps. This might be anytime, anywhere, like at the doctor's office.

"It's a *lake*!"

Giggle. Run a lap, fingers held high in the air in front of face. Examine fingers from all angles as though they have just sprouted. Wondrous hand. Fascinating fingers.

"It's a *lake*!"

Giggle. Run a lap. Marvel at fingers some more.

"It's a *lake*! It's a *lake*! It's a *lake*! It's a *lake*! It's a *lake*! *IT'S A LAAAAKE!!*"

Like fireworks, there is often a burst at the end.

And then he might sit down and thumb through a book, back in near-neurotypical mode. I cock my head. Where does autism stop and Erik start? Where is the seam? Is there a seam? If he can do one mode—like us—why then, the other? Are they co-dependent? A balance? There are so many questions I cannot answer. There is so much to know, to find out. I default, again, to the old Ontario licence plate: *yours to discover.*

People stare. Some quickly look away. Sometimes I feel too tired to try to Grinch the laps and the fingers and the random whoops, to blend it, to normalize his behaviour, so I let it go. I let Erik be Erik. Without explanation. But sometimes, like in the lobby of the National Arts Centre, we need to rein it in, divert the flow or move the show outside.

As for the printing and the journalling, we have a trickle, but it is molten. Words dissolve into each other; sentences bump and overlap like irregular ice floes. Forming each letter is a big deal, traced and retraced, and the result is an ooze of letters. It takes a forensic eye to parse and decipher what Erik is trying to say. Words become liquid, an alphabet tide. I watch, fighting the urge to grab the pencil and scribe for him. It's hard not to, like watching a child put together a puzzle, knowing exactly where the pieces go, hand hovering, but resisting the itch to reach over and click the pieces in place. I let him do it himself and then try to make sense of what it says.

"Yikes!" I say to Frank one afternoon, holding open Erik's Grade 1 journal: "wewere buzyonthe week end wenitrainedand i pleyed insid."

"This is going to require surgery." But Erik is trying his best, and to this I think of "Just do your best" and "Always do your best." I know that Erik is doing both.

We teach him to use his left index finger as a spacer and this is helpful, but he often forgets. In contrast to his burbling speech, written output is glacial. I wonder how we will possibly keep up.

But Erik is unfurling. There is no doubt about that. We press on. *I will do everything eventually, Mommy!*

IN WEARING MY HATS, I discover that Erik is literal. What comes across as deadpan humour is autism playfully at work, painting the world in absolute black and white strokes. Erik interprets at face value. His world is this or that; nothing in between. There is no figurative.

One day in the van, where we have our best conversations because eye contact is not required, Erik's shrill voice punctuates the air between us: "What I wanna know is, *who* is Paula C., anyway? Every day Mr. Berry talks about her. Why do we talk about Paula C. so much?"

I ask a few questions. Over the morning announcements, the school principal reminds the students that the school practises a hands-off policy. There is no Paula C. There is no plea to give her space, just a literal mind conjuring up a mysterious little girl, Paula. Another aha. There will be many.

Big brother Scott delivers, too. His language is straightforward, without filters. I am running with a friend one morning, the mother of a Grade 4 classmate of Scott's.

"Did Scott tell you he was over at our house last week?"

He did.

"It was the first time he had seen our house. Did he tell you about that?"

He had. Now I am worried. She continues. "He walked in and looked around and then said, "Geez, when you see *our* house, you'll think *your* house has been *robbed*!"

I am not sure whether to laugh or to apologize. I will need to rehearse something in between.

CHAPTER 25

Countdown Meltdown

ERIK IS SEVEN. POPPA IS dying. My world is caving, folding onto itself, but I need to attend to my chickadees. Heather is in kindergarten and loves the social stimulation. Scott is in Grade 4 and is making friends, finding his people. He has begun a district gifted program, a once-a-week pull-out called Challenge, and he is thriving in the deep layered teaching and learning. As for Erik, he is settling into Grade 2. His teacher is traditional, and in this she is orderly.

Warmth is present in the form of a nurturing education assistant, Mrs. Power. "Fitting," we say to Erik, half-joking. "Like a personal power pack!" Mrs. Power is the bridger of gaps between teacher and student. And she's fun! I know Erik's days at school are good because unlike in kindergarten and Grade 1, Erik wakes up ready to roll. I need this because things are rolling badly off-course at home.

In November 2005, with our three children beginning to know their Poppa, he succumbs to cancer. I am heavy with grief and disbelief. Like the autism diagnosis, emotion strikes in waves. In fact, the diagnosis is still delivering waves, as is Mary's passing, as is the death of our wee ray of hope, baby Sunflower. And now this: the loss of my father. My template for learning and love and perseverance and belief has evaporated. Poppa is gone, and with his death, a light is extinguished in Erik's corner. I imagine a *pop* as the oxygen disappears.

These waves, all of them, feel compounded, as though they are rushing in from every direction—because they are. Throughout this turmoil, ordinary life persists and tugs. I know that I need to show our three how to grieve. To honour. How do we take

Nana's and Poppa's life lessons forward? How do we learn from loss? What do we do with death?

I think of my father in every waking moment. *The vault is full. We have made our memories, our lifetime deposits. There are only withdrawals now.*

I move through my autism to-do lists mechanically, on automatic. When I am not overcome by the void, I am buoyed by the words that linger at the rim. "There's nothing wrong with Erik!" and, "Erik will surprise you." We are wrapped in my father's belief, dimmed only by degree.

IN THE WAKE OF POPPA'S passing, things falter at home. Erik needs to off-load his school day, and home is where his composure times out. When he becomes overwhelmed, he transforms from quiet, bottled boy into the choker, face enraged, taking a running leap at whomever is closest and pressing his slender, pale fingers deep into our necks. It is painful, frightening and startling. It seems out of character. Gentle Erik is on the attack! Why?

Around this time, Erik is also in the habit of counting down. Everything. His favourite activity revolves around the microwave. When I place items in, he revels in counting backward from the thirty-second mark, all the while running tight circles and clapping to the beat. If I stop the microwave before the countdown is complete, Erik goes berserk and switches from counting to choking. Times are rough.

What I do not know is that numbers are comfort companions. Counting and clapping and laps are Erik's coping and calming mechanisms. Countdowns are predictable and offer structure and solace. In the midst of a chaotic day, Erik has latched onto something he can count on: numbers.

Letter combinations irritate Erik. He despises "th" sounds, "f" sounds and "p" sounds because of the way our lips and tongues form these letters. For him, a "th" with the tongue thrust between front teeth is ludicrous, and an "f"—a beaver mouth—unbearable. A "p" as in "Please pass the pepper" at the dinner table puts him over the top. He simultaneously shouts and places his hands over his ears to block out the vulgar attack. We are on word alert, and we are aware that we might unwittingly use the wrong letter combination. Years later, Erik will delight in hearing about this forbidden letter stage, laughing until he cries when I tell him that the days of the week became a challenge after Wednesday . . . that Thursday and Friday ceased to exist for a year. And as for his father's name, Frank? Well, that was tricky, too.

WE ARE EATING DINNER AND talking about our day. It reminds me of dinner tables from my childhood. Scott is Leslie, the entertainer. His movements are flamboyant; his voice, loud, and his stories, comical. Classroom chaos is a favourite. I feel for the teacher, but I join the laughter.

"And then she lifted her coffee cup, and we all stopped what we were doing because we *really* wanted her to drink . . . *Drink it!* We all thought . . . and then she did! And she *spit* it out . . . right in front of us. She spit out her coffee . . . because . . . ," he says, eyes wet with rolling tears, "it was full of staples! Before the morning bell we pointed the stapler . . . *Plink! Plink! Plink! Plink!* right into her cup!"

I imagine it. This woman delivers verbal barbs and sarcastic volley, daily. She is confusing and hurtful. Though wrong, filling her cup with retribution, Bostitch barbs, must have been satisfying.

It's Erik's turn, but Erik doesn't remember his day. He cannot recall it. So he shows us what we have seen many times before, his "What's not allowed?" books. He shows us as though they are new. Frank and I play along, but Scott and Heather do not. Kids don't tolerate nonsense.

"We've seen those books a *million* times, Eriky!" Scott sighs, unimpressed.

But Erik is not concerned with what we think. Smiling broadly, he flips through them as we eat.

Heather is next. Before she can speak, Erik jumps up and launches a happy dance, a singsong trot, and circles the carpet adjacent to the table, running, hands held high, laughing at a phantom joke or remembrance that he doesn't have the words to describe. But he has claimed the stage, and with it, our attention. It is then that Heather bolts, and her tearful exasperation as she thumps down the hall will be repeated in the year to come.

"You. Don't. Appreciate. Me." One angry word per thump.

Her words hang in the air, four words that I will need to tame. Another hat. I will need to carve space for the siblings of a child with autism. How many hats will there be?

Heather will leave the room in tears again and again, and she will hide in the house and shout from her new secret corner. She can offer Erik support for only so long, and then the young child kicks in, needing light for herself. I understand that.

Erik will keep running, chanting the phrase of the day, possibly, "It's a *LAKE!*" louder and louder and Heather will shout above his repetition and Scott will throw back his head and laugh, wildly, because he loves upheaval. And Frank and I will look across the table at each another and wonder how dinner has unravelled. Again. We will try to eat, but Heather will keep up the "You don't appreciate me!" and Scott will hoot because with each distress call, she signals her location, even though she intends to hide. Scott finds this hilarious, and he finds Erik's running and shouting ridiculous. In the midst of the mayhem, our dinner goes cold, and the chef does not feel particularly appreciated, either.

In time, I will add appreciation to the standard autism duo, awareness and acceptance. *What about autism appreciation?* It takes Heather's stamped out words to suggest this.

"Did you enjoy swimming with the humpback whales today?"

The voice is eager, warbly and high-pitched. The speaker wears a plastic purple and white Hawaiian lei and a speckled fur coat. This is somehow okay in the Maui heat.

"Oh, yes, *I did!* It was exciting to see those whales come so close to that sailboat!"

The other speaker wears a multicolour lei wound on his head like a crown. He rests in a deck chair; the Maui sunset highlights his freckled fur.

I follow along, caught up in the performance. On each trip and car adventure, we pack five plush harbour-seal puppets we have rescued on our west coast treks.

"Another one?" That is Frank. He was okay with two; surprised at three; incredulous at four and resigned by five.

"Now we have a Hedley family of seals," I explain. "And besides, these puppets are beautiful and realistic. I can use them to teach."

That is my standard line, my justification for gift shop splurges. But the fact is, Erik, Heather and Scott adore these soft creatures they refer to as the *memmays*. Erik, especially, speaks prolifically with them, through them. Puppets are unexpected points of entry into Erik. *Portals to potential*, I begin to call them.

I learn that puppets, like costumes, shift the spotlight from the speaker to the medium. Wearing a harbour seal on his arm, Erik's word output quadruples. Like costumes, there are no rules with puppets. You go for it, speak, express and create. Seal puppets do not make social blunders or grammatical errors, and if they do, who cares? It's okay to experiment. The memmays travel with us and become part of our entourage.

On this late March afternoon, as we stretch out on deck chairs a few metres from the rhythmic Pacific Ocean, it is the seals via Erik and Heather and Scott that recount our day. It is the seals that keep Erik present and out of the periphery. For five years, our plush narrators become a point of connection and access.

CHAPTER 26

The Dress Detective

WITH ERIK, DIAGNOSIS OR NOT, he is friendly but without lasting friendships. Kids like him. Little girls want to care for him, and it is to the mothering females that Erik attaches.

There is one girl, Megan, who is drawn to Erik. She and Erik are inseparable at school, indoors and, thankfully, outdoors, where Erik has a hard time knowing what to do and how to fill his free time. Work is play, and play is work. There are so many choices, and each is arbitrary as are the playground rules. It's hard to be structured in fluidity. But with Megan to make sense of the mayhem, Erik finds his way.

The office secretary reports that the big-eyed twosome regularly request the long-handled pinchers used for plucking garbage. Erik and Megan scour the playground, racing between wrappers and ridding the yard of that which should never have been discarded.

"What's not allowed?" is a powerful compass. In their quest to tidy up, they are leading the way, but that is never the intent. Erik does what needs to be done, and he does it without expectation. He doesn't expect to be noticed; he doesn't expect to be thanked; he doesn't expect to be rewarded. He lives without an agenda. In Megan, he has found a like force. "Just keep being you," I tell my three, "and you'll find your people."

One day after school, I approach Megan as she helps Erik cram his lunch kit into his backpack.

"I want to thank you for helping Erik out," I say. And then as an afterthought, "Did the teacher ask you to do this?"

She replies brightly to part A, my gratitude, but to the notion that she has been forced to help Erik, she clouds over.

"No one *asked* me to do this!" she responds, defiant. "I *like* Erik. He's my friend. He's funny and he makes me laugh."

I want to savour this moment, freeze it and preserve it. Megan has seen beyond the label, and for that, I want to hug this girl, bring her on board as our campaign manager. "See the good!" will be our slogan. She does, and their relationship flourishes.

Megan visits our house after school and dresses up as Jungle Girl, delighting in Erik as he emerges from the bathroom wearing his pointy green hat and beloved Peter Pan costume. She is jubilant, as though her little prince has hinted at a secret identity, and she is here to witness the transformation. He is her Jungle Boy and she, his Jungle Girl. They romp around after school, sometimes with Heather as an adjunct jungle girl, sometimes alone, content and oblivious to all that swirls around them. Like young love, in tune and in sync. I feel great hope, both for the present and for the future. There is someone for everyone. We don't need a handful of friends. We just need one. Megan is our Grade 2 proof.

And then the unimaginable happens. Erik's bright puzzle piece moves away. Her father has been transferred, and she is plucked from our lives as swiftly as she appeared. Erik does not mourn the loss of Megan. *But of course he does*. He mourns, but it is unreadable. He feels but does not show, cannot express, what he cannot comprehend. Is this another inaccessible slice of the brain? The work of autism? The Megan months have been so very good. Will he connect like this again?

ON THE PLAYGROUND, WITHOUT HIS feisty sidekick, Erik is solitary but content. He seeks the solace of the forest and hits the trails each recess and lunch, endlessly running, pounding up and down the pine pathways. The playground imp.

I am passing the school in the noon hour, and I pull over to observe. A playground can be heard before it is seen, and this one is no different. It is a screech of output, of bodies in motion, collaboration and mostly, joy. I notice the impromptu pairings. It looks easy at a distance, the casual connections, the games, the coming together, the moving apart, the freedom. But it is not easy for my son, and this is why I pull over, to see how he manages. To spy.

There he is, body light on the trail, feet skimming, face a mask of something. Is it pain or pleasure? His lips are moving; his eyes are wide, alert but somewhere else. It's like he's conversing with air, a precursor to Bluetooth. The effect is mesmerizing and spooky. He is at once immersed and removed. No one bothers him. *Do they notice him? Has my son become invisible? Or accepted? Or tolerated?* He is the lunchtime runner, and this is understood. I pull away from the curb because I have seen enough. I am relieved but heavy-hearted. This is not the way I thought it would be. My son is the playful pixie, the enigmatic forest gnome.

BACK IN THE CLASSROOM, THERE are incidents that perplex. Flip the lens and absurd is absolved. Everything is obvious from the shoes of the doer. Henna gaijin. There are no strange foreigners. There are simply divergent operating systems.

For around a month, in the spring of Grade 2, Erik begins to lie on the floor and gaze up his teacher's dress. Not good. When asked why, he giggles. Fortunately, this phase doesn't take years to figure out. Back at home in the comfort of his jungle bedroom, Erik explains that he is investigating, checking to see whether the teacher's upper half and lower half match "on purpose or by accident." Are skirt and top attached—a dress—or deliberately coordinated? He is curious, and he wants to know.

"I am being a dress detective," he explains, matter-of-factly.

Once he outlines his motives, it seems logical, not ideal but understandable. Well, sort of. I pull on translator and buffer hats and return to the school. I explain Erik's motives to his distressed teacher. She is not amused.

"What do you suggest I *do?*" she implores.

She is ruffled. I feel for her, but I also see the humour. This phase is purely innocent, driven by a brain juiced up with curiosity and a passion for patterns.

"Wear pants till this blows over?" I offer. She does not laugh.

I will spend years explaining Erik to others.

THERE IS ALSO *THE BLEND*. The blend requires Grinch-like cunning, the ability to think quickly and to incorporate the nonsensical into any context and to have it make sense. This is a feat bordering on sleight of hand.

Case in point, a class barbeque. It is Scott's class, and because Frank is out of town, I must take all three children. This makes me nervous because I will be stretched, and the likelihood of a reasonable conversation will be nil. But I take them all because I have to, and we are lining up along the backyard buffet table serving up dinner when Erik activates a download. Today's topic is Pluto. Erik feels Pluto got the short straw. So he jumps in, out of the blue, out of context and completely out of sync.

"Oh, I'm so sad about Pluto! Knocked out of the planets. Poor Pluto. But I'm still going to count Pluto. I'm going to keep Pluto in. Pluto will *allll-ways* be a planet!"

Talk of hockey halts and the serving line goes quiet. All eyes are on the Pluto professor, and it is then that the blend kicks in. How to integrate and normalize Erik's narrative is always my tasking and the tasking of siblings of children with autism. *How do we make Erik seem regular and worthy? How do we take his comments and move them from left field to centre field?*

I do what I would do around adults: I show respect and interest, even if the comment is random and out of place. I have learned that the way I react to Erik affects the way others react to him. I am a mirror. If I scorn, others scorn. If I praise, others see worth. So I launch in, embracing his planetary passion. *Fake it till you make it.* I'm prepared to give it a try.

"You know, Erik, I've been thinking the very same thing. It doesn't seem fair, does it? Kicked out because of size. Who would want that? Certainly not you guys," I say, gesturing to Scott's classmates. "Kicked off a team because of height. It would feel wrong, wouldn't it?" They nod.

The secret, part two, is making a connection to the audience. If it matters to them, it's worth discussing. We have covertly moved from planets to players, to what they know and care about. Making a connection saves us. Failing parts one and two, I keep talking. Bamboozle your audience. That works, too.

I am Erik's mirror, and I am Erik's deflector.

I can exhale and serve my food. Another Erik-moment merged, melded and mollified. And like Scott explaining away the red reflector, the blender hat is my ace.

CHAPTER 27

Untangling the Christmas Lights

WHAT ARE WE TRYING TO achieve with autism? This is my big question. I need clarity. Why are we feeding Erik into the therapeutic mouth? How do we wish him to emerge? Like us? A version of himself? And for whom do we therapy him? For Erik? For us as a family, to smooth out this anomaly? What are we trying to create?

I attend a conference in Vancouver, a large gathering of parents, professionals and paraprofessionals, spanning three days. It's the first time I hear and consider this notion: "Defeat Autism Now!" There is a group of doctors that call themselves DAN! doctors: those bent on eradicating autism because they believe it is a treatable, biomedical disorder. I sit, somewhere between intrigued and perplexed, and take it in . . . something about a poorly firing immune response and an abundance of environmental toxins. There is more. A cure? Hyperbaric oxygen chambers. Supplements. Chelation. While somewhat plausible, this feels extreme. Risky.

I am beyond surprised. I am flabbergasted. Defeat your neurology? I understand what these doctors are getting at—the need to groom the best attributes and cast the rest. Do we achieve this by beating back facets of ourselves?

Confusion offers good lessons. Eliminate wrong to illuminate right. Like attending a job interview and realizing that the position is not a good fit, learning what we don't want hones what we do want. I ponder the fallout while crossing the Strait of Georgia back to Vancouver Island. I stare out the ferry window, allowing the ocean to do its work. I am processing autism intention. What are my objectives?

I do not want to knock down segments of my son's neurology. I want to build him up, nourish him, sculpt him. I do not want to erase; rather, I wish to embrace and illuminate so that he can see himself. I want to show him the secret, the mirror, and I want to feed him to him. "Erik, you are an astute individual." I will tell him that.

But I don't realize all of this in the moment. Just fragments. I learn as I stumble. I am not privy to knowing the answer to the big question. Not yet. It takes time to translate looking into seeing. Emotion must fall away first. Emotion clouds and obscures clarity.

Fourteen years later, my childhood friend Karen will text me, and she will say, What I don't really get is what any parent of a child with autism is trying to achieve. Are you trying to hide autism or trying to draw it out?

She wants to know what I want to know. Conceal or reveal? One day I will have journeyed long and far enough to be able to tell her.

I HAVE ANOTHER LOOMING QUESTION. How much of Erik is Erik and how much is autism? How much of what I am seeing is Erik before the label intervened? Can these halves be cleaved? Extricated? What if in therapying Erik, we rob him of who he is? This is blurry and confusing territory. It's slippery, like separating an egg and a yolk. Do we want to do this? And why? Because whatever has shadowed or veiled or consumed Erik is pervasive. A bit like untangling Christmas lights.

My mind pumps out analogies as fast as the questions form. My brain operates in its comfort zone, processing at a distance, via simile and metaphor. I am as visual as my son, not surprising because I have helped to create him. I am left with no answers, only questions, and the sensation of not knowing what I ought to know.

One thing is clear. We will build our son up before we take him apart. This makes sense. We will project the good. And later, we will turn to the tangled and confusing lights.

I HEAR ABOUT KIM BARTHEL through the autism parent group I belong to. "Teresa, you've got to meet the phenomenal occupational therapist I heard in Campbell River last weekend. Her name is Kim Barthel and she is *such* an amazing speaker. I think we can hire her to come and work with our kids."

The mother reporting is Jan, a savvy and pleasingly hippyish mom with two bright kids on the spectrum. If Jan says Kim is good, she's good. We decide to hire Kim and invite her to come to our small town and assess our children, one at a time.

There is something about Kim's manner, a mix of competence, curiosity and confidence that feels sacred. Her presence is grounding, hushed. I am hopeful. You feel that she gets your child. Like a medium peering into a glass ball, she sees beyond what anyone has seen, and each word she speaks is uplifting. In my reaction, simultaneous sweat and goosebumps, relief and disbelief, I realize I have been starving for such language. She feeds me what I need: hope. And best of all, she makes Erik feel worthy. Capable. He turns to me and says, emphatically, "Kim is a believer."

Kim carries with her a bag of tools and treasures that mesmerize both Erik and me. From a large, multicoloured carpetbag, she pulls out bits of occupational therapy gear like finger fidgets, muscle stimulant tape, tinted glasses and modified therapeutic music CDs and tries them with Erik. She pauses, peers, pokes and smiles, jotting down what she observes. Erik purrs and I sit, transfixed. I tell her that she is an intoxicating blend of Mary Poppins and Oprah, a mix of magic, wisdom and hope such as I have never before experienced.

She tells me that there is brilliance in there . . . and that, yes, I had better dare to believe. If I do not, who will? She challenges me to tune in. I do.

THERE IS SO MUCH TO know. I want to know *now*, so I can react now, in the best possible way. I dig and discover conferences, workshops, hands-on training, everything to do with autism and everything remotely to do with autism. Autism Awareness Centre's Maureen Bennie, a music specialist turned autism mom turned autism advocate and educator, is the source of our out-of-town illumination. I take a line from Scott, and I sign up for a little of everything, near and far.

Hundreds of parents do the same. It feels good to know that we are not alone in the climb, because that's what this is—a blind ascent. There is consolation knowing that there are others wondering how this will all turn out; others who celebrate fundamental feats like shoe tying and teeth brushing; others with the same worries, similar resolve and yet all of us, diverse. We are autism-aligned, united by this enigmatic sliver of ancient Greek. Autism shapes us and threatens to break us, but the more we talk, the better we feel. Sharing is therapeutic, an unexpected release. Despair recedes.

HE STIRS FROM SLEEP IN the hospital bed and brightens when he sees us. He perks up and sits up, gazing from one of us to the next. His reaction, this lucid reception, is not what we expect. We expect nothing because we have been told he is unresponsive.

The dying know when death is near. Sometimes they pull out all stops, as though supercharged for the grand finale. Frank's father, Grandpa Harold, is this. His blue eyes blaze; his mind is fired up. He is energized and he is present. He wants to know our plans. We have flown 4,560 kilometres to see Grandpa; our plans are him, to sit and talk. He will have none of it.

"Go out and have an adventure!" he commands, punching a frail fist in the air. "And then come back and tell me all about it!"

And so we do. After an emotional day camped around Grandpa's hospital bed, we take the kids to Canada's Wonderland north of Toronto. The following day, we are ready to return to report back, when we receive a phone call. Grandpa has died.

Six months after Poppa's death; twelve months after the baby who died; sixteen months after Erik's diagnosis, and eighteen months after Mary's passing, another light is extinguished. Ninety-five years are spent seizing the day, and now Grandpa's eyes have closed. This is inevitable, but it is hard. This is Grandpa.

"Here we go again." I hear myself say it out loud soon after we receive the news. Here we go again. A move back to my home town was supposed to be the easy posting, but it has turned into a blur of decline and death. I pull on the departure hat and explain Grandpa's passing. Everyone important is dying. I need to reassure them.

"Remember how Grandpa told us to go out and have an adventure? Well, while we were gone, Grandpa also had an adventure. Only, he can't tell us about it. We will have to imagine it ourselves . . ."

We talk about what it means to die and about Grandpa's life and spirit. It is Erik, solemn in the middle van seat, clutching his green felt hat, who speaks. "Grandpa said to have an adventure. We did. I think he is happy."

CHAPTER 28

The Dollar Store Deviant

ERIK IS EIGHT, GRADE 3. We have much to celebrate. He has a teacher who gets him, and she enjoys his offbeat manner. With Mrs. Reis and Mrs. Power, school feels like a celebration. At last.

This changes everything.

Because Mrs. Reis projects positivity onto Erik, others see Erik this way. Erik feels good about Erik, and I feel good about hanging around, talking to the other parents. What a difference an enabling mindset makes. Same person, different projectionist. I have the Reis-Power duo to thank for this: *you get what you project*. It is a gift.

There is a corollary: *you project what you get*. You become what you are given, and in return, you deliver it back. If you are made to feel good, you will pay it forward to others. This is how cheery circuitry works.

Erik and I feel positive because these ladies project positivity onto us. And because I feel this, I project positivity when I describe my son to others, offering optimistic descriptors, adjectives to try on and for Erik to become.

This has not always been the case. I think back to Grade 1. Same us, different projectionists. Different fallout.

~

WAITING OUTSIDE ERIK'S GRADE 1 classroom, I chat with other parents, but the talk goes to where we are not—to baseball, to hockey, to the latest toy fad. I smile and pretend that we have a foot in, but we do not. Through Scott and Heather, I know this world, I am a part of it and I know the vocabulary. But I am aware that I have one foot in each camp: Brownies, Cubs, skating, horseback riding and windsurfing with two children; and with Erik, occupational therapy, targeted social skills groups and after school academic tutoring. These parents bond over their kids' activities and the associated driving. I feel the unintentional squeeze. It is as though they have enhanced cable and watch the most remarkable shows; I watch reruns on a basic bundle. They have moved on. We run out of shared space.

~

THOUGH GRADE 3 IS A turnaround, there are hitches and glitches, the not-so-good-at-the-time but funny afterward moments.

Erik and I are at the Dollar Store, selecting birthday party favours for Heather's Hawaiian party. The tiny paper parasols and the crinkly grass skirts hold his attention, but what really draws him in is a bank of light switches hidden behind the bouncy balls and the water guns.

Erik finds the secret switches terribly funny, their random and ordinary position a surprising contrast to their function and importance. The laughter is only the start of it. Before I process his intrigue, his hand darts forward, hits the switches and casts the store into darkness.

I hear it when I can no longer see it. *Click! Click! Click!*

There is a lovely, hushed "Ohhh!" as customers fumble in surprise.

Delighted, Erik reverses the flow and casts us in light once again . . . "Ahhh!"

He dances on the spot and yelps out loud. His eyes flash. He feels scientific. Ecstatic! Powerful. Before I can react, he repeats his experiment, and again, delights in cause and effect. Ohhhhhh! . . . Ahhhhhhh! Little Erik is in control. This is so easy!

He has seen what we have seen, but he has thought something completely different. Ludicrous light switches! And he has acted. He is, by now, running the length of the aisle, eyes wet with laughing tears and wildly alert, lips twitching, incredulous and wondrous.

After three rounds, we hear the advance of feet, fast feet, furious feet. A sweaty employee huffs around the corner and lays into us . . . mostly into me for allowing it. Although embarrassed,

I can barely contain my laughter. I nod solemnly as we promise to behave. Once she retreats, Erik and I look at one another and erupt in giggles, recalling the dramatic and sweeping "Ohhhh-Ahhhh!" but understanding that it is a one-time event.

We laugh about this. *The Dollar Store Deviant*, we call it, proof that you don't need toys to play.

ALONGSIDE HOME AND SCHOOL THERAPY, Erik is participating in social skills groups and in occupational therapy. He is learning how friendship works and how his engine runs. He is learning to self-regulate.

At home, in a rainbow row of plastic baskets in Erik's bedroom, rest widgets and trinkets called fidget toys. We learn that busy hands calm and focus the mind. I think of Lori and of smuggled body parts. "Everything is connected," she explained, and now, in the context of autism and neurology, I am immersed in connectivity once more: occupy the hands and you regulate the mind.

In surveying the tangle of rubbery, flabby, squishy, lumpy, bumpy, bendy, twisty, leafy, knobby, creaky, squeaky, whirring and purring gadgets, I am reminded of the Grinch yet again and the oddball Whoville toys piled high on his sleigh. Erik's hands will never want for quirky companionship; and it is to these fidgets we defer, toting Ziplocs full of squishies with us whenever we leave home.

This need to squeeze spills over onto human surfaces.

Crawling through a Lycra hammock one afternoon, Erik reaches out and presses his fingers deep into the soft, fleshy arm of the local occupational therapist. As his pale fingers sink into her velvety upper arm, he lingers and grins, "Wow!" he marvels, delivering his trademark lopsided smile, "Margaret, you're just like a GIANT fidget toy!" I gasp and fill the space with awkward talk. We will add tact and delivering compliments to our very long to-do list.

THEY SAY THAT KIDS WITH autism have a hard time generalizing learned behaviour: it's tricky to pluck life experience from one context and insert it into another. I hope, in the context of teacher squeezing, that this is true.

We debrief after the giant fidget toy episode and talk about respect and the need for personal space and appropriate language. But I am not convinced that what happened at the Child Development Centre will stay at the Child Development Centre.

In the classroom, I spy Erik scoping his Grade 3 teacher's bosom. Anything bigger than Mommy's is an anomaly and a curiosity. I become worried. I want to nip the temptation to touch, especially where he is focussed. I can tell by the fixed expression on his face and the tilt of his head that something is in the works. He is sizing up his teacher with the tenacity of a sharpshooter, and I fear for the target zone. In his defence, when he stands in front of her, he is exactly as tall as her chest. His eyes meet her cleavage, not her eyes.

Song brain cheekily summons the Steve Miller Band: "The Joker." *I really love your peaches, wanna shake your tree.* This is no consolation.

At home, I express my concern to Frank. "I'm worried that Erik will surprise us again, and this time, it could be way worse than the dress detective. I get the feeling that one day soon he's going to reach out and . . . touch something."

To this, Frank throws back his head and laughs a whole body laugh that reminds me of my grandfather, Jack King. In the context of "autism the austere," *this* is funny. But not to me. As frontline buffer and blender, I will be there to witness, to mend and to mop. *The touch* is ticking.

I am not sure whether to snuff it by talking to Erik, or whether a talk will be mistaken for a strategy session and will stoke his interest. I'm stuck, and the thought of spending time on this topic is absurd, but also not. Just as I suggested to the Grade 2 teacher to "wear pants till this blows over," I want to do the same in Grade 3: "blouses, please, till he moves onto something else." But I don't want to alarm her.

We play by the rules and create a body parts "What's not allowed?" There is a silhouetted, clip art buxom teacher and a reaching hand, encased in a red circle with the slash. Erik is thrilled! Another "What's not allowed?" for his collection and a new rule, reinforced: we do not touch our teachers. We reintroduce Paula C. and review Valley View's hands-off policy. Everyone's hands. Everywhere. Got it? He says he does. I hope so.

In creating a paws-off-the-teacher sign, our normal shifts again. I begin to convince myself that everyone has these concerns and makes these signs. I almost believe it. Another part of me knows that we belong to an exclusive club, and that "normal" is elastic. When something bounces or stretches, it is said to have . . . ? What we live: a life stretched off-course, extinguishing hot spots. It is also a life stoking sparks. *Buddha's hands*, I remind myself.

CHAPTER 29

From Frustration to Fascination

AGE NINE. GRADE 4. THIS year's teacher is not a believer. When Erik does well on a test, the triumph is tainted by caps lock: large, lopping, red letters scrawled across the top of the page, WITH ASSISTANCE.

We take a step back. The projection is flawed, and like the careless breath that scatters the dandelion cotton, Erik's persona is cast in a disabled light. As the fluff floats and settles, I stop waiting outside the classroom door with the other parents after school. I duck back into the wings, out of sight. I sit and read in the van until Erik emerges, because wearing the coping smile takes too much effort.

What a difference a year makes. The student has not changed and neither has the parent, but the teacher has, and in a single projection, mother and son are diminished. Mindset matters. Its effects seep and bleed like the blur of watercolour on wet canvas.

ERIK PORES OVER A MAP of the Comox Valley he discovers in the van, wedged between the front seat and the console. "Have you been on this street?" he asks, jabbing the map.

"Uh, no," I say, glancing sideways as I drive.

"How about this one?"

"Nope!" I say, and on it goes, street by street, road by road, avenue by avenue and lane by lane.

"You mean, you grew up here and you haven't explored *every* road?"

"No," I say. "Why *would* I?"

In his reply, I begin to understand the difference between our neurologies.

"*Why would you not?*" he shrieks, shaking his head.

Autism is about endless curiosity. Complexity. The rest of us are about endless complacency. Simplicity.

My map takes me where I need to go; Erik's map takes him where he wants to go. I begin to question who is disabled and who is enabled.

I have not thought of the map, my hometown, this way. I go where I need to go. I have never felt the need to plot out and explore the entire town, side roads, dead ends and all. I feel bland, lacking an adventure gene, low on the curiosity scale.

"Hmm," I begin. "No, I've never had the urge to go off track. Until now. I have a feeling you want to explore, check out these unknown areas?" I say, my hand hovering over the well-studied map.

Erik lights up, utterly, entirely.

"Can we? *Really?*"

Our after school adventures begin. I pick all three kids up from their schools, and we set off according to Erik's plan, plotting out roads whose names I have never before encountered. As we drive and check out rutty ocean-side lanes, we imagine our lives and routines if we lived on each of the roads. The just-imagine game launches all sorts of fun, wistful conversation.

"We could come home from school and have a snack on the beach . . . and make rafts, or poke around in tidal pools . . . or fly kites on the beach!" I offer, recalling my days spent roaming Miracle Beach with Mary and Jack.

Suddenly our own routine seems a tad dull, but no matter, visualizing is fun, and the chatter is rich and animated. Erik is chiming in without prompts; he is with us and not lost in his own space. He has drawn us into his world, wholly outside the traditional function of the map. This fascinates me because we are solidly in our world, but we imagine it through Erik's eyes, through curious, thirsty, other-worldly eyes. We have shifted to his intent. This is about as close as we get to stepping into the shoes of autism.

WE VISIT THE LOCAL FISH hatchery and befriend Chinook salmon as they bump and jostle in tanks, just inches from our faces. Their worn out, bloated and battered bodies draw concern from Erik. He taps at the glass and chats with them, encouraging them, congratulating them for a job well done. When the salmon phase is over, I miss it. Standing behind Erik and gazing at the swirling mass of fish is hypnotic. Listening to Erik-the-devoted-salmon-coach exclaim and console is both heartwarming and uplifting. We are colouring way, way outside the lines. I feel privileged to be here. After years of looking, we are starting to see.

"TEN, NINE, EIGHT, SEVEN, SIX, five, four, three, two, one . . . *BLAST OFF!!"*

There is a great rumble, a blip of dramatic music and a seven-year-old squeal. The expedition has begun!

I stand outside Erik's bedroom door, and head bent, I listen. I have heard this narration so often, I could recite it. Erik, too. He knows it by heart, but each time he hears it, he responds as though it is new. There is talk of the sun, a pause, more music and then a high-pitched beep. I know what's happening: Erik is pulling the slide strip through the projector, adjusting his 3-D glasses and stretching himself back out on his bedroom floor. He does this every afternoon for months. It's as close as he comes to living in a planetarium, and it's about as good as it gets, swapping public with private, social with stars.

Some nights we all lie on our backs in the darkness, covered in blankets, on Erik's bedroom floor. We each pull on a set of cardboard glasses, the sort with one blue tinted lens and one red lens, and we wait while Erik readies the projector. There are two shows. One is planetary; the other is undersea. In one moment, Erik's bedroom ceiling is the firmament, peppered with constellations. In the next, it is sparkly blue and alive: the ocean. The device responsible is a child's 3-D projector. We purchase a blind for Erik's room to blacken it and then allow the device to transport Erik to the heavens or the seas. There is nowhere else he would rather be. The ambiance is soothing, informative, spellbinding. It is an escape from what is hard—the neighbourhood kids.

I wonder what is right. Offer Erik this or guide him toward that? To where he eventually needs to be. 3-D is easier for all of us. I admit that I default to easy. We can exhale. But exhalation gives way to guilt. We are avoiding what needs to be done, but for now this plastic orb and these massive D batteries offer a needed respite.

ONE NIGHT WE ARE READING one of Erik's favourite chapter book series, Magic Tree House. "Ha!" he scoffs, jabbing at the page, "The author's used that chapter title before."

"What do you mean?" I am confused.

"Chapter one in book nine has the same title as chapter ten in book twelve," he gestures. "She repeated the title 'Master Librarians'!"

It takes a moment for this to sink in. There are twenty-eight books in the growing series, and each book has ten chapters. Two hundred and eighty titles. "You mean," I begin, "you know all of the chapter titles in every book?"

"Yes, pretty much."

"Pretty much," Heather tells me, is Erik-speak for *entirely*. It is then I learn that autism is modest.

Autism doesn't know when it's blowing the rest of us out of the water.

I test my suspicions. I hold up a book in the series and call out a chapter number. He supplies the title. Another book . . . three random chapter numbers. He spits out titles matter-of-factly, without pride or excitement, and he answers each correctly. Shaking, I run to get the video camera. We all gather around and watch as Erik recites chapter title after chapter title, all accurate and from memory, without ceremony. He is unaware that there is anything to flaunt.

With autism, the easy stuff is hard and the hard stuff is easy.

Erik cannot tie his shoes (in Velcro we trust), initiate a conversation or bat a baseball, but he displays savant slivers that send shivers. He is like us and not. In many ways, he is better than we are: he shows no pride, no jealousy, no competition, no prejudice, no judgment, no boastfulness, no ego. Erik just is.

We are moving from frustration to fascination.

And once again, we are moving, pulling up the carefully tentacled arm that is our Vancouver Island life and moving on, destination Ottawa.

CHAPTER 30

The Naked Lady

SIX MONTHS BEFORE DEPARTURE, WE fly to New Zealand and Australia. Erik surprises us in ways unanticipated, offering random richness when we least expect it.

The planning for this adventure begins one year before our November 2007 fly date. Drawing from past treks long and short, Erik needs plenty of advance warning: he needs the trip mapped out geographically and chronologically, and he needs upfront pre-teaching. In short, he needs seeds sown early so that he can grow into the trek. I have learned from whiney, unglued adventures to plan from Erik's perspective. If he can visualize it, he can do it.

We set up a mini-schoolroom in the basement, and we study all things Kiwi and Aussie: geography, coat of arms, icons, maps, local sayings, fun facts, our travel route and our travel friends. We record everything in travel binders before we leave home. Seeds sprout in familiar soil.

Erik flips through his Down Under book, anticipating our adventure. Because he is part of the plan, he becomes swept up in the trip long before we take to the sky. Closer to departure, we construct and hang a vibrant paper countdown chain. Step one: anticipation.

Step two is the doing. We aim to follow the plan, but we also plan for change. I am reminded of Lori, decades before, teaching me to land before I am hurled. We talk about travel glitches in advance, and we script possible scenarios. We are as ready as we can be.

What we are not ready for is the gifts that autism packs.

The international dateline is one such celebration. Erik sleeps little on the fourteen-hour flight from Vancouver to Auckland. He is fixated on the monitor in front of him, to the sphere that is earth and to the imaginary timeline: the international dateline. He reaches out and reverently traces the dotted path with his index finger. It exists. The idea that we could bisect it and magically gain a day blows his mind. Time not only flies, but it expands and vanishes. While the rest of the aircraft sleeps, Erik keeps watch, his face tinted a ghostly green by the glow of the screen—a little boy on night duty, awestruck. When our aircraft intersects the line, he yelps and looks around. Nothing has changed, but everything has changed. It is tomorrow in the Southern Hemisphere. His grin is visible even in the dark.

The other autism encounter is on New Zealand's South Island. Our circular driving tour of the island begins and wraps up in Christchurch. As we exit the city at the outset, we pass a voluptuous statue of a naked woman. Erik whoops and insists we stop and gather around her for a photo. We do. A week passes amid glaciers and exhilarating outdoor adventures in Queenstown, and then we re-enter Christchurch through the back door. Just as I am about to plug in the GPS, Erik starts to giggle. Loudly.

"Cover your eyes because heeeere she comes!"

In his exhilaration, I imagine *The Tonight Show:* "Heeeere's Johnny!"

From the backseat, "Heeeere she is!" I am certain Erik is perseverating again, overstimulated by a phantom image. "She's only two blocks away now!!" Erik is flushed, wiggly. He breathlessly counts down to hips and breasts, his lopsided grin cranked up to full brilliance. "On our left! . . . *I think I see her!*" He is shrieking.

More giggles, hysterical now, and from the back of the van, this: "Heeeere's *THE NAKED LADY!*"

And sure enough, there she is, the naked lady. And here we are, delivered back into unfamiliar territory one week after departure via Erik's Positioning System—EPS, as we come to call his mysterious sense of direction. Behold, Erik-vision: open, authentic, observant and otherworldly.

BACK IN THE NORTHERN HEMISPHERE, we are uprooting and moving on, this time Ottawa-bound on Erik's tenth birthday. We celebrate as a family on the road. The pressure is off; the open highway is our backdrop, and for ten floaty days, the van is our mobile home.

Upon arrival, we are served up a fresh start and a new playground. We are reinventing ourselves. Everything that delights me about uprooting—the possibilities, the change, the newness— daunts my son. I remind myself to step into his skin and walk in it.

Before autism arrived, moves hinged around pinning down the big three: a family doctor, a dentist and a hairdresser. With autism, our needs list mushroomed. The big three became the insignificant three. Hair, health and teeth bump to the back. Autism eclipses all.

I HAVE A GOOD FEELING about Grade 5. Earlier in the year, on Vancouver Island, Gayle, the learning support teacher, devises a plan. She fills out the standard needs profile for Erik's new school, but she goes beyond and creates an illuminating snapshot DVD for the Ottawa school, *A Day in the Life of Erik*, showing Erik moving throughout a typical school day on Vancouver Island. It is brilliant.

A year later, the receiving school tells me this: "We were shocked and surprised to see how our expectations were so out of sync with what we were watching on the DVD. The boy on paper was difficult, a challenge, classically autistic. The boy we were watching on the TV screen was sweet and funny and intelligent. It taught us to keep our preconceptions, our judgments and our expectations in check."

I am reminded that paper and practice are often mismatched. Ottawa prepared for disruption but were delivered, instead, delight. Erik *has* autism; Erik *is* not autism.

There is one other thoughtful detail. A few months before we head east, we receive a packet in the mail. Buoyed and inspired by the Day-in-the-Life DVD from the west, Erik's new school in Ottawa sends us a class list and student pictures to match. As we drive east across Canada, Erik sets to work memorizing his new Grade 5 classmates. He hollers from the second row of the van, rattling off the names like St. Nick summoning his reindeer: "Marley! Jessy! Rebecca! Ian! Dustin!" By the Great Lakes, we make it a group chant. Erik will later wow his classmates by greeting each by name on day one.

Grade 5 is a very good year. We falter, but like the Grinch knotted in the sooty chimney, never for long. The tone is set by the classroom teacher. She creates visual schedules for Erik and other helpful anchor charts, recording rules, expectations and guidelines that are appreciated by all of the students. She arranges play partners for recess and lunch. *Hallelujah!* We have structure for the unstructured part of the school day. Erik is rescued from haphazard meandering and awful uncertainty. The forest imp is invited to integrate.

ONE DAY, DRIVING BY THE school during the lunch hour, I spy a boy immersed in a pack of girls. Immersed is accurate because as I glance out the van window, I see a boy's legs being held by the tallest and strongest girl in the class . . . and swung upside-down by the running shoes. My eyes are attracted to the movement. I gasp. Not until I pass by do I realize the wiggly human pendulum is my lanky, fair-haired son. But Erik isn't being bullied; he is being buddied. My heart soars!

Grade 5 is also the year Erik takes to the stage. His teacher is into Greek mythology. Lo and behold, the tales appeal to Erik, and he morphs into a bearded Greek Zeus. Just as Jungle Boy has transformed him years earlier, the bed-sheet-Greek works its magic: on stage, in his new skin, Erik is animated and extroverted. Theatre is an astonishing portal into Erik.

CHAPTER 31

Good Throw, Good Catch

ERIK AND I ARE SIDE by side, reading a book about a school with a celebrated football team. There is a buzz around the quarterback: because his throws are accurate, the receivers are able to catch the ball effortlessly. The quarterback's ability allows the receivers to shine.

"Erik!" I exclaim. A lightbulb analogy flashes through my brain. "Football is just like school! If the quarterback is good, the players look good. If the quarterback is poor, the receivers are going to have a hard time catching the ball. *The ability to receive depends on the ability to throw.* And in football, we talk about this. We look for it. Replays show good throws and good catches. Replay and analysis also show that a poor throw is nearly impossible to catch, and then the receiver is excused. Good throw, good catch!"

He nods because this makes sense, but he isn't sure about how it relates to school. I'm about to add a part two.

"If a teacher teaches the way a student learns, a student understands the material and does well, looks good. Good throw. Good catch. But if a teacher does not understand how a student learns or if he or she uses the same teaching method with the whole class, there's a good chance that some students won't do well, that they will not catch the information. We say that they do not *catch on*, you know, *get it*."

I pause to check that he is following me. He seems to be.

"But when this happens in school, we look at the student and say, 'They didn't understand' or 'They're not so smart' or 'They failed.' We do not look at the throw, the teaching, to see whether it was a good throw. If we did, like they do in football, we would see the relationship for what it is: Good throw, good catch. Bad throw, fumble. It makes perfect sense!"

Erik nods, processing. I think about it some more. Our football analogy changes everything. *It changes where we shine the light.* Who has failed whom? The paradigm shifts the focus, and to me, every student and every teacher needs to be reminded: Good throw. Good catch.

At the end of the school year, Erik receives the Grade 5 French award. No one is more surprised than I am when Erik's name is announced. Erik? He arrived in Ontario ten months ago repeating a single French word, *moi*. Coming from the west coast where French is exotic, our children arrived in Ottawa woefully behind.

But in Ottawa, Erik loves French at school. Curious, I pay a visit, and I learn why. It is not the language nor the location that captivate him; it is the methodology. His wise teacher has figured out that if kids can move and assign gestures, moving visuals, to language, they can learn it. Monsieur Morrissette is kinesthetic. This is a perfect teacher-learner fit. Good throw. Good catch.

Can we take it a step further? I make a phone call to funky and upscale Bowen Island off West Vancouver in British Columbia, where the innovative language program originates. I pretend I am a French teacher attached to Erik's school, and I arrange to purchase the French gestures DVD program and have it shipped to the school. I bring it home and place it on Erik's bed.

"Just like at school," he breathes as he turns the half dozen DVDs over. He does a series of happy claps, and he lines the jackets up on his bed. He has the whole set, and the completeness of this and the lining up and the familiarity soothe and please him. He likes the randomness of school colliding with home and somehow landing on his bedspread. This strikes him as funny.

He inserts a DVD into the player, closes the study door and then leaps and twists to the music he has enjoyed at school, learning hand gestures to represent French vocabulary. He draws his hand forward in an exaggerated flourish and bows low, "Madame." Laughter wells up and spills out. "Madame! Madame! Madame!" He is a giddy bowing machine.

As he mounts the stage at the end of the school year and accepts the award, I speak a silent thank you to the teacher whose movement-based methodology has made the difference to a young boy with autism.

OUTSIDE OF SCHOOL, ERIK PULLS on rubber boating shoes and climbs a worn out, docile horse at the local therapeutic riding barn. He loves *voltige*, circus on horseback he calls it, and finds draping himself over a horse's hairy torso, arms pitched like a superhero, ridiculously comical. What he doesn't know is that Superhero Erik is strengthening a floppy posture and is building core strength. I am relieved to see him interact with the horses, the instructors and the other riders—pretty much in that order. Erik has found his creature of choice.

We have our share of flops, as well.

Wishing to integrate Erik into local recreation programs for those with autism, I sign him up for a stay-and-play program. When I pick him up the first day, his opening question is telling: "Why am I here? Everyone is so . . . so . . . ba-aaad!" he whispers loudly. "William shouted the whole afternoon because someone messed up his crayons," Erik continues, tittering, as we step out into the parking lot. "He had them in a row, like a rainbow, and someone wrecked the rainbow. He went . . . crazy . . ." Erik shows me in the van with flailing arms, laughing until he cries.

Just because you have a label, you don't necessarily fit the course code.

I will investigate more thoroughly in years to come. I will find the right fit. But there is value: Erik references William and the precise row of crayons. We talk about the need for control, order and predictability, and the pristine Crayola rainbow is the best illustration we know.

WE MAKE A VISUAL, A sequence of sketches on a small laminated rectangle of construction paper, to guide Erik after school. Every step in the flow—hanging up backpack, cleaning out lunch kit, nibbling a snack—takes a long time. In between each there is a buffer, a running of laps, a quiet corner with fidget toys. Transitions are treacherous.

You cannot hurry an individual with autism.

There is no good time for homework. After school, Erik is too burned out to look at it. After dinner, he is too tired to attempt it. After is never a good time to begin.

But it has to be done. And so we do, side by side, son and mother, in his bedroom. Most of the work is what he did not get done at school either because he didn't understand what to do (mostly, how to start) or because he got distracted or because his output is excruciatingly slow.

Time works with and against autism.

He sits and grinds away at geometry, and I flit from Erik's room to Heather's, setting and keeping the homework pendulum going. I spend most of my time with Erik. There is endless prompting; endless erasing; endless task reduction; endless re-teaching; endless cheering and endless coaxing. There are sometimes tears and often staggering fatigue.

We have squeezed this day, gone beyond its limits. But we get it done, knowing that tomorrow will be the very same. And so will next week and next month and next year and the year after. For better or for worse, I relive the elementary curriculum day by day, year by year.

Be careful what you insist upon. I recall Erik in Grade 1, slow to start, and my insistence that his program not be modified. It would have been much easier, but to turn the tap then? It was too soon. So on we go. I need to know how far we can take this. Erik needs to know, as well.

"TERESA, YOU'RE LUCKY."

This is the voice of child psychologist Dr. Yolanda Korneluk, and she has been working with Erik, updating his diagnosis, helping to propel him from child to preteen. They click. She loves him, he her.

I don't know what she means by luck. Working alongside Erik for years with no end in sight, I do not feel particularly lucky. Not hard done by, because I know everything could be *more*—more pronounced, more profound, more taxing, much more—but not lucky. I also feel that with Erik, it has been a slow and steady chisel toward what we have achieved. We have earned the present version. Erik has been hewn.

Years later, I will understand her version of luck. In Erik, we have *willingness*, a boy with autism, yes, but a boy open to self-awareness and self-improvement. And a hardworking boy. In Erik we have the Energizer Bunny, and like the reliable TV rabbit, Erik keeps on drumming; he never gives up. Yes, she is right. We are very lucky.

It is at this time, as Erik turns eleven and heads into middle school, I notice his voice and body changing. He is sprouting hair, height, hesitancy. Puberty has come early, and with it, social challenges I cannot begin to imagine. More hats emerge—*Pop! Pop! Pop!*—and with these, more resolve.

I transition from cultivate to capacitate. I need to lengthen the puppet strings, to hold back and to pull back. In Erik, a cautious self-advocate begins to unfurl as a so-named helicopter parent decides it's time to stow the chopper in the hangar. But I leave the door ajar, just in case.

CHAPTER 32

Worst-Case-Scenario Machine

PUBERTY FEELS LIKE AN ARRIVAL. Like we have made it this far, together. Autism is like that: each age and stage is shared. It is as though, like Peter Pan's shadow, I am Erik's outer skin, stitched in place, part of him, invisible but protective. I am Erik's barometer: I can look at his face and read his anxiety before it registers with him; and because I am me, I am able to articulate those emotions long before he is able, *if* he is able. As skin and barometer, we arrive at life's pauses side by side, hand in hand and breathless. Autism's journey aspect never goes away. Neither does the shared part. Autism is a lifelong odyssey, forever together, scaffolders and scaffoldee.

Puberty also feels like a switchback on a path. We are about to change direction moving forward. I imagine driving up a mountain to a ski resort. In order to ascend, we need to snake back and forth. Erik's climb is remarkably the same: steep, sure—but cautious and gradual. Measured. It's the only way to move forward when the climb is vertical.

Puberty is a good place to pause, inhale and exhale very slowly. I need to take stock of this journey. I want to appreciate the rear-view before we push on. I need to learn from what I have seen.

I am a hiking guide. An experienced guide stops to ensure that the hikers have caught up, explains what has been seen and what is about to be seen. A competent guide checks in frequently because, otherwise, there is nothing learned along the trail. There is only a relentless march to the finish line. And that is not what this is about, this autism journey. It's about savouring and understanding the scenery along the path, looking back and anticipating what is to come. I want to become that guide, for me, for Erik, for my family.

And so, as Erik becomes hairy and spotty and greasy and mercurial, I pause, and I reflect. I rewind to diagnosis. I revisit roadblocks and detractors, but I also rejoice in our believers and supporters. I want to process the childhood trail before Jungle Boy grows into something much bigger.

~

MUCH OF LIFE, I HAVE discovered, exists in the mind. We anticipate, we fret, we conjure, we project, we reject, we rehearse, and we believe the worst. Or we expect the best. New Year's Eve will be amazing because that's what New Year's is supposed to be: packed with pageantry and promise. But it's all practice. It's not real. We do it so much, and we do it so well that it seems real. It becomes life. But it's not. It is virtual, life in the head. It is construed and at times, it is embellished. But in the end, it is imagined.

I allowed virtual reality to seep into my autism life, to shape it, to project it and to have it influence my emotional state and my decisions. My biggest autism detractor early on was my mind's eye.

But to be fair, I think it all started with *The Book*.

Given that knowledge is power, when I was handed the autism diagnosis, I went shopping. I bought books about autism, and I began to read, obsessively, voraciously. I wanted to understand, to contour and to control the entity that had gobbled up my son. I thought books would be my ally, my comfort and my compass.

This was a good thought, but I was hasty. I chose books in desperation. I read what I could get, and what I found was primitive, calamitous and destructive. If I was inclined to believe (and how was I to know otherwise?), an autism diagnosis was utter doom and gloom. It was static and scary: a sentence.

And the worst part was, I read these books—one in particular, *The Book*—before bed. After a long day puzzling out autism and autism therapies, I sat up in bed and I read, heart tight, fretting and projecting how our lives might play out. It was a lousy way to cap the day. The autism portrait was dismal and damning. *The Book* was harsh, heavy on the worst-case scenario, light on insight. Everything Erik would never do was itemized, and the list was long. It was one-sided reporting at its best and at its worst.

Sitting there in bed, solemnly taking stock, I unwittingly programmed my psyche to conjure up the poorest possible outcomes. I was feeding my dreams and creating havoc in my head. I allowed it.

THE DREADED WORST-CASE-SCENARIO MACHINE BEGAN to rev up at 2:30 a.m., nightly, and in the wee hours, everything seemed dire and doomed. We were the family in *The Book*, and the prognosis was not good. Try as I might to staunch the stories, they kept coming.

One day, it occurred to me that perhaps the author of *The Book* did *not* have all of the answers. Perhaps this doctor was wrong or perhaps he was only partially right. Who is in charge of "will never do"? This mindset did not factor in growth and pruning and neuroplasticity; this mindset was primitive and narrow and inert.

And then came the reframe: how ridiculous! This detractor has omitted the most important variable—change over time. This model is flawed: it is a snapshot in time, spread out over time. It does not anticipate growth beyond the moment. There is no Miracle-Gro.

The more I thought about it, the more unreasonable it became. Surely, autism or not, Erik at sixteen would not closely resemble Erik at six. I would neither accept it nor allow it.

Fast forward ten years. I will be handed a book that will validate my early reaction. The book is *Mindset*. Author Carol Dweck illustrates the construct *growth mindset* to show that a can-do model of growth nurtures progress. We are ever-evolving. The idea that intelligence is predetermined and fixed is its antithesis. It is this stagnant forecast that I was fed early on when my son was six and freshly diagnosed. And it is this fixed, static mindset that I could not and would not allow in. Long before I read about the transformative power of a growth mindset, I knew, I *felt*, I had choices, and I chose to reject that early autism book, to toss it and to eliminate that detractor.

Of course, there would be many more.

But here is the key. Detractors can be denied. A detractor can only detract if you allow it to do so. So I laid that book to rest at the bottom of the blue bin.

The Book, I discovered, fed my mind's eye. Eliminate the book, eliminate the worry, right? Not so. The words and the dismal landscape that leapt from the pages persisted. I would lie in bed rehashing everything in my head: the predictions, the probabilities, the prognosis, the limited possibilities. At 3:00 a.m., the brain conjures up bleak outcomes. Why is that? A primal brain? Survival? Does the brain think, *If I can manage this, I can cope with anything*? Perhaps it is a primitive mechanism solidly at work, and maybe this is another "you never know what's good and what's bad," one more inverse power source, but the process gnawed at me and it exhausted me.

I googled "worst-case-scenario night brain" one morning after a restless night. I learned that my despair is the result of a natural dip in my circadian rhythm, and at this time, my cortisol levels are low. I read on. Cortisol is an adrenal hormone that helps our bodies respond to stress, regulate blood sugar and fight infections. Too little cortisol and I am defenceless and prone to invoke the worst. Good to know. Hard to stop. In any case, I would wake up tired, worried and beaten before I had even begun my day.

I needed to dump this cargo, too.

CHAPTER 33

Ominous Input, Optimistic Output

I TOLD MYSELF I WOULD make an effort to surround myself with practical people. Those who saw the good would help me to bring out the best in my son. I prefer possibilities to dire outcomes. With the former, the future is ours to cultivate and create; with the latter, the future is handed to us, tarnished, and set to mediocre. *No thank you. I will create my own future, and I will work hard to shape my son's future, thanks very much.*

I vowed not to allow my mind to become cluttered with negativity. I vowed to steer clear of the worst. I would default to positive or neutral. But never negative. Like most things in life, however, you eliminate one annoyance, and another little fire pops up, hot, bright and challenging. There is never a shortage of detractors.

Beyond the autism books, disparagers came in many shapes and sizes, ages and outlooks. The detractors offered words, predictions, condolence, recommendations, damnations, outcomes and advice. I listened, weighed, tucked and tossed at my discretion. I learned to filter. But still, I was prone to falter.

When I am well rested and feeling balanced, I am an adept detractor-detector and deflector. When I am tired, stretched and operating on too little sleep and with too many balls in the air, I allow the words in, and I allow them to have an effect. I feed the worst-case-scenario machine. It fires up, and even though I know better, exhaustion invites anxiety, and anxiety permits acceptance.

Exhaustion lowers the bar and throws open the gate.

Here is some of what I allowed in—the words and thoughts I permitted to permeate, the memorable stings, the sobering and often unsolicited bits of input, prefaced, in each case, by the source:

The Anxious Gut: This is a marathon, a long-haul job. Are you up for this?

The Pediatrician: I'm not sure what we're looking at, but I can tell you this—you don't want it to be autism.

The Speech and Language Pathologist: You will *always* have to be Erik's scaffolding.

In hindsight, he was accurate, but the *always* felt like a sentence. It was too much, too soon. Years later it would dawn on me that he was being kind and that scaffolding is a good word. Scaffolding is temporary, put in place during construction and growth. It is meant to be taken down. But in the moment, I saw metal bars: infinite, heavy metal. "Always" felt like a yoke.

The Grade 2 Classmate: I know what Erik is! He's *autistic!*

The words ricochet from child to child and from parent to parent. The diagnosis is out. Erik has been reassigned from classmate to category.

The Grade 2 Teacher: Erik will *never* be able to work without an aide.

The Individualized Education Plan: Autism is a *severe, pervasive* neurological disorder.

The Fringe: The lack of invitations; the lack of eye contact; the lack of yearbook signatures. *The silence and the invisibility.* Life on the periphery.

The Looking Glass: As a parent, looking in from the other side. Nearly neurotypical. But not quite.

That is a glimpse of the continuous input, a fraction of it, representative of the early journey. It was a kaleidoscope of worst outcomes, heavy on *never* and *always*. All told, if I allowed it,

Erik's future was cemented, cast in doubt and narrated by a potpourri of detractors. I needed to remind myself to step back and to decide what to do with the information. *It's not what happens to you, it's what you do about it that matters most.*

I BEGAN TO CULTIVATE A personal collection of guiding lights. Like a smart wardrobe, I assembled a set of go-to mantras for every occasion, something to pull out and wear that would allow me to reframe, massage and manage the weighty words. The process became a game. In my head, I saw it as a flow chart, a computer model with ominous input and optimistic output.

Controlling the flow of words and their impact on me felt powerful.

These were and remain my go-to mantras. I consider these *The Transformers*, my comfort words and the sensible thoughts that seize the alarming input, work it, sculpt it and deliver a workable, breathable output.

Where there's a will, there's a way.
Just do your best.
You don't ask; you don't get.
If you don't like something, change the way you think and speak about it.
You never know what's good and what's bad.
It's not what happens to you, it's what you do about it that matters most.
We can make that.
There is no real failure; there is only failure to meet expectation.
When you think you know, you stop thinking.
It could have been worse.
If it was easy, anyone could do it.
It'll all work out; it always does.
Continue is the power.

IN MOVING BEYOND, I TURNED to those walking in my shoes, to the autism parents in our community. We were initially a group of five like-minded undeterred mothers of children with autism. Shared experience and shared emotion comforts and connects. It binds us; it motivates us; and it allows us to move forward together. There is incredible relief in sharing the load. And for me, there is synergy in pooling brainpower. I paid attention to how I felt after each of our meetings. Uplifted. Empowered. Inspired. It was a compelling trio.

We moms discovered that time heals and time offers perspective: it allows us to climb out of life and view it from a distance, objectively and without emotion because with time, reaction settles and flattens. It is then that clarity comes, followed by lessons and then, wisdom.

The lesson learned in the context of autism is never to act in the moment.

"Put it in drafts," Frank tells me. Good advice. I've read that one should never promise when happy, reply when angry or decide when sad. Give it time. I've since added a corollary: do not react when tired. Fatigue derails. Emotion blinds. But time softens the blow, diffuses emotion, makes sense of events and offers renewed hope, new beginnings. Trust time. It is often kind to autism.

IN TAKING STOCK, A CATEGORY four disparager bubbles up. Ah, yes. Great Big Emotion, the sum total of the autism diagnosis aftermath: that nebulous knot of disbelief, sadness, incomprehension, denial, rejection, awe, appreciation, sadness, fear, joy, confusion, determination, hesitation, triumph, fatigue, fear, belief, disbelief, anger, pride, worry . . . packed into a tight and relentless orb. Early on, it immobilized me, taunted me, embarrassed me and surprised me. Years past diagnosis, this one continues to challenge me.

Emotion persists.

This recurring detractor was ever-present early on, cutting in like an unwanted dance partner, provoking me and diminishing my purpose. When I needed to be articulate and advocate for my son, tears welled up, uninvited, and my voice betrayed me: shaky and high-pitched are neither convincing nor helpful. When I intended to work collaboratively, the combatant would surface. Great Big Emotion can do that. It can spoil deliberate plans.

In time, I discovered I could harness GBE and use it purposefully. A friend offered me this realization: "Teresa, I see that these deep and sometimes painful emotions actually power you. Whether you realize it or not, like water falling from a dam and turning the turbines, your emotional response is the force that propels you forward. I see it clearly. You are driven by raw emotion. You've made it work for you."

He was right. Perhaps I had my detractors to thank: the damning predictions, the books, the emotions, the worst-case-scenario mind, combined to shape resiliency and to keep me moving where I needed to go. Forward.

THERE IS A GLARING DETRACTOR that has been hovering, hidden in plain sight. Words. Not the night thoughts or the words spoken directly to me, but the words spoken *about* autism: the autism adjectives. A constant flow of words, like water, has the power to erode over time if we allow the flow to sculpt and shape. Words meant to help elucidate autism are double-edged. Flip them and those words damn and dictate, predict and paint. They are sticky, unwanted but undaunted. They just won't go away.

There is a danger of becoming what we are told. I fear this for Erik.

It starts with the diagnosis and the adjectives around autism: pervasive; disabled; anxious; isolated; alone; different. Limiting adjectives. Tell me something good. It's a nudge from song brain, demanding clarity and balance. Isn't there anything good about this? I thought, too, of a poem I had read years earlier, about being cautious with words, about words wearing big heavy boots and stomping off, loudly, making noise, having an effect. Words last. Once unleashed, you can never take them back.

If words can do this—shape and dictate, can we not dish up better words for autism? If we can demote through projections, can we not balance the equation with words that promote? If we can manufacture anxiety, can we not, instead, build positive self-esteem?

IN THE MIDST OF CONTEMPLATING autism detractors, my unicycle-riding friend, Karen, texts and describes a personal hurdle.

It wasn't as bad as I imagined, she tells me.

I text back, Well, there you go. There's your guiding light for the rest of the month created for you by you: it wasn't as bad as I imagined.

Don't think too much, I add. It might be simpler than you imagine. Or it may turn out completely different. There's no use hauling yourself through versions. We both create scenarios. I'm trying to stop that. My imagination is too vivid. Yours, too!

I explain my new outlook to Frank over morning coffee, how I plan to move forward with less expectation and more celebration . . . with a plan but without scenarios preprogrammed in my brain. I'm not going to overthink.

I get through my spiel and look up to find him smiling broadly. I know why. I am describing what it is to be him: pure in-the-moment experience and the absence of preconception. I could have tapped the source.

In his reply, Frank is—as always—frank: "Think like a guy and don't."

CHAPTER 34

Overwriters of Prediction

DETRACTORS SHADOW THE LANDSCAPE; SUPPORTERS invite me into the sunlight.

I think about the lifelines. Many have been unexpected, like brilliant sunshine after a heavy rainfall. These gracious and giving people have offered us buoyancy, partnership, understanding, inspiration and hope. Their resonance is compounded when you factor in the effect on Erik.

Supporters allow me to reframe and to keep the frame a positive one. Instead of despairing all that is going wrong, supporters invite me to notice all that is going right. They teach me autism gratitude.

Supporters get the ball rolling; they start the positive cycle of belief. And then, like cell division, it builds, slowly at first, and then exponentially.

If our detractors are our reactive fuel and provoke a response, our supporters are our proactive spark, offering faith without judgment and encouraging us to carry on. Our detractors knock us off track; our supporters keep us on course. Our detractors fire us up, and our supporters offer us light.

In life, we need both fire and light.

Like our detractors, our supporters came in many forms. Sometimes they fell into our lives out of the blue. Sometimes they were not the types we would have pegged as sources of strength. One never knows where the rays will emerge.

There were little girls like Megan. "No one *asked* me to play with Erik. I do because I like him. He's funny and he makes me laugh." Blessed girl.

And there were one-on-one autism respite workers like Kylie, who, at the end of the day, did not look exhausted and beaten after an afternoon with my son. Instead, "We flew kites at the beach and we talked about objects and their shadows. Erik took pictures of our skinny shadows on the wet sand. He said we looked pulled like putty. He's a poet and his photographs are art. Truly."

You only lose sight of your child if you buy in to the detractors' mindset. Stick with the supporters, and they will feed you what they see, not what they are told to look for. They will keep your perspective intact: child first, autism a distant second.

"Erik will surprise you."

It is the guiding light we turn to daily. It is our default, the glimmer that carries us through. It is proof that we become what we are fed. We are what we eat.

THERE WERE FIRST RESPONDERS, THOSE like Miss Sarah who were swift to sweep in and catch me after the diagnosis.

One day, shortly after receiving the autism stamp, I received a packet in the mail. There was a stack of papers: neat, detailed, handwritten notes from an autism conference and two books. *My Kitty Catsberger*, clever and light, likening autism to quirky feline smarts. This was the uplifting stroke. The other was classic Temple Grandin, *Thinking in Pictures*. It was the first I had heard of Temple, and it was my introduction to autism through autism, a good place to start. With these treasures was a note: Miss Teresa, I'm sending you these bits and pieces to help you begin your autism journey. With you beside him, Erik will shine. With love, Miss Sarah.

Sarah and I met in Germany in 1993, and back then, neither of us paid much attention to autism. As a speech and language pathologist, Sarah had autism on her radar, but it was not yet on my scope. Sarah would later work closely with children on the autism spectrum. As a mother and consultant, so, too, would I. Our overlap continued to grow. We playfully imagined combining forces: Miss Sarah and Miss Teresa's School for Unlocking Potential.

Unwrapping and drinking in the package became indelible. Holding the note, I knew that, like Mary and Audrey, I would get by with a little help from my friends.

BY CONTRAST TO THE EDUCATED and the wise, there were and are the little people, the wee family members like Scarlett and Layla, who squeal and delight when Erik chases them and hops after them as though he is a giant frog. "Ohhhh Eeerrik!" they shriek. They do not judge; they do not see autism. They have not acquired limiting filters like preconception and stereotype. Their vision is clear and it is pure. They see what they see. They *like* what they see. And perhaps they don't even see Erik. Perhaps they see Erik the frog and they see the best babysitter ever. In their midst, he is adored and he is cherished. And in their company, Erik becomes how he is made to feel.

Among the tiny and medium-sized, Erik says he feels helpful and admired. Each summer, we connect with family at the cottage. There in the wilds of Georgian Bay, Erik, Heather and Scott interact and play with cousins half their size and one quarter their age. In Carwyn and Rhys and Leo and Margot, Erik is esteemed. He's the big guy; the one whose team they want to be on; the one who hoists them for rides in cardboard boxes. There is so much laughter. The effect is uplifting, even from a distance.

"How did that make you feel?"

"I feel energized by them but also like a role model . . . *like I'm doing the right thing.*"

Erik beams as he speaks, and the radiance is as telling as the message. In an existence devoted to therapying out the wrinkles, it must feel to Erik that he is constantly doing the wrong thing. To be made to feel the opposite, not by experts but by youth and through the purity of not knowing, must feel like a blessing.

THERE WERE PRINCIPLED PRINCIPALS WHO created quiet spaces for Erik in their schools. The Mr. Berrys and the Mr. Lees and the Miss Linens walked with Erik in their hallways, noting what he noticed, captivated by what enthralled him. They revelled in his unconventional interests—heat registers leading where? Light switches that powered *what?* They hadn't realized how many fire hydrants surrounded their schools until Erik brought them up to speed.

These principals stretched borders, concocting mini-challenges, like speaking over the loud speaker, at first after school when the hallways were empty, and then over the morning announcements. What a thrill! The effect on Erik was radiant. He stepped up. He shone, basking in their light. These leaders were among Erik's early supporters, and he knew it, felt it and became swept up in their conviction.

Alongside the principals was the handful of teachers who helped to sculpt Erik's inner dialogue. These unassuming heroes understood their role: allow Erik to be the only thing he knows, the person he is. Authentic Erik.

Their genuine reaction to Erik became the reaction of choice. Students, teachers, parents, custodial and office staff started to buy in and mirrored our supporters. "Emotion is contagious," writes Malcolm Gladwell. If this is true, then so, too, is reaction. *Reaction is contagious.* And when it is good, it is very, very good. And when it is bad, well, yes, it is dreadful.

OUTSIDE SCHOOL, OUR FRIENDS AND their homes were our seren-dipitous sanctuaries. There were the Annes and the Leahs who did not flinch when seven-year-old Erik pushed buttons and flicked switches in their houses, dimming lights and triggering ice cube avalanches in their kitchens. Instead, they looked on amused, open to discovery. Their expressions showed Erik that they appreciated his need to know. He told me later he felt respected.

And there were friends who applauded from afar; those, like Karen, who validated Erik's artwork: "I love his choice of colour and how he uses positive and negative spaces. He understands what appeals." Erik's confidence soared. This is the transforma-tive power of belief and believers: they take us and they catapult us forward. They make us better first in our own minds and then in our actions. Erik told me her words made him feel like an artist.

There were visitors to our home and to our family members' homes who gravitated toward and talked with Erik, seeing around and beyond autism. There was Ping, entrepreneurial, worldly and big thinking, who cradled and tickled and tuned in to toddler Erik. Years later, there was Lyle-with-the-smile, the rule-breaking, poetry-writing cop, who sat on my mother's sundeck and engaged Erik in animated, man-to-man conversation about music and life's quirky moments. And there was the mushroom-picking, bare-foot wood carver, Courtney, who invited Erik for beach walks and talks; who taught Erik the art of jewelry-making and who saw in Erik what we see: "Erik is an awesome, cool guy with good hands and a huge heart." There was also the rock-collecting, body-building surfer, Will, another of the unlikely and unexpected devotees: Erik is like a 1000-piece puzzle, he texted, . . . taking longer to figure out, but the image is often brighter and more beautiful.

The enablers are proof that those with autism are as capable as their environment allows them to be. If you are an open and able sculptor, the clay will take shape. Erik becomes your projection and your creation.

THERE ARE AUTISM OASES THEMSELVES—THE family support centres and the therapy centres where there is no judgment. *People see things for what they are and not for what they are not.* Nothing needs to be explained. When Erik flicked the light switches, he was not a misbehaved kid; he was simply curious, a junior scientist working out the electrical circuits. Having others see in our children what we see is a relief.

Supporters changed the way I saw my son. Our cheerleaders shook up the developmental trajectory I had etched in my mind. They sketched a more promising picture. They dared me to believe. They stretched my thinking and the possibilities for my son, and like an artist's hand over my own, they encouraged me to dabble and to explore and they taught me how to paint a better, brighter, more beautiful picture. They rewrote boundaries, and in some cases, removed borders. Supporters pulled me from the detractors and allowed me to transform messages of doom into messages of hope and resilience.

The fallout of support is immeasurable. Effect is what we carry forward. Effect shapes. Effect transforms. Effect affects.

Supporters keep us afloat. Emotion *is* contagious. I have a choice.

~

CHAPTER 35

Hormones and the Number Line

THE STORY REEL IS POISED at puberty. The mountain is high, the road twisty. Switchbacks are us. We are moving forward. Up and out.

Up and out of what? Up and out of expectation; out of the shadow of the word that consumes my son and, evidently, me; away from sticky adjectives and the damning predictions; far from the lowballing; above the scrawling red letters and beyond the numbing prognosis. We need to distance ourselves from the "will nevers." And while I do not expect a miracle, I do expect growth, continuous growth. I need to see how far we can take this. On we go, up and out.

ERIK IS ELEVEN. LIKE A premature frost that tints September leaves, puberty appears earlier than we expect. It goes to work on Erik, and the transformation begins. An accompaniment, "Sunrise Sunset" is set to repeat: "When did he grow to be so tall? Wasn't it yesterday when he . . . was . . . small?"

Erik's voice changes, from elfish to gentle giant, deep and resonant. His body erupts with hair, fuzzy at first, and then wiry and resolute. And he grows, quickly, from danger zone, perpetually in line with Mommy's chest, to taller than Mom, approaching Dad. Our playground pixie is no more. He is entering middle school, and we are on a new trajectory.

The school is familiar territory. Big brother Scott broke ground when we moved to Ottawa: the hallways and the gymnasium and the lockers have been explored. The school is comfortably travelled. We visit in June before Grade 6 and take pictures: Erik's new teacher, his classroom, the halls, the lockers, the change rooms, the library, the gym, the office, the office staff and the washrooms. All of the usual targets.

We cover curiosities, too. This is when I hand the camera to Erik. He knows what he wants; I know what I think he wants. There is a difference. So he goes at it, snapping drinking fountains, light switches, heat registers, on hands and knees at times, recording what the janitor's mop might see. Perspective changes everything. We return at the end of the summer, and Erik photographs the classroom floors and walls once more in case anything has changed over the summer. He is tenacious. Digitally, he is ready for week one.

But we have not anticipated the effect of hormones.

It is most noticeable in the girls. There are curves; there is height; and there is effort to blot T-zone shine. And with awareness, the social scene tilts. Girls are no longer interested in buddying with Erik. They have moved on to boys with brawn. The boys are noticing the girls with curves. Erik is mesmerized by the number line that borders the blackboard and how it is the same and different from that in his elementary classroom.

"I didn't know you could turn *left* at zero!" he gushes one day after school. I feel negligent for not having told him about negative numbers or having linked the outdoor thermometer with the classroom number line. Old numbers. New value. He can't stop talking about them.

Erik is in his own space. Those around him have evolved. There is heat in these hallways, preteen exhibition, nuance and flirtation. Erik hovers at the classroom door, beaming, faithful to the number line and to the classroom anchor charts. *Good name.* These charts are grounding. Order is salvation. Order is reassurance, rescue and recovery.

Erik's teacher is attentive, visual, positive, encouraging and organized. We could not ask for more. But this is middle school: hormones crowd out pedagogy and hijack help. Recess and lunch become murky drop zones. Erik's peer group has scattered and Erik free-falls.

SCOTT IS IN GRADE 8, and while he is not prepared to care for Erik, his eyes are open. He comes home one day and spills it out. His report stirs the beast. Great Big Emotion is awake, and the tears trickle.

"And there he was, Mom, sitting *all by himself* at lunch recess, cross-legged, staring at a brick wall. Just sitting there, rocking, facing the wall."

Erik had been left to wander during recess. He couldn't figure out how to insert himself into the throng, so he chose the next best—to block it all out, to give himself a blessed time out. He knew what he needed, but this was not what others needed to see. Hats in hand, I rush to the school.

"During recess and lunch, *Erik needs help*!" I am frustrated that I have to ask *again.* "He needs structure during the unstructured time. You know, 'work is play and play is work'?" Just as traffic lights are installed after an accident, I am in to mop up, to put it right.

"The brick wall incident?" I continue, ". . . can we not do better than this?"

The learning support teacher is losing patience with me. "Oh . . . well . . . that," she pauses, gathering air. "That's just *autism.*" She is backpedalling and reminds me of the Grinch caught stuffing the Christmas tree up the chimney.

Autism hangs in the air between us.

But I am not little Cindy Loo-Who. I know better. "No, that's not autism." My voice is quiet. "That's *neglect.*"

We stand together, silently facing off. My thoughts are defiant. *And what if I didn't know better? What if I put my eggs and my trust in the professional basket? What if I bought in? Believed this?*

"It is not . . . uh . . . *normal* . . . to have a mother here at the school in the noon hour . . ." The LST crosses her arms. Unaware, I do, too.

"Believe me, I'd rather *not* be here, but I *will* be here, every day, until we get this right. For Erik."

The thoughts tumble before the words are carefully formed. The words have surfaced like a geyser, mushrooming when I least expect it. The pressure release feels good.

The result of the hallway standoff is the puzzle room. It is the brainchild of a learning assistant, Mrs. O'Reily, who notices the anomalies, the enigmas and the social square wheels. The teen-aged puzzles. She fills her learning resource room with treasures: books, comfortable nooks, noon-hour bingo, movies, popcorn, and puzzles, plenty of them. For Erik and others, it is a sanctuary in a bewildering teenage play yard.

OUTSIDE SCHOOL, ERIK REMAINS FRIENDLY, but with few friends. His social life consists of skill-building sessions where he partici-pates in infinite role-play—an endless warm-up for the real thing. I am impatient, but I notice the role-play soothes Erik. Practice is perfect; he isn't ready for real. He also rides therapeutic horses once a week. He is happy with this schedule because it is struc-tured and scripted. Life with lines is pleasing. Safe. Predictable. Social spontaneity makes him anxious. With Scott now thirteen and Heather nine and both very active, "life scripted" is all we have time for.

Life is about meeting immediate challenges but being vaguely aware of broader goals. Autism scaffolding forces me to think ahead. Like the store owner who stocks shelves with swimsuits in February, I am the mom anticipating the next autism hot spot to be cooled and arranging the therapy to temper it. Scaffolding is an ongoing magic act.

CHAPTER 36

The Birthday Masher

BIRTHDAY PARTIES ARE ANOTHER BALANCING act. Erik's, yes, but Scott's and Heather's, as well. What to do with Erik while caught up in the celebratory swirl?

During Heather's fairies-go-bowling party, nine seven-year-old girls strap on gossamer wings and hurl bowling balls. Jungle Boy copes by patting and polishing the dimpled balls, but he soon finds it too much: too noisy, too drawn-out, too hot, too confined. Too many *toos* tip and tilt the boy. Frank steers Erik out into the sunlight, agitated, and I continue, solo and sweaty, consumed by fluttering fairies, mask in place but mind in another.

We live with rehearsals and contingencies, perpetually prepared to bail and re-muster. Plan B is our default.

Two years down the road, we stage a treasure hunt in our backyard forest. Heather and I have spent many hours planning this party, sending out riddles and treasure maps a week in advance. September thirtieth is upon us, and the girls arrive, poised, maps in hand, memorized (this is a motivated bunch). They are hungry for the loot, rumoured to be glittery, fashionable and buried somewhere in the forest behind our house.

Erik, meanwhile, is taking stock of the changes that have transformed the backyard into a desert island. There are walk-the-plank activities; pirate basketball; something involving water balloons (a cannon ball throw); necklaces to bead and room décor to fashion. He pokes around the set, wiggly and ecstatic.

Heather convinces Erik not to wear his Jungle Boy outfit today. He complies, distracted by the importance of the camera dangling around his neck. He is the birthday photographer.

As we build to the treasure hunt, Erik forgets to take pictures. I am vaguely aware of this, but my focus is on my young audience. We are gathered around the edges of a green fleece picnic blanket, finishing up a snack. I am delivering instructions. The girls are giving me their full attention, but out of the corner of my eye, I spy offbeat fluttering.

Erik is running delirious circles, arms flapping, his delight spilling out, overwhelming him, exploding from him. This wasn't part of the rehearsal. I keep up the instructions, but I see that the circles are now loopy: he is performing an odd lunging dance, and like a punctured balloon, he is wildly zigzagging, gushing air. There is a hoot of laughter. The girls think Erik is putting this on, but Heather catches my eye. She knows what it is. So do I. Erik has short-circuited. He is on ecstatic overload. Autism is here, full on.

"Erik!" I call out. Nothing. The wildness continues; the laughter is uncontained. Heather's brother is hilarious! But a few have noticed Heather's face, horrified, and have caught on. Something is amiss. I shout again, sharper. He stops, freezes, and I ask him to sit so I can finish the instructions. Of course he cannot, but he tries.

The girls turn to me. The show's over. I continue speaking, warily confident that we have weathered something. But then it evolves into something new, this orb of excitement, and what it looks like beyond rolling and wiggling is not good.

"Look!" someone shouts, "He's . . . *mashing* the grass!" All heads swing back to the lawn show, and to a backdrop of shrieks and laughter, there he is, performing something face down in the grass that looks like a rap dance turned lap dance. How do you Grinch *that* away?

And in that moment, our beautiful and detailed backyard treasure map is wholly hijacked by the rapturous birthday masher.

I HAVE BEEN TO PARTIES like this, events upended in seconds, sometimes by the birthday girl or boy themselves.

There was Kelsie, three, without autism, who stopped unwrapping presents, ran and hauled her potty into the centre of the gift circle, squeezed mightily, got up, straightened her expensive party dress, held the potty straight out in front of her and announced, matter-of-factly, "I just did a poo-poo!" She seemed more surprised than her stunned gallery. But she wasn't done. Like a chef on cable TV, she made the rounds with her product, tipping it reverently for all to admire. I looked. It seemed rude not to. Her mother was speechless.

Jessica, five, with autism, slam-dunked a hunk of her birthday cake, *SMACK*, onto the kitchen floor. The boys at the party were enthralled and began imitating her, joyously clawing and slamming cake. The euphoria ramped up when she paraded out of the kitchen holding her dress up around her waist. She wasn't wearing underwear. Dilemma: demolish the cake or ogle the anatomy?

And there was my mother's eighty-fifth birthday celebration, planned in infinite detail, except for the collapse of an elderly gentleman during the group photo, dropping with a colossal *CLUNK* and passing out cold.

"Somebody call 911!"

Erik heard it first, and I heard his intake of breath followed by "HEH!" his random delight sound: an abrupt, unfiltered whoop of joy at life's pure randomness. "Somebody Call 911!" is also the title of a popular dance mashup. He had never heard the words shouted in real life, outside the dance floor. Neither had I, and I admit to thinking, for a flash, of the song title.

For me it was a blip, the recognition. For Erik it was an inclination to lock onto a captivating detail in the big picture, which is good if you're a forensic detective but bad if someone is in distress and you're stuck on and enthralled by the cry for help. I didn't want the party-goers to see Erik's half smile, to judge my son because of that unlikely and inappropriate response. To know Erik is to know the look and the reason for it: it was not about the event, it was about a random feature attached to the event.

Erik defaults to laughter in emergency. It's the easiest release: nervous, giddy laughter is his safe zone. So while I called 911, Erik paced, smiling, processing how life can become a song and how everything can unravel in seconds. In the scheme of random chaos, to Erik, this is Oscar-worthy.

Meanwhile, a paramedic team sweeps into the stunned festivities, attends the fallen man and wishes my mother a happy birthday on their way out.

Autism or not, you cannot plan for everything. With autism, the likelihood for the unexpected and an adventure within an adventure is much greater. In fact, it is probable.

EIGHT YEARS AFTER THE BACKYARD masher, I will be vacuuming in Heather's bedroom, and I will notice a set of cue cards on a shelf. I will recognize the scenario that launches her high school speech about perspective-taking. It is the birthday masher in her words, via her sibling perspective:

> When I was in fourth grade, my family and I hosted a party to celebrate my ninth birthday. I was beyond excited. I had moved to Ottawa all the way from Vancouver Island just a year before and was thrilled to celebrate a very exciting day with my new friends. We'd go swimming, play some games and go on a scavenger hunt around the yard. We had it planned to a T. When the time came that all of my friends were over, we were all outside sipping on what was probably Five Alive juice boxes. This had been the first time I had friends over all at once since we moved, so there was an overall buzz of excitement throughout my family, including my older brother Erik, who was eleven at the time.
>
> As we were all snacking and munching away, I look beside our picnic area and spot Erik rolling around in the grass, laughing excitedly. Now my friends saw Erik at the same time I did, and they all began to laugh. There, in the grass, was Heather's older brother, a sixth grader, doing something we would've done years and years ago. My friends were laughing, which encouraged my brother to continue rolling and rolling. I was so embarrassed. An older brother isn't supposed to be doing

that. He's supposed to be playing video games in the basement or something, right?

What if I told you my brother has autism? Does that compensate for what he did? Can we understand why he was doing what he was doing? Can we see things from his perspective now? Rolling around in the grass was Erik's way of expressing just how excited he was. Sometimes it's easier to express actions rather than words. Perspective is everything.

CHAPTER 37

Venus, Goddess of Love

IN 2009, WE BECOME HOCKEY-GOERS, Ottawa Senators fans. We each have our reasons for going beyond hockey.

I want to relive the Montreal glory days and my time with my father. Frank is vaguely interested in hockey; he especially likes that you can drink beer in the stands. "Civilized," he says. Heather is pumped because she longs to be *discovered*, to appear on the JumboTron, twirling her blond ponytail in helicopter-Heather mode. Riding on the Zamboni between periods will do, too (we stuff the ballot box with fifty-three entries but never win). Scott is mesmerized by numbers, by stats, by plays and by strategy. Erik is captivated by the swirling lights. I am worried that the sensations may overwhelm him, but he is instead transfixed and transformed.

This constitutes our family fandom.

On this particular pre-season night, we attend this sound and light show, and lo and behold, a hockey game breaks out. We climb up to our nosebleed-level seats and prepare to make our way into the row when Erik stops, yelps, and grabs my arm. I assume he is excited to be here, so I continue, swishing past bent knees into our row. Erik whoops again and bumps into me, hard this time; the rest of the family follows, *BANG, BANG, BANG*, thumping into one another slapstick-style, like a family of stooges.

I look up and see the object of Erik's eye, the thing that has distracted him from the spinning lights. It is a very hairy man sitting where we are headed. All I see is eyes and masses of dark hair—face, arms, hands—and a wide dazzling smile. I sit next to our bushy row-mate, nod and say something as Erik tucks in beside me, wiggling wildly, wary, watchful, waiting for the furry face to speak. *Funny how hockey can be trumped by lights and how lights can be diminished by hair.*

Erik sits beside me throughout this game, beside himself with glee, peeking through me at this man, shrieking and peeking, shrieking and peeking, writhing, the entire game. I try to normalize this giddy seesaw, quiet him. The man notices and pretends not to notice. I try to divert Erik, but he won't be distracted. I am the sweaty fulcrum in this peep show, the middle man, the traffic cop and the two-way filter. Metaphor is rampant. Where did the hockey game go? As usual, hijacked by autism.

It strikes me that *filter* fits well: without me, autism is incomprehensible and hair is outrageous. With me positioned between the two, two-way understanding is possible.

To Erik, this shaggy intrigue is way better than objects and their shadows and what's not allowed—combined: Mom is sharing an armrest with a near-Neanderthal! I know he wants to interview me, ask me how it feels to be so close, *touching*. This is a classic *trip character*, Erik's term for what he considers an outing anomaly. Trip characters delight him because they stand out; they are rule-breakers, daring to step outside of culture and expectations. They speak their mind and they are courageous in action and appearance. It strikes me that life is indeed a mirror: Erik loves what he also is—original.

Back in Row R, Erik is mesmerized. He has never seen a face like this. I am afraid he may grow brave and lean past me and gape, or worse, touch.

He does not, but he talks about that hockey game (what hockey game?) for days, months, years beyond this. Right now, we need to focus on "He shoots; he scores!" and on convincing a young boy with autism that this Sens fan has not broken any hygiene rules, and that it's perfectly all right to have copious hair—and to take it most anywhere.

WE DO ONE MORE THING before 2009 gives way to 2010: we sponsor a boy from Malawi named James Malunga. There is something about James' picture that we like, this snowy night when we choose it. We are Christmas shopping at a local mall, and we pass a World Vision display. We begin talking to the representative, and before long, we have a photo of a big-eyed boy in our hands. He wears a blue work shirt, and he stares through the lens, startled, directly into our eyes. His first photo? The bio says James was born in 1999, right between Scott and Erik, and that he likes maps and running and sweeping the floor. "So do I!" squeaks Erik. And so it is sealed, this link with a wide-eyed boy from Malawi.

We all write to James. Back that up. The kids write, and then after a year, the task is Mommy's. I am also feeder of fish. James and our koi fish belong to me now. We send James pastel muscle shirts, just like the boys and Frank wear, and James declares that he feels like a Hedley man. We also send him a deflated soccer ball and a pump and a whistle. James tells us these riches have made him popular. I fear, like *The Gods Must Be Crazy*, that our trinkets may disrupt the social order, but James is adamant that the ball is a source of joy for his village and full advantage for him. James has an inflated soccer ball, an inflated status and an improved self-concept. Like Erik, environment has shaped James.

Erik is twelve, in Grade 7. Heather is in Grade 5, her last year of elementary school, and Scott is in his first year of high school. Bigger picture, Vancouver is hosting the 2010 Winter Olympic Games, and we are all hooked on the theme song, "I Believe."

I volunteer at two of three schools that year, to help out and to keep an eye out. Erik has another fabulous teacher. We have been fortunate—three for three since our arrival in Ontario. This year's teacher invites me into the school during the first week to talk. I arrive ready to explain, defend, illuminate, but it isn't necessary. This woman wants me to know that she is excited about having Erik in her class; she wants to know more about my son so that she can tailor her teaching to his interests, talents and inclinations. I think I might cry.

It is not often that everything lines up beautifully in life: the teacher is in tune; the academics are gelling; and the puzzle room is filling up with a lively assortment of kids. Erik has comrades, if not friends. He also has a girl interest, and it is mutual.

One day, I am volunteering over recess, and I investigate the puzzle room. Erik is at a reading table with this girl, Jocelyn. They are head to head, flipping through a book about astronomy. Cute. I venture closer. I hear him laughing as he points out the planets, and hovering over Venus, he cuts to the chase: "Venus," he purrs, gazing at Jocelyn, "Goddess of Love . . . "

I nearly choke. "Erik?!" I manage, and his head snaps to attention, equally surprised.

"My *mother?*"

We both wish the other away. He later tells me that "Goddess of Love" was an attempt to dress up the book, to breathe some fire into it . . . only to look up and discover . . . *his mother?* It was his first foray into flirting, and Mother was hovering, incredulous. Go figure.

But I needed to see it. Erik is teenaged Erik first. Autism, please take a number.

ERIK IS READY TO LIVE without lines. Weary of endless social skills classes, Erik is eager to "live for real," he says. Just Kiddin' Theatre is our science lab. We find our people.

The director, Andrie Nel, is in our shoes. As a mother of three teens, one of whom has autism, she gets it. Spirited, cheeky, sensitive, in tune and existing somewhere between the box and the fringe, she writes the scripts, penning parts with each young actor in mind. No one is excluded, and everyone is welcome. There is a string or two involved, one being the need for parents to stay and volunteer. Eager to learn about blocking and props and set design and prompting, I sign us up.

For Erik, the experience transcends theatre: he feels what it is like to be part of a collaboration, a team that needs you. This feels like home. He makes the happy sound here. The purring begins as soon as we pull into the parking lot. The happy sound is Erik's on board indicator.

Makeup artists slather thick stage makeup on Erik's face, and he doesn't baulk. I am stunned, and he is captivated, transformed into something he is not—or perhaps into something he is. He likes this concept: it feels deceptive and exhilarating, he tells me later, like running through chaotic streets on Halloween night. Everything is the same and different all at once.

"I am free on the stage," he says one night on the way home.

I find it fascinating that his reaction is 180 degrees from his measured daytime persona. It is also the inverse of most: public performance lifts him up and out. Public speaking does not frighten him; it becomes a portal to his soul.

Like Jungle Boy, these roles that he plays—an alien, a surfer dude and a husband—allow him to step away from himself and from autism. He can reinvent who he is, and there is no preconception, no judgment. In costume, diagnoses do not exist, and social rules are suspended. You cannot be wrong incognito.

Opening night and he is on stage, lines memorized, eager face tilted toward the glittery stage lights. Erik does surprise us. Tonight, in this darkened theatre, the autism adjectives fade to black.

CHAPTER 38

Niche Cramming

THIS IS THE YEAR WE will not only discover portals, I will force them.

My mother records a made-for-television movie about twin teen boys with autism. What strikes her about the movie is the mother's determination to have the boys fit in, to discover and nurture their loves. Audrey says I must see it.

I tear up as I watch because it is also me, my current life. What I discover is that these boys love to run. So does Erik. He always has, the ubiquitous tight circles, as a way of processing information, of self-regulating. The twins in the movie turn out to be exceptional cross-country runners.

Convinced that running is a natural fit, I persuade Erik to join the school running club. Scott is no longer at the middle school and Heather has yet to exit elementary, so I have no in-house spies, no one to report Erik's progress. He tells me little about the practices beyond, "Ya, I went."

With zero feedback, we press on. The theatre group worked, why not this? But maybe by his avoidance, he is telling me something. Erik communicates by reluctance, rarely exuberance. If I pause and observe, perhaps I will see what he likes. But I do not. I experiment and I force.

When the cross-country event consent form comes home, I sign up as a driver, a chaperone, a detective and a cheerleader. I want to see how Erik fits in with his new friends-by-club-association and witness his transformation to runner-boy, just as it had unfurled in the movie.

Life seldom imitates the screen, and in fact, the outing is a disaster. The kids' snacks have been left at school, so I scramble to purchase nibbles for the six runners in my care. They grab with teenage detachment and shark-like fervour.

I notice that Erik is outside the group. The others talk, laugh, warm up and mix. Erik hovers at the periphery, pacing, looking pinched and panicked. I suggest that he may wish to stretch his muscles, and he looks at me darkly. I wait for the running aura to descend; he waits for the air horn, looking agitated. It starts to sprinkle. I find a good spot to view him and to photograph him, to record the moment when he sails by at the halfway mark (this is a five-kilometre run). It starts to sprinkle harder. It's raining.

I wait at the bend. There are lots of runners, lots of high-fives, lots of pictures taken mid-race, but none by me. And then no one. Minutes tick by. Is he lost? In the movie, one of the boys gets lost. Maybe Erik has gone off-trail. We rehearsed the route, walked it, just like in the movie. Maybe it looks different in the rain?

And then I see him approach. Walking. (Not like in the movie). Muddy. It is his expression that is conspicuous. It is undisguised fury. As he gets closer, he attempts to run, to trot, but he does not smile. To my astonishment and embarrassment, he instead bares his teeth, snaps his head my way and growls at me.

"Errrrrr," is all we hear, those of us remaining.

I try to patch it, to cover it, to spin it. "He must be having a bad run," I suggest lightly, as though he often has good ones. "The rain . . ." What the others do not know is that I have cajoled him into this. In wishing to find a portal, I have crammed a niche. Running doesn't work. It isn't one of them. I have also done what I despise: I have lumped Erik into a stereotype for autism. "Kids with autism often like to run to release their anxiety." I assumed. I tried the buy in when I knew the tune in was the right thing to do. I was wrong.

I am at the finish line, waiting, mostly alone, and I get my confirmation: "Never again!" he hisses, once more through clenched teeth, as he labours past. He does not talk all the way home and for two days after that.

BEYOND THE RUNNING, WE SEEM to be in a good, supportive groove: theatre, academics, a school social oasis and a budding love interest. Erik wears a giddy glow.

One January morning, as we are waiting at the end of the driveway for the school bus, I ask about Jocelyn. "Sooo, what's happening with you and Jocelyn?" I venture. I am expecting a planetary update. Instead, in a matter-of-fact and measured tone, Erik pulls the rug.

"Well, she holds my hand, and on the way to the bus she tries to nibble my ear . . ." Noticing my wide eyes, he adds, "I know I'm a little young for that . . ."

His bus has arrived, and I exhale as he moves forward to board. Just as I relax, he turns with a slow smile. "But I kinda like it."

Wham!

School dances take on a whole new twist this spring. He is dancing. He apparently never stops. But just as magnificently as the magic builds, it vanishes.

"There's a dance at school tomorrow . . . ," says Scott, now in high school. "I'm really not into them; could you come and pick me up early . . . take me out for lunch maybe?" At fourteen, food trumps females.

Before I can reply, Erik chimes in, "Me too . . . Can you get me, too?"

"But I thought . . . Jocelyn . . . ?"

The boys start a discussion . . . Subway or Lebanese shawarmas? Jocelyn has been supplanted by subs. I learn later that she has moved on. I pull on my consolation and explanation hats. I hadn't expected this so soon.

JUST AS WE ESTABLISH A breezy rhythm, we derail. Autism is like that. We can never fully relax—none of us. I ask too many questions, I know I do, but there is one that is bothering me, plaguing me, especially at night. I am conjuring more worst-case scenarios.

"Erik, what time does your bus arrive at school in the morning?"

"8:05."

"And what time does the bell ring?" I know that the kids are not allowed in the building until the bell rings. I also know that Erik finds small talk excruciating, especially pre-teen talk, especially so early in the morning. He is not warmed up enough to fake it.

"It rings at 8:25," he replies. "Why are you asking me these things?"

"Oh, because I'm curious about what happens between 8:05 and 8:25." For Heather, this is bliss, this free time; for Erik free-range is as bad as it gets.

"I line up at the door and wait. Eventually it opens. They let us in."

I picture my son staring at the door, just as he had the wall. I am reminded of a bargain-store shopper, camped outside, waiting for the opening bell, only that is a hopeful scenario. This is not. It is a coping strategy.

I head back into the school when my emails go unanswered. I am back to bridge the gap between overlooked and looked after, and it is not just about Erik. There are other free spirits for whom this morning limbo is agonizing.

I approach the learning support teacher again—the standoff woman. I am back to plug another gap. Her expression says "you again?" and her voice is weary, wary, "Yes?" I ask whether the outside door can be opened early for those wearing a hallway pass. I am told there is nowhere to put these kids. No supervision. The outside-till-the-bell rule cannot be relaxed, no matter how painful for some. I go home and puzzle out how to make this work. Solutions are within reach. A creative compromise is always possible.

I return, animated. "I've got it!" This one can be remedied. "You know how at airport gates there are TV monitors and special shows to pass the time, to offer a distraction? How about wheeling a TV up to the window beside the waiting door and give those gathered something to watch. A focal point. A common interest. We do it for adults. We could do it for these kids, yes?"

The plan is acknowledged as possibly viable, but the idea is never adopted. It is too something: too much work, too much responsibility (to wheel the TV to the window each morning), just plain too much trouble.

Is it too much trouble to stand in my son's shoes?

CHAPTER 39

A Bad Rash

I USED TO BE SHY. I tell myself this so I don't lose touch with the inner girl. I tell Erik so that he knows that words will flow in time. His words, his timeline.

I think about what I have become, this spokesperson for my son, for others who cannot speak for their needs. I did not intend for this to happen. It was necessary. I want people to know that what they see was not a choice. Autism chose. I would rather not be intervening, interpreting, asking, forever asking . . . repeat, repeat, repeat. This is not how I thought things would go. Most people do not plan for what they get. They step into it. There is need.

Sometimes I wonder how I must look. Determined? Desperate? Dogged? How do I come across? I'm not certain I want to know. Sometimes we drown and hibernate in our children, and for better or for worse, the effect is transformative. *Consumed* fits, and it is seldom a choice.

"Who will you tune up *this* week?" Erik titters, eyes bright. To him this constant vigilance and intervention is humorous. He is keeping tally. He sees me like a piano tuner, forever tightening the strings on his teachers, on the administration. This has become my duty, and it makes him laugh. It makes me tired.

I think to friends from Germany who visit us in Ontario. We are immersed in Little Tikes and other kiddie branding. They had known us in our medieval castle, throwers of parties, drinkers of wine. The travellers. Now we look like we run a Montessori school in our kitchen.

"The Hedleys . . . *with toys?*"

They can hardly believe it. We can hardly believe we've been anything but this.

And now I cannot recall being anything but relentless. I'm not fond of this version. I'd like to revamp it, foist the responsibility, but there are no takers, so I wear it. This is not what I ordered, but this is what I am being served. I accept it and go at it with the tenacity I would have devoted to any other path—the paths I thought I might live.

I was not always this person attached to autism. My life used to be simpler, freer. But now I hardly know how to live without it, without Erik, constantly watchful, offering options and drop-down menus, directing the flow.

A few years down the line, an administrative assistant will let slip that she and her team refer to me as *a bad rash* (let's just say I will have written many emails until things work in our favour). "Your video really added to the conference. Thank you! It worked out so well . . . ," she will say to me. And as an afterthought, with a quiet laugh, "You're not actually *a bad rash* after all."

Her hand will immediately cover her mouth, but like the poet's boot-wielding verses, the words will be out and marching. *Bad rash.* Imagine! Frank, for the record, will howl. "You always say that you never aspire to be beige," he will sputter between peals of laughter. "You got your wish!"

I will also find it funny; mostly that the words spilled out. The two little words do their work. They make me think, as words are meant to. I do wonder whether I need to ease back. I see it clearly in my head: the relentless spectrum. It is rosy, attractive, but as it intensifies, it becomes a harsh red, and to the far right sits the rash, bumpy and irritated. It looks prickly. I never intend to be this.

Like it or not, I will toss bad rash onto the post. Like horseshoes ringing a metal stake, I see the projections stacked up, and with each pitch, I can hear the *clink* as new words hit, metal on metal. These ringers never go away, but that's okay; they make for something better than beige.

Fast-forward further still—to a beach community on Vancouver Island, 2018. A neighbour will ask me what I think my life would be like if Erik were not in it.

"Weird," I will say. And after a pause. "I'm his tour guide for life. I'm not sure how to be any other way."

WE LIVE WITH ANXIETY AND advocacy. The little stuff rolls, accumulates layers, snowballs and becomes the big stuff. It is time to exit stage left and refresh the slate.

We are in Mexico, peering into a cenote, a vast, underwater cave. I feel panic, not for me, but for Erik, unprepared to be lowered into this cavern, ten metres of winching in darkness toward the clear, cool water below. As we peer down, the water winks back at us: a flawless circle of glittery turquoise, spot-lit by the sun. The periphery is inky black. I shiver. Can Erik do this? Will we need to abort this mission? Do I go first and pave the way or do I linger and reassure, coach and monitor him from above?

We split forces: I follow our mavericks, Scott and Heather, and Frank stays behind to flank Erik. I am lowered into the shadows and admit to feeling thrilled, perhaps how Indiana Jones felt entering the Temple of Doom. The music booms in my head: "Dunt-da-*DAAA*-da, dunt-da-*DAAA* . . ." and I revel in the descent, jerky but joyous. The cave world approaches and envelops me, and soon I am dangling just above the water; toes dip and I am unhinged and released like an eager salmon fry into a stream. I swim; I love it; and then I look up. Erik is by now en route down.

"Why, this sound isn't *sad*, this sound is *glad!*" Song brain is fired up. Erik's face is exuberant, not tortured. "Why, this face isn't *freaked*; this face is *piqued*." He's enjoying this!

I notice something else. Erik is doing what no one else has done before him and what no one else will do after him: he is looking *up* on descent, not down. He does the same in life: endlessly looking back, reviewing photographs, reliving vignettes, and looking up, capturing the sky.

Erik later tells us that the walls of the cave were plastered with bats. Families of bats caked the walls, sleeping, hanging, fluttering and jostling. He says it was amazing, "like a kaleidoscope of wings and pointy faces." But only if you looked up. None of us had. None of us saw what Erik has seen, but we are used to that.

Autism asks us to look elsewhere. And to notice.

WHERE DOES ERIK STOP, AND where does autism begin?

The Mexican cenote rehashes the old questions, brings them into focus. They never go away.

My Big Three are these:

1. How much of Erik is Erik and how much of Erik is autism? What would Erik have been like without autism? How much of the intriguing bits of Erik are autism or coloured by autism (mostly, the noticing, like the bat cave)? Is it possible to separate the strands? Would we want to, or would we destroy the whole?

2. What are we trying to achieve with therapy—a different Erik or a polish on what we already have? As my friend Karen articulates so clearly, "I don't get it. Are you trying to hide autism or applaud it?" In truth, I don't get it either, but it does become a little more obvious with time, the great elucidator.

3. What is success for you for Erik? This is also Karen, a text this time. She likes to ask the hard stuff, to poke, and I welcome it, encourage it. She makes me think and I need to. I expand her poke. What is success *for Erik* for Erik? I realize somewhere along the line that I need to be asking him.

Untangling the Christmas lights—Erik and autism—is always right there beside what are we trying to achieve with this? And mostly, have we ever asked Erik whether he wants this? Indeed, what *does* he want? These are my questions, fodder for my 3:20 a.m. brain. There are many more. These are the biggies.

I MENTION OFTEN THAT ERIK is friendly but without friends. This is not completely true. There are some fleeting and flickering friendships, but they do not last. In some cases, we, the family, do not allow them to thrive because they are too painful. We extinguish them.

The Jason Experience (TJE) is one of the friendships we snuff, vigorously and unanimously. TJE becomes a shudder-with-laughter family fable, at once funny (time can do that, too) and also so uncomfortable that it's hard to go back because the emotion returns, and the heart pounds. TJE is a one-time event, never to be repeated. It all starts with four words.

"Erik, are you medicated?"

The voice is high-pitched and the body is small, taut, perpetually in motion. This is Jason, Erik's sleepover guest. He has arrived at the foot of our driveway to work on a Grade 7 project—a salmon dip net (drilled by Father Frank and threaded by Mother Teresa . . . what will *our* letter grade be?).

Back that up. Jason has been dropped off. From where I am bent over weeding in the side garden, I can hear the squeal of tires in the street. Mom or Dad has released the son, flung the torch our way, and the bushfire has ignited. I had hoped to chat, to be briefed, but it doesn't go this way. Instead, I hear a car door slam; the eager tires spin off, and then the boys gather Jason's belongings and walk up the driveway. From behind the bushes, I hear the question about medication. What follows makes me very nervous.

"No, I'm not," says Erik.

"Well, I *am*!" squeaks Jason, "Only, my parents don't agree about that. My mom thinks I need medicine, you know, to slow me down. My dad, he says he was *just like me* when he was a boy and he wasn't medicated. 'And look how I turned out!' my dad says . . . so I figure he's probably right. That was my dad who dropped me off. I took my pills this morning at my mom's house, but pretty soon you'll see *the real me* because my dad didn't pack any pills."

He sounds pleased about this joke they have played on Mom. I feel sweaty and anxious. The clock ticks. How much time before a hellion surfaces? How much time have we got to get this social studies project done before the transformation begins? I imagine a green Hulk-type deal, growing, exploding from within, popping buttons and roaring from somewhere deep in the basement. My imagination is stoked. I tell myself to relax. How bad can this be? Really?

Well, quite bad. There is a trail of destruction, and that is only what I can find. Erik tells me, breathlessly, that there is more hidden carnage.

I take stock and discover that in his desire to see inside, to discover how things work, our revved sleepover guest has beheaded a cat toy; ripped apart a stapler; torn my beloved ceramic Prague marionette puppet from its moorings and pried open its jaw in the name of oral surgery; jammed a CD into a player; whacked a Wii remote so hard against a wall that it has been knocked senseless; and for his final act, has hauled our prized hornet's nest from its perch in a cedar tree and hacked at it with a hockey stick on the outdoor rink—dissection by demolition.

"Noooo! Not the *hornet's nest*!"

That is Scott; he thinks Mom might blow a gasket with this one because I love this dried nest, its honeycombed perfection, and he's right.

"Okay! *Enough!*" I bellow from an upstairs window. I run downstairs, two at a time, and corral them off the ice. I police the boys until bedtime and Erik is relieved. The show has gone beyond thrilling; Erik is now feeling thrashed and worn. We all are.

Later, as I lie in bed willing my heart to relax, I hear it. Flushing. I awaken again in the night to more flushing, but I convince myself that it's worst-case-scenario prime time. Chill.

Two weeks later, a plumber comes to adjust a malfunctioning sump pump in the basement.

"You've got to get your kids to stop flushing Ping-Pong balls," he tells me. "Here's what's wrong with your system." And he moves aside and reveals a dozen little balls, some of them the yellow smiley-face variety, bobbing and sloshing in the reservoir.

When I peer in, I see Jason's face on those smiley balls, smirking up at me, getting the last laugh.

"Ohhhh," I gasp, as it all sinks in. "That's not *my* kids. I know who did *that*! A friend of theirs . . . ," I explain, the anxiety I felt during that sleepless night returning, the uneasy knowing but not knowing.

"Ya, right," he says, grinning broadly now. "It's always somebody *else's* kid . . ."

CHAPTER 40

On Becoming a Stereotype

July 16, 2011. Erik becomes a teenager. Thirteen! He can't believe it.

"Now I've become a *stereotype*!" he informs us, big-eyed, pimply. He thinks all teens are a certain way, but he doesn't feel that way. It's confusing. Like his teeth, he is braced, but he isn't sure for what.

"When you finally get to an age, it doesn't feel like that age," he muses. And then the adjunct, "You don't have to act according to the stereotype for your age." He, no surprise, does not.

If you see something, say something.

This line flickers onto my awareness, brightly, one morning. It is something that our three children spotted in Australia, a crime prevention sign that charmed and challenged them. The wording, in its ambiguity, struck all three as funny.

"See what? Say what?"

Now, four years later, autism advocacy has delivered those answers. When something doesn't seem right, you need to speak up.

In Grade 8, our teacher fortune runs out. Erik's eyes tell me we are in trouble. After a week in his new class, he sports a deer gaze. He tells me I'd better go into the school for meet-the-teacher night. He tells me to be ready. I am not.

The new teacher is a talker. I sit in stunned silence with the other parents. We are hushed; he gushes. Teacher thumps on desks as though issuing a battle cry. He means well, I do think so, but he is pure ad lib, without a plan. He is hard to follow, and his thoughts and speech are rapid-fire. I try to imagine Erik here. I shiver.

We are handed a timetable, but it's the wrong one. It is the cryptic copy meant for staff. The kids have also been given it a day or two before. They reckoned themselves code crackers, puzzling over teachers' initials and course codes. The students were never meant to have this version. This is part of the bundle of bright red flags. By the end of the evening, I feel confused, sweaty, heart racing. No wonder Erik comes home wide-eyed each day.

I speak to the new learning support teacher on my way out. I request a student timetable for Erik. She glances at the staff copy, blanches. Her face registers that the teacher has handed it out to the students in error, but what she says is this: "Yes, Erik has problems with things that aren't literal." And with a patronizing smile, "*Autistic* children do . . . I'll give him a copy that he'll find easier."

I feel myself tighten at the word "autistic." I never use it, and the way she says it, hanging onto the letter "s" comes out sticky sweet. I feel something between a shiver and a shudder. She views Erik by the book, not alongside it. As his primary support person outside the classroom, this is less than ideal.

"Please give him the *correct* version," I say. Inside I am furious. It will never be about the teacher. The special education student is unable to read what he should never have been given. The red flags unfurl, fluttering and snapping. I pay attention.

Fast forward a month. The assignments are pleasingly creative and thought-provoking. That part is hopeful. The concern is the how. There is no blueprint, zero organization. If this were theatre, it would be an impressive bit of improvisation; but it is not, it's a middle-school classroom. There are too many words and they are spewing, unrestrained. The kids are drinking from an unruly fire hose. The class is chaotic and never the same on any given day.

Erik is unravelling, and he is not alone.

I visit the principal, and he is a stellar fellow. This is delicate. I tell him what I see. He also has eyes, and he is pedagogically astute. He sees but he cannot say. I speak for us both. "The emperor isn't wearing any clothes. I see this clearly for what it is."

If you see something, say something. Prevent the crime.

I tell him that the classes are chaotic. I tell him that for a change, we will not shine the light on the special education students and assume that they are not getting it. We will turn the light and shine it where it ought to be: on the educator. There are kinks in this flow. The students are not receiving the information in a way that works for them. Good throw. Good catch.

The principal does his best to engage the teacher and offers professional coaching and mentoring, but things do not improve. Erik unravels further, and as a family, we are forced to absorb the shock each day. Emotion is extremely contagious. Our days are tinted by a child wound so tightly that he cannot speak, so he runs and he shouts and chokes and he cries out in frustration instead. Dysregulation is us.

I MOVE UP THE CHAIN of command and speak over the phone with a district superintendent. Now we ought to make some progress.

"I'm not sure I can conjure up this pedagogical marvel you describe . . ."

My heart races. I had not expected this. I thought I had an ally, someone who would understand what it is to be Erik, to be me, and a pedagogical partner to boot. But the inference is that I am asking for perfection when it does not exist, that I am asking too much. But I am not. I am asking for competence. I am asking for planning, predictability and professionalism. I take a breath. I try not to flinch. I try to keep Great Big Emotion out of this.

"Good news! No conjuring required," I begin, kneading my thigh, suppressing the emotion that will surely come. "This pedagogical marvel *does* exist. There are two of them at Erik's school."

I feel vaguely bullied, as though I am meant to back away and fold, say "Okay, okay," and hang up so that he can tick off his to-do list and get on with his day. But he hasn't done anything useful. And I cannot go away. I must keep him on the line. We reach acceptable ground, and further professional support is offered to the teacher. Nothing changes.

I am aware that Great Big Emotion has leapt aboard and that my reaction and my interpretation of the superintendent's words are bathed in deep, churning emotion. Maybe he is trying to relax me, inject a bit of levity. I'm not certain. Encased in concern, I feel only surprise and deep disappointment.

And then one morning, it happens. After another chain of spiralling emails to the teacher, I set my coffee cup down hard on the desk, and I hear my voice: "That's *it!*" The words hang.

This is not the encouraging or the eureka variety of "that's it!" It is the fed-up version. We will step up and speak up. Song brain calls up a lyrical accompaniment, "If you don't stand for something, you will fall for anything." We are not about to fall.

A voice is born out of disbelief. I would rather not be speaking, but I will. If I do not, nothing changes. Erik comes home, twisted, tormented, and we are a family on alert, forever untangling the knotted version Erik becomes at school. I cannot allow this.

Erik and I decide to write about it. Writing allows moments to crystallize; words make sense of what happened. For us, it is a mighty and overdue catharsis. A letter to Erik's principal and classroom teacher, originally meant for the school, makes its way to Autism Ontario. Entitled "I Have Autism and I Need Your Help," the letter becomes an article, and this article becomes the basis for a mother-son autism article series that will span six years. "We always need to be positive, purposeful and practical," I tell Erik. It becomes our creed.

"Erik, if you see something, you must say something."

We look back over that tortuous school year and laugh. Almost. Our family mantras resurface: it's not what happens in life, it's what you do about it that matters most; you never know what's good and what's bad. A challenging year provides the seed for collaboration, and like a warm summer wind, the words waft and float, settle and become lyrics for other families like ours.

"Erik," I say playfully, "Imagine if you had had a good teacher in Grade 8?"

CHAPTER 41

The Accidental Messenger

MY FRIEND NATALIE CONTACTS ME. She is the red-white-and-blue-swimming-ribbon mom, and she is also a lawyer: sharp, quick, intuitive, tuned in and relentless. She tells me she is the representative for autism on the Ottawa Catholic School Board's special education advisory committee, and that I might consider doing the same for the Ottawa public board.

"What do you actually *do*?"

"Well, mostly just listen," she tells me, "and speak when necessary. Kind of like being a parent," she laughs. "No really, you speak for students with autism when the school board comes up with new policy and programs. You are the shoes of autism. Also, you are the liaison between the board and the parents. As rep you are a public advocate."

I am interested.

I join the Ottawa-Carleton District School Board SEAC— Special Education Advisory Committee. As a representative for Autism Ontario, I sit with others around a massive woodgrain table once a month at the school board office, also vast. The elongated table is the largest I've seen: expensive, expansive and austere. You get the feeling that important things go down in this room, or at least, there is the potential for that.

Dotted around this enormous table there are others, a mix of policy-makers, advisors and advocates. The latter are mostly parents, speaking up and looking out for those with speech and hearing impairments; with Down syndrome; with learning disabilities; with visual impairments; with giftedness and with a myriad of other conditions. I advocate for the voices of autism, but what

I am most keen to do is connect with families. We walk the same walk; it makes sense that we collaborate on shared concerns.

I sit up well into the night, hunched over the keyboard, writing to these families, learning their stories and listening to what is not working for their child in the classroom or on the schoolyard. I know these narratives because their glitches are also our own. I have an urge to cocoon them and tell them what they are feeling is normal, and it's okay to be emotional and concerned and that I am, too. So I do.

There is something else Natalie and I tell them, these caregivers so tangled in autism, in bureaucracy and in emotion, and it's this: when you go into the school to talk about your child . . . when the meeting starts, pull out a 5 × 7 school photograph and slide it forward on the table. A small face sends a big message. We're talking about this person, not a problem to be solved. Faces humanize issues. As with televised news, we remain removed until we see faces. The pictures draw us in, let us know that the tally had lives. Like us. When it becomes like us, we are more apt to act with compassion. "Don't allow anyone to remain removed," we tell them. "Humanize your concern."

We are not often thanked for our efforts. Many assume that our communication comes from a cubicle in an office when, in fact, it comes from the heart, late at night and around the corner from our sleeping children and husbands. But that's all right. This feels right.

"Teresa, you've become an autism advocate," a middle school principal remarks. And so I have. Autism chose this.

IT IS AROUND THIS TIME that I decide to expand professionally, and like the Ottawa Senators bumper sticker, I go "All in, all red." The only tweak is a colour change: blue for autism.

"I'm here to tell you that you can *do* this." The speaker is knowledgeable and genuine. Tuned in. I don't register much after that, because that's what I have come to hear, to know.

I approach Dr. Korneluk after the presentation. I thank her for her intuitive words and arrange to have Erik meet her to refresh his diagnosis. Erik visits her office three times, and after each appointment, he wears the same look: one who has been validated. With Dr. Korneluk, Erik is not something to be fixed or corrected; she approaches him with sensitivity and leaves him celebrated and released from whatever it is that has snagged him. I notice, and this is what draws me to her practice. Erik's endorsement is my green light.

Emerging Minds diagnoses and treats children and youth with autism. However, the multidisciplinary team is missing one link— an autism parent consultant. I become it. My role, as we see it, is to help parents untangle sticking points in the home around self-care, family integration, forays into the community and family vacations. Later on, we tack on school support and advocacy. No surprise, this one mushrooms to the forefront.

"It's a bit like being an autism supernanny," Dr. Korneluk jokes, ". . . the person who goes in and untangles the thread."

Untangle. There's that word again. Untangling requires bags of props because, like basic navigation and clunky airplane parts, to learn about autism is to see it and to hold it. My sensory props are not housed in a kitchen cupboard; mine are portable, tucked inside a shiny, brightly coloured Picasso suitcase. I arrive at doorsteps, luggage in tow: autism handywoman.

ONE OF THE THINGS I do for Emerging Minds is create two large bulletin boards for the clinic foyer. These displays are loaded with visuals detailing autism supports and services in the Ottawa area. The idea is to offer parents a menu of choices, much like the toy menu we have devised for Erik at home. Before these panels are delivered to the treatment centre, they rest in our front hall for a day or two.

I come downstairs one morning and discover Erik poring over the colourful laminated visuals tacked onto the boards. I pause on the stairs, midway, and watch. Will Erik make an association between the words and what he knows about himself? Will he wear these words? He touches them, reads them, head tilted. I see that he recognizes some of the therapy centres because we have visited them. Some are our favourite places to hang out. He doesn't back away.

I watch and he stares. We stay like this, suspended, for several moments: he who reads; she who barely breathes. And then he spins around, seeming to know I've been there all along, hovering.

"Just like me!" he declares. He gets up and swishes past me.

I am floored. "Pardon?"

"It's me. I must be that because this," he gestures at the bulletin boards, "is all about me."

His reaction is no-nonsense. Factual. This is not how I imagined it. But in reality, the air has been slowly seeping from the hot air balloon. We've been floating downward for some time now. So the bump, when it happens, is gentle, not harsh. And Erik seems okay because he already knows the contents, just not the title page. And now he knows the word.

CHAPTER 42

LD, That Doesn't Feel Like Me

HIGH SCHOOL IS UPON US. Just as we get comfortable with our surroundings, we have to move on. Erik and I start talking about high school while he is in middle school, around halfway into Grade 8.

"Imagine," I say to him one icy January afternoon driving home in the van, "by this time next year you'll be in high school. And by January, it will be familiar to you, your new home."

This sort of talk comforts him. It soothes me, too. I am sowing seeds for both of us, but first there is the business of finding the right fit high school.

I start making phone calls and feel a sense of déjà vu. School shopping. I've done this before. The sensation is familiar, but that does nothing to ease the uneasy knot. I speak to a handful of learning support teachers to get a feel for school philosophies and support for alternate neurologies. "How do you breathe life into the Individualized Education Plan?" I ask, again and again.

I have discovered that the million-dollar question is not how to land a great IEP; it is "How do you make sure it's *used*?" How do you give legs to a fine plan, mess up a pristine Word doc with coffee stains? I imagine a closet full of beautiful clothes that are never worn. Impressive but useless. This is when coffee stains are good.

In the midst of these phone conversations, Erik's middle school psychologist steps in and suggests having Erik tested for the LD program. I flinch at the title, Learning Disability. This descriptor goes against my instincts. Honestly, why fixate on the glass half empty? Why not focus, instead, on the process . . . toward a glass brimming: Learning Enabled?

Connotation aside, we have Erik tested. We have no choice. He is too high-functioning for the autism program; his expressive and receptive language skills don't qualify him for the Asperger program, and regular high school will eat him up socially and academically. With its small class size and nurturing instructors, LD is our best route.

When the acceptance arrives, we rejoice a program whose title we oppose. It's the language that trips us up. Erik looks at me with big questioning blue eyes one evening, asking once more for clarification.

"Tell me about that LD name again . . . ," he says. He thinks about it, and eyes shiny, he whispers, "But LD . . . *that doesn't feel like me.*"

We embrace the four years by renaming the program. We drop disability and refer to it as Learning Enabled. We lean on a family mantra: *When you don't like something, change the way you think and speak about it.* We do, and we go a step further. We write to the school board, reminding the experts that the way we think and speak about our children becomes their inner voice and that inner voice guides our children's thoughts and actions. Even though I sit on the special education advisory committee, and I know these people, it still feels as though we are speaking into a shadowy chasm, as though addressing an elusive Oz.

We eventually receive a reply. There is sage agreement that this label is potentially damaging, but there are no changes. It would be too costly to change the board documentation, to scrub and redress the LD. But the cost, we implore, to a child's developing self-esteem? Who wishes to publically attach themselves to *disability*? Who would choose it?

It is ironic that the "no" comes from the same room I learn about growth mindset. I imagine what it must be like to be a superintendent, knowing what is pedagogically precise but having to answer to something larger.

Students are rarely consulted in the naming of programs. What would you name it? You have to wear it; what would you like to be called? Imagine being asked? To catch a fish, think like a fish. To cater to a fish, consult with the fish.

In June of Grade 8, we arrange a tour of Erik's new high school, a small school by Ottawa standards, constructed in the 1960s. Driving up, it feels like a *Get Smart* film set, Cold War era. It is low and stout, bunker-style, as though if pressed, students could hunker down here and survive. It feels historic, museum-like, and this fascinates both Erik and me.

Together, like our childhood games of *I Spy*, we list all things '60s: the occasional circular window; small swirls of outdated orange and brown bricks; an inner courtyard to invite the outdoors inside; low-ceiling underground hallways crammed with lockers; a fully functional home economics lab equipped with spotless, IKEA-like kitchenettes; a modest cafeteria and a cavernous, velvety auditorium with theatre-style seating. Erik and I heave open the massive door and peek inside: it is dim and silent. I imagine Grade 12 Erik somewhere in here; the idea seems mirage-like, theoretical and very distant. I am happy about that.

In my head, Elton John sings my thoughts, faint, a backdrop. I turn it up because I need to hear it, to have my feelings vocalized. "Don't wish it away; don't think of it like it's forever . . ." I know it's not. School shopping is my reminder: we've sailed from elementary to middle and now to high school alarmingly quickly. Time can do that, too.

Erik calls this June 2012 visit *Sweaty Wednesday*. We have unwittingly chosen the hottest, most humid afternoon of the young summer to tour his new school. We show up with our iPad, ready to record anything of interest or consequence. I cover the latter, and as we have done in the past, Erik takes care of the topics of interest: lockers and drinking fountains and club signage and hallway plaques. As we hand the iPad back and forth, our eyes meet.

"I feel like we've done this before," I joke.

"Ya," says Erik. "My schools in iPad folders . . ."

He adores these snapshot tours. With each click he gains control, because that's what this is about: the translation from foreign to familiar. The pictures reassure him and later reaffirm what we have come to understand: prime the mind and the body will step in line.

His photo list is not my list, but this is Erik's school. These images need to address and soften Erik's anxiety, not mine, so I trail sweaty student and heavily perspiring education assistant along humid hallways. Erik's photographs and short video clips will become his go-to transition toolkit throughout the summer. If he can see it, he can start to imagine it, and if he can imagine it, he can eventually do it. He is partway there.

The script starts in the mind.

WE DO NOT ATTEND GRADE 8 graduation. We cannot pretend the year has been anything but difficult and trying. We cannot fake it, sit and watch as the graduation scroll is handed from teacher to student, as though passing an enabling torch. It hasn't been like that; it has been a flame very nearly extinguished.

It strikes me that time is a great renderer, an impressive sorter and distiller of negative and positive. In the present, the negatives loom large and outweigh the positives because we have to do something about the hard stuff. As present becomes past, the positives are largely what we recall, not the tough stuff. *It wasn't that bad* is the default sentiment, and this is surprising, because it often was *that bad.*

I think about this on a late-summer night in the hot tub. I sit outside in the steamy, bubbly water, surveying the house. Some rooms are dark; others are bright with light and activity. I feel like a voyeur watching an animated home movie: my family, in silhouette, scurrying around, doing their Sunday night business. Lights click on and off and my eyes travel with it.

In the kitchen is teenaged Erik, bent over his lunch kit, adding items, arranging things carefully on the counter. He is efficient and not: for each task he completes, he circles the kitchen island. There is a great deal of pacing and circling, pacing and circling. I am mesmerized; my eyes cannot move from this room.

His mouth is in motion, silently speaking, appearing to over-enunciate and smile at the same time. His eyes are open wide, and like his mouth, they seem exaggerated, animated, over-the-top. His face expresses a strobe of emotions. If I didn't know Erik, I would think something was wrong. This looks like a supernova, a short circuit, like he is about to glow very brightly and then burn out. But I know what this is; it's a shard of autism, and it's what emerges when no one is looking.

This surprises me on this summer night just before Grade 9. I haven't seen autism flow from Erik like this since he was seven or eight when he would come home from school and run, hands fluttering, "thundering velvet hands," as though conducting and orchestrating his thoughts. I assumed these behaviours had been—what is the word? Extinguished. But no, they exist during private time, and this is one of those moments of heavy-duty self-regulation, not just the transition to the first day of the school week: it is the start of a new school year and a new school. High school.

As Erik circles the kitchen island, over and over and over, he reminds me of an aircraft spooling up, performing rotations until his engine is ready to roar. I understand what I'm looking at, but I am surprised that this takeover has survived, as though Erik has been possessed. I thought he regulated in other ways now. Seeing him from the outside inside, I realize that there is so much I don't know about autism and about my son.

The voices begin to flow, a throwback to my dusty Greek class-room, my students educating me as I sought to educate them: "Miss, it's a *Greek* word." Autism, Greek for *self*. Gazing into the kitchen, autism is there on display: a teen reaching into himself, into his own space, because that is what he needs to do to function in our space. "It's a Greek word, Teresa. You need to learn the language in order to understand the culture." I soak; he spools. We prepare for high school in our own way.

PART III

FROM BOY TO MAN

CHAPTER 43

Humbled by Hormones

GRADE 9 ARRIVES, AND WITH it, its soundtrack: The Barenaked Ladies' "This is me in Grade 9 . . ." Erik cannot believe it: he's a minor niner. He is fourteen, in *high school*!

We are now eight years into the autism odyssey, and we have become just-in-time advocates. *You don't ask, you don't get* prompts us to ask, but at times, we still don't get. "We might be planting seeds, though," I tell Erik. "Sometimes it's better if the idea comes from them, not us." We are learning diplomacy.

There are so many questions: Where is the quiet room? Is there a sensory room? How do you integrate students into school clubs? Why is this year's IEP exactly like last year's? Why isn't the IEP being used? How does Erik ask for accommodations when they aren't happening? How do we access a laptop for Erik?

The questions are similar each year. This is strangely comforting and predictably alarming. My bigger question is this: what if we did not ask? I imagine the tide rushing back in and everything we have worked so hard to achieve washed over, filled in and smoothed out. What if we did not advocate, continuously re-sculpt the sand?

IN GRADE 9 MATH, SOMETHING is percolating beyond pedagogy. Erik is struggling over a word problems unit, and I put his poor performance down to language. Too many words. Kids with autism struggle with too many words. I also wonder whether the teacher, who via her website seems exceptional, is explaining via diagramming. Erik is visual, and he needs to be taught this way. I go in to check out my theory, convinced I know the answer before I have seen the evidence.

I discover I am wrong. Completely and utterly wrong.

What I see has nothing to do with math or methodology. I see before me a pretty teacher. I also see my teenaged son heated and flushed, absorbed not with numbers but with smooth, pale skin, pinkish lips, soft reddish-brown hair and a scented sexuality. She bends over his desk and her hair falls forward, eclipsing part of the word problem, which *is* the problem—and to Erik, the solution. Oh joy. I thought I knew. Now I *really* know.

This cascade of hair might put him over the top. My mind flashes to the birthday masher and to other energy bursts that seem to take hold and detonate my son. I can hardly focus on the teacher-student demo, wondering what liftoff might look like in the heat of arousal. Erik, meanwhile, is rapturous, vacantly acknowledging her efforts with glazed smiles and mumbled yeses when I know for sure he has not been listening. The only input is sweet and feminine. He isn't absorbing anything numerical. How *can* he be?

It is then that I notice his gaze, away from the flow of auburn hair and beyond, to her jeans. I trace the path and notice it, too: the patch, the tiny red embroidered heart sewn onto her jeans. It is a delicate and pretty little patch and would be innocuous except for where it is: adjacent to the zipper on her jeans. All I can think of at that moment is real estate: location, location, location. Why is it there? Is it covering a hole? *There?*

Stop your thinking, Teresa. I feel like I've stepped into Erik's head. We are both locked on, rapt, wondering what the heck the miniature heart is doing there and why it has come to school, riding this pair of jeans. Does she wear these often? Does he cherish these heart days? I cannot look at Erik, or the jeans, or the teacher. Somewhere in the background, math swirls. She keeps up her explanation and does try her best to untangle the words. Erik floats higher and higher, and on multiple levels, the problem is never solved.

In the van on the way home it bursts out, as I knew it would. I am feeling a Dr. Wuuu-ah déjà vu. Erik, erupting in laughter, says, "Did you see the *heart*? Where it *is*?"

"Yes," I say. "She wears a heart; I did notice." Do I downplay or laugh along, but possibly escalate the heart to perseveration status? "She wears a heart," I say . . . and with a quick glance in the rear-view mirror I add, "and it's not exactly on her sleeve, is it?" I peek at the mirror. He lights up at the wordplay, face euphoric.

The little patch lives on and becomes our meme for clothing choices. It is also put to rest, down the line, in something we call the *finished box*.

The math unit is a bomb. No amount of diagramming and academic accommodation is going to solve this. We are up against sweet-smelling hair and a hormonal surge. I go home and report to Frank.

"Too many words?" he muses.

"Nope. Curves!" I reply.

He throws back his head and laughs. He likely had a *math-dish*, Erik's term, at one time or another, too. Go figure. I had been so focussed on autism that I had forgotten who Erik is more than anything else: a teenaged boy. My respect for hormones as a change agent is cemented.

I am humbled by this lesson. Humbled by hormones. And this is good for me, this human comeuppance. When I think I know, I become vulnerable to knowing little.

IT IS ALSO IN HIGH school that we are told a story that resonates. It is an astonishing tale of transformation by error.

We have arrived at an awards night at Erik's school, and we sit comfortably in the very theatre we photographed one year ago. A teacher addresses the parents, and her talk about the power of positive projection reverberates. Sitting in the darkened auditorium, I feel like she is speaking directly to me.

"At midterm, a teacher is in the process of adding comments to a student's report card and, by mistake, clicks on an exceptional comment for this average student. Instead of remarking that the student needs to work on dramatic timing and expression, the teacher's annotation reflects that the student is, in fact, *gifted* in these respects. The comment is completely wrong, but the report cards have already gone out. What to do? Turns out, nothing at all. What happens next is remarkable. Because the student *thinks* the teacher considers this ability to be true, the student begins to *believe* it, embody it. Inner thoughts create an inner voice; the inner voice drives actions. The student's performance improves. People notice. The student eventually goes on in dramatic art and does very well.

"Turns out what we project upon students affects what they become. In this example, the comment was made in error. Imagine how much we can achieve if we knowingly apply this formula? Belief is ours to give."

CHAPTER 44

Spinning Plates

CONTEXT IS CUMULATIVE. IT SNEAKS up on you. Context, like hindsight, is also 20/20. It will be clear to me in years to come that I have heaped too much on my plate, and the result is many plates, varied and loaded, demanding huge swaths of me. I feel carved, and I also feel revved, on fast-forward and at the same time exhausted. A teacher friend, Nanci, describes it this way:

"M.T. [her name for me, Mother Teresa], I see you with all of these spinning plates, you know, those performers who have plates on poles, spinning, all at once . . . so many plates, all spinning at the same time. That's you."

I'm not sure whether this is a compliment or a caveat. I accept it as the former, but maybe she means it as a caution: be careful, you'll burn out this way.

I like being busy, but even I feel things ramping up beyond what I can get done in a day, a week, a month. My lists are ongoing, never-ending. After a while, I stop dating them. They are continuous, and like a chore triage, only things with deadlines get done. Items like health bump down to "nice to do." As I allow this demotion, my blood pressure bumps up. My life, I realize, has become what my friend Sarah calls ATA—all things autism. I have not consciously allowed it; it just happens. Autism seeps. Pervasive hijacks the rest. We all feel it, Mother pulled, but no one so much as me.

I decide I need to reshuffle and trim. Like endless items streaming into our house, if I don't skim the bottom, it fills up. I need to eliminate some plates—let some drop. There is not time for everything I want to do.

I START WITH **SEAC,** THE Special Education Advisory Committee. I miss the little faces. I have floated up too far beyond them, and while this policy-making is for them, it is not *with* them. I fear, pulled up to this enormous table, we have become tangled in words. We have lost sight of our purpose: enabling children. This is a constant hashing out of complex issues. It's weighty. I need to cut this string. And so after two and a half years, I do.

Next, the autism consultations. I love them, and I dread them. I love them for the connection to families, for their stories, for their courage and for our shared paths. I love nudging parents toward understanding and toward practical strategies. And I love meeting their children. One non-verbal and highly expressive little boy hugs my Picasso suitcase. He chirps because it is on wheels, like his beloved school bus collection. He presses his face up against the smooth plastic exterior and runs his hands along the swirly, colourful surfaces. He looks like a harp player, in sync with his instrument. I have never thought of my suitcase this way.

What I find difficult is reliving the diagnosis. It is as though I am revisiting it, picking at it, allowing it to bleed. I am unprepared for this, how it rises up and how it spills over: all of Great Big Emotion rushes back, as though first-hand. Triggered.

Another bit of weightiness is something I feel as I give. Drained. After each consultation, I arrive home too exhausted to be much good, but there is still plenty to be done to keep the plates whirling. Sometimes fatigue knows no bounds. So, after much deliberation, I let this hat—this plate—go, too. Trimming comes with equal parts relief and regret.

I keep the article writing going because this is cathartic for me and for Erik. We learn as we talk and write and draw. The words we write echo back, letting us know what just happened.

Erik-advocacy. Here is one I can pare without entirely dropping. Erik is in Grade 10; he needs to be doing the asking. He begins to write down his requests in his agenda, and he schedules time to meet with his teachers. While Mother can be dismissed, Erik never is.

Homework help. Large, capitalized red letters stand between Erik and me: WITH ASSISTANCE. I realize why the careless scrawl annoys me even now: because it's true. Erik does need help. Reading on his own, for example, is next to impossible. Words go in, but meaning gets lost. By the time Erik gets to the end of a line, he has forgotten the beginning. Little details linger, but the big picture dissolves. I imagine icebergs calving, floating off.

We purchase a book reader, but Erik is not caught up with reading; he is tripped up by meaning. What he needs is a book translator and summarizer. But he has one of those already: me. We bump along, side by side, each night. With each school year, I hope that this will be the last (so does Erik, no doubt) elbow to elbow, but it never is. Erik sits on the bicycle; Mother pedals.

Don't wish it away, Teresa . . . Don't think of it like it's forever.

I remember when all three kids used to pile in bed with us. We thought that would go on and on. It seemed to, and then it stopped, by degree, and then forever. I tell myself the reading and tutoring will be the same. One day I might even miss it, feel a void, sadness, and wish it back. Perhaps.

IT IS AT THIS TIME the silver screen takes over our lives. Heather decides she wants to break out. She is talented, and I don't want to deny her her dream, so we sign her up at a local modelling and talent agency. The upshot is a new series of hats for me as well as for her. She gets calls for auditions in television series and sometimes in Hollywood movies that are frequently shot in Montreal, sometimes Toronto. This means we have to travel there for auditions, but mostly, that she needs to memorize lines in a day or two. Everything is astonishingly last minute in this business. It also means we need to shuffle life to make this work. The topper is catching up on what she misses at school during these filming frenzies, and I am needed, sweeping up, catching up.

The Scott hat is relatively light. He dashes off homework on his knee on the school bus and does well, but the big picture is demanding, worrisome. He needs help knowing what to do with his life. We attend counselling appointments and try to puzzle out a way forward. To parent is to expand, and Scott is the ultimate mother stretcher. "When something bounces or stretches, it is said to have . . ." Elasticity—me.

The plates spin and some fall. We seem to get everything done just in time, which is not me or Frank. Frank, for the record, is now DCO (deputy commanding officer) West, no longer practising dentistry or commanding a dental clinic but in charge of keeping all of the military dental clinics in western Canada functional. He lives with immense spinning platters. We perform side by side; we used to perform together. Life tugs. Divide and conquer is the logical way forward.

Autism has competition. But I never worry about autism: it jostles and rises to the top. It is me that concerns me, because I am also rising. And what goes up must eventually come down. Or do something.

CHAPTER 45

The Logic Behind Strange

LATE FALL. 2013. GRADE 10. Erik is fifteen. High school has so many rules, mostly unwritten. He learns some the hard way.

The phone rings. It's one of Erik's high school special education teachers. The consensus is that things are going badly off track. I listen and bite my lip.

"Erik has been acting, well, *strange*, lately."

"Oh? Tell me." I used to pull on my armour at this point but not now. I no longer recoil or apologize or agree. I listen and I attempt to illuminate.

"Well, he just sat there today," she begins, "and would not leave his first class. But it wasn't really his first class. He sat in Learning Strategies even though no one was in the classroom. He just sat there. He should have been in Art. Everyone knew that. His behaviour was very strange."

"Why do you suppose he did that?"

"It was definitely very odd!" She pauses, waits for me to chime in, agree that my son's behaviour is strange, but I will not. "He wouldn't move! Everyone knew it was day one. Day one starts with Art."

"Day one?" Now, I am confused. Hmm, I'm beginning to slip into Erik's skin without much effort. Yesterday was day one. How could there be two day ones, back to back?

"Oh, don't you know? The days follow the calendar days—odd calendar day, day one; even calendar day, day two. Yesterday was the thirty-first; today is the first—two day ones in a row."

"Does Erik know this rule?" It's new to me.

"Yes, the principal announced it to everyone. He would have heard that."

Evidently, he did not, or could not in the morning shuffle, or could not process the information quickly enough. "Words float and evaporate," Erik tells me. His behaviour is not strange. It's logical. Day one is followed by day two. He simply doesn't know the exception to the rule. He is operating according to his understanding, and to him, that makes sense. Erik thought he was doing the right thing, as did a blond teacher in Tokyo. Henna gaijin. Strange foreigner. I know it. I have lived it, too.

There is always logic behind strange.

FALL 2014. GRADE 11. ERIK at sixteen is halfway through high school. Already.

It is now ten years since Erik was diagnosed with autism. We have moved from a child preoccupied with signs and symbols and absorbed in the movement of his own fingers to one focussed on and dedicated to his own self-improvement. And through necessity, Erik has become a self-advocate.

One night, arriving home late from a meeting, I discover three pieces of paper on our kitchen island. On each page is written a brief message, and beside the trio is a note: "Which one is right? I think the middle one? Goodnight, Erik."

Puzzled, I begin to read. I am confused: three letters written to one of Erik's teachers, and aside from slight changes in wording, they are all essentially the same. I ask Erik about it in the morning.

"Well," he says, "these are self-advocacy letters, asking for more details so I can start my Careers summative." He pauses, smiles and then carries on, picking up the paper on the far left. "This one seemed too vague." He sets it down and reaches to the far right. "So I wrote it again with more detail, asking more . . . but then I thought it seemed too pushy." He makes a face and discards it to the far right. "But *this* one . . . ," he begins, reverently selecting the middle page, "this one is *just right* . . . not too weak and not too pushy. This is the one I'll take to school."

"And how long did this take you last night?" I ask, gesturing at the three letters.

"Most of the night," he admits. And brightening, "But it's important to get the tone right. It's not what you say but how you say it," he reminds me, offering something we've been telling him for years.

"Kinda like the three bears of self-advocacy?" I ask.

"Yes!" he says brightly. "Just like that!"

And that is how we refer to the art of advocacy: a three-bears approach to getting it just right.

At school we advocate for inclusion. While the special education staff has worked hard to provide students with a lunchroom safe haven and a handful of specialty clubs such as weaving, cooking, anime and crystal growing, students with autism remain, for the most part, segregated. I am struck by this as I leaf through Erik's unsigned yearbook. He is not in any candid photos because he was not in the hallways. Erik and others like Erik remain on the periphery, observers of high school, bumping up against but forever skirting neurotypical. We have seen progress, but there is still much work to be done.

OCTOBER 22, 2014. OTTAWA IS under attack. My mother emails me at 10:30 a.m. and keeps it brief. You might want to turn on the TV news. (She knows I don't much.) Ottawa is under attack.

At that moment the phone rings and the answering machine picks it up. It's a call from Erik's school. They are in lockdown. The phone rings twice more, immediately. It's Heather's school: lockdown. Scott's: lockdown. I imagine them all hunched under their desks wondering what's going on. Heather and Scott will absorb the calm and direction of their teachers. Erik may not. What is he thinking?

I switch on the TV and sit glued to it throughout the day. I suspect most of Ottawa does the same. The city fills with national and international news crews, special police teams and the army. What's going on?

We soon hear: a lone gunman has shot and killed a soldier at the National War Memorial. The gunman has been taken down in Parliament. The gunfire, as it ricocheted off of the stone pillars and walls, was earsplitting. Ottawa?

Two and a half weeks later, we take our three teens out of school, and we attend the National Remembrance Day ceremony downtown. Typically, Frank and I attend together, he in uniform and I a civilian observer. We have never done this, all five of us, because it's not a day off school in Ontario. This year we make it one because we think it's important that our three attend.

Police snipers line rooftops. This is not our Ottawa, but it is the new Ottawa. A sermon is read and the words are riveting. I pull out my iPhone and begin to tap the message into it. Scott frowns. "You're *texting*? Now?" I flash him, NOTES.

"Recording," I whisper.

"Everything has changed, but nothing has changed. We are now all guardians of peace."

I love these words. But what remains with me on this solemn day are the four words spoken by one of our nation's finest, former CBC anchorman Peter Mansbridge. Each year I am among the gaggle of middle-aged women who gather to see him—to hear him—after his Remembrance Day broadcast. This year is no different except that I haul the family over to observe, to gawk and to soak in that voice. *That voice.*

To my surprise, this year we have an opportunity to take pictures with Peter and to chat. And this is where I am struck by four words that I do not expect but that I ought to have expected. He is clearly surprised and pleased to see three teens have taken the time to attend (they are among a very few). Instead of lecturing them on the event, he does what he does best. He looks at our three standing in front of him and he asks, "What did *you* think of the ceremony?" He wants to know. Inquiring minds do. Imagine being asked. I think of autism support and of Erik. Imagine being asked what he thinks, what he wants.

That moment stays with me. "What do *you* think?" Four words that speak so much.

CHAPTER 46

Autism and the Astronaut

ERIK'S HEARTFELT PROJECTS ARE HAPPENING outside school, in life. Many of these are forays into videography alongside Heather. Team blondie is back.

To backtrack, Heather and I spend two years commuting to Montreal and Toronto, showing up for movie auditions. There always seems to be someone shorter or taller or blonder or more ideal. The process is humbling, and you learn to expect nothing and to rejoice at the occasional something. When it happens, a callback, there is a rush and a tiny thrill to discover a dressing room with your name on it. There is that. But the cash flow is mainly out, not in, so after a couple of years, Heather decides *enough*, and she ponders her next move. It turns out to be closer than we think: YouTube.

Heather auditions, and at thirteen, lands a spot on a British-based all-girls collaboration channel. A new machine is in motion, and we pump out a mini-movie a week: me, scriptwriting, arranging props and designing sets; Heather as the primary actor and film editor; and Erik as the devoted cameraman, gamely trailing her during weekly filming, hauling studio lights and a tripod around the house and occasionally taping up a green screen at the entrance to the living room.

For four years, our house becomes a film set: any and every room is potentially *live* and we live on alert, playing a bizarre version of freeze tag on filming days. "FILMING!" halts everything: no noise, no movement, no nonsense. Moments later, we may exhale, unfreeze and resume. It's novel for a year, life in lights; beyond that, we play along. It beats the trek to Montreal.

I smile as I observe Heather and Erik, side by side, Heather directing, Erik faithfully recording. It reminds me of *Dog and Owner* in Halifax. Now the nearly grown-up blondies morph into an eclectic collection of online characters. Erik pulls on an indigo wig and an upside-down moustache and makes appearances as Curious Carlos, a quirky character he invented. Carlos has a dedicated group of little girl followers, worldwide, who create chat rooms and knockoff skits, *The Best of Carlos.*

"Hey look, Erik! Two six-year-old girls in Australia . . . with blue wigs and upside-down moustaches . . . trying to be *you*!" No one has tried to be Erik before. He is celebrated.

In YouTube, we have an unwitting therapist. Video collaboration and production becomes something we call *a birth a week*. It is a way for Heather to involve Erik, to assign him multiple roles so that he can experiment and improvise and polish talents he didn't know he had. Serendipity sculpts.

ERIK AND I ARE STANDING on Ottawa's Parliament Hill. We do this every April on or around World Autism Awareness Day, April 2. The event is marked in our nation's capital by an annual gathering that is the brainchild of an Ottawa grandmother turned autism advocate and events coordinator, Suzanne Jacobson. Suzanne calls this coming together of those with autism and those supporting autism, aptly, Autism on the Hill. It is here that I have stood in Aprils past and have listened to Member of Parliament Mike Lake and Senator Jim Munson describe how they are taking autism forward inside our federal Parliament.

It is here that I bend to Erik and whisper, "Could you ever imagine yourself up there, speaking?" It is here Erik gives me a side look that says, "Are you *kidding* me?" And it is here, on these steps overlooking the Centennial Flame, that Erik will address those gathered, exactly a year to the day later.

But today is not that day. Today we are honoured to be invited inside. Mike Lake's assistant, Breanne, gives us name tags, and we hang them around our necks as she explains parliamentary protocol. I smile as I read my card. Today I am "Mother of Erik."

Later that afternoon we sip refreshments and stand at our assigned station—a round, raised cocktail table in an ornate and historic inner chamber. We are exhilarated, but there is work to do. Beyond nibbling and sipping, we are teaching. About autism. Of course.

"It's a bit like speed dating," Mike Lake explains. "Members of Parliament and senators will circulate around the room; those with autism, their families and autism leaders will remain at their tables. You'll get around ten minutes to mingle and talk, and then you'll switch up. I'll announce that. Ready?"

Our third customer is someone whose name I instantly recognize: the Honourable Marc Garneau, our astronaut turned politician. My heart starts to pound. I'm not ready for this. How do I connect an astronaut and autism? Because I must make a connection, get this rolling. And then I know.

"Mr. Garneau, Erik's favourite movie is *Apollo 13*."

Two faces light up, I step back, and I observe the magic, because to me it is that, this connection between boy and man, student and politician, autism and astronaut.

They start talking about perspective and what you can see from space with the naked eye. Erik is transfixed. He loves perspective. Mr. Garneau is noticeably pleased to be asked so many questions. At one point, they start talking about Uluru, formerly Ayers Rock, in Australia. It can be seen from the International Space Station, and we listen, fascinated, as one of our country's great space explorers tells us how it appears, a bird's-eye perspective from the heavens.

Erik interjects, "And I can tell you how it feels from the earth." We hiked around Uluru a few mornings in a row back in December 2007, in the scorching outback heat. Erik tells Mr. Garneau what this was like, how his shoes were powdery outback orange for weeks afterward.

I take pictures, capture the moment, but I hardly need to. This is indelible, this connection between two incredible perspectives. It's like out-of-this-world squared, and for me, it doesn't get much better than this.

ALL GOOD THINGS MUST COME to an end. Cinderella has proven this. But Cinderella also teaches us to seize the moment, to enjoy it and to live with less expectation and more celebration. On this day, inside Parliament, Erik meets Cinderella but then she slips away.

As soon as Marc Garneau leaves our table, both Erik and I sag. We have expended a lot of energy keeping the ball in the air—on our best behaviour—and we have been standing for many hours. I can see Erik stifling yawns. He is about to TX (time expire, a Frank-military term). I suggest Erik sit on the padded wooden bench that skirts the lavish banquet room. He does, and I relax and keep going knowing he can also relax. Still, I am concerned. TX can be, well, unpleasant. I glance over to see how he's doing there on his own. And it is then I see he is not alone. He is sitting alongside Cinderella.

This is the part in the story where the protagonist seizes and enjoys the moment. Hollywood uses shopping music and has the characters sail through vignettes set to inspired tunes. If I were to choose a song for what I now see, it would be "Blinded by the Light," for Erik is bathed in it. To be fair, he is also beaming; they both are and they are clearly enjoying each other's company, Erik and this mystery woman.

I ask him about it an hour later once the speed dating has wound down. "Who *was* that?" He shrugs. He doesn't know. "What were you talking about? Suddenly, you didn't look very tired," I say to him.

"Suddenly I didn't *feel* very tired. It's like she gave me energy. She said she was also tired of standing at the tables, and I was relieved to hear this. I don't know what else we talked about, but I remember she was nice. She made me feel relaxed." He thought for a moment. "I'd also like to know who she is."

To me he sounded a little sad, as though the fleeting happiness had vanished, here and gone. This is the part where Cinderella slips away. Erik is the captivated but clued-out prince. He doesn't know how to locate her. She forgot to leave a glass slipper.

As the event winds down, I ask around. No one knows exactly, but someone says they think it was a representative from Autism

Speaks Canada. Once home, I email and ask (you don't ask, you don't get). My subject title is Seeking Cinderella.

A day later, we get our reply: Esther Rhee. It's me, Cinderella, she writes. Erik lights up. Esther is the national program director for Autism Speaks Canada, and she is also a social worker, hence, a people magician. An angel. She has worked her charm on my son, and he on her. Esther embodies what environment and respect can achieve. Erik confirms what Esther knows about autism: that it is authentic and that it exists without ego or intent. It just is. And they just are, connected and in sync.

Cinderella lives. We know her, and her outlook makes a difference in our son's life.

CHAPTER 47

Did You Pack the Aliens?

AT SCHOOL, ERIK IS LEARNING that environment sculpts. He gravitates to a particular teacher's classroom because around this teacher, Erik feels good. He tells me this a lot, and for a boy who doesn't talk much about his school day, this is significant.

"I go to Mr. Breadner's room first thing in the morning and at lunch sometimes because I feel relaxed there . . . like whatever I do is okay." I listen and he continues. "You know how when you like someone . . . it's mostly about how they make you feel . . . ?" I nod. Erik knows when the feeling is right.

In this class, Erik is asked to create a multimedia project that is a culmination of the year's work. He knows exactly what he will do: research and design an outdoor walking tour of one of his favourite places—Ottawa's Parliament Hill. Erik's choice reminds me of something he stumbled on by accident at EPCOT in Florida, an engraving in the cobblestones: "Discovery consists in seeing what everyone else has seen but thinking what no one else has thought." Erik saw it; the rest of us walked on by.

Autism, merged with intense curiosity. Or maybe intense curiosity because of autism? . . . How many sixteen-year-old boys care about the statues outside Parliament?

On a warm May evening in 2015, Erik and I haul a script, a map, a toy microphone on a pole and a video camera around Parliament Hill. For six hours, we film and we improvise, running off-script, becoming brazen as we troupe along. Lifting the microphone toward bronzed faces, Erik playfully gives them voices and has the statues offer their turn-of-the-century wisdom. His palette of falsetto for the Famous Five surprises me and makes me laugh.

He's really into this! He smiles fully as he becomes a suffragette, holding back welling laughter, but his message is serious: "Women are persons, too!" he squawks into the microphone, struggling over the pronunciation of the word *women*. "Weeeemen," he says. We practise a short i—wimen, wimen, wimen—and reshoot until it's right. Off-camera, he looks reverently at these coppery leaders and half-whispers, "If you see something, say something."

I had never thought of the Hill in statues and stories. It takes Erik to want to do this. Just as he has opened my mind to what's not allowed, to objects and their shadows and to wacky woods, he introduces me to Canadian treasure that is mostly ignored.

Autism elevates the everyday—every day.

"This is the best thing I've ever done!" Erik announces, joyfully, as he presses SAVE on the edited video. It is pure Erik: artistic, aesthetic, enlightening and accurate. I will never view the Hill in the same way. It feels like ours.

EACH SUMMER WE PACK FOR the cottage, a modest pine cabin Frank's father built in 1947 in the wilds of Georgian Bay, north of Toronto. Heading there is healing: there is the nature-nurture aspect (it worked for the Group of Seven); but what beckons and pleases us is the retro feel, like warping back to the '50s or '60s. There are *Chatelaine* magazines detailing how to satisfy your man and cook a ham—in the same evening. There are stacks of teen magazines with splashy neon bubble lettering that spell words like *groovy* and *hip* and *sock it to me*. The cottage is a Wi-Fi free zone. We need to talk here to survive. Some pay for a device-free experience; it is ours each summer by default.

Here at the cottage, Erik can relax. There are no expectations aside from sweeping the cabin floor and closing the outhouse door. The wilderness is a place, simply, to be and equally, to be simply.

These summer treks are also an occasion to plan and to pack. I used to do it for everyone, but I'm letting the air out of the balloon on this one, too.

"You're all OYO," I tell them. "I'll do the groceries and the gear; you pack your own bag."

OYO equals *on your own*. This began as a joke (likely out of frustration) and later became code for *figure it out*. You won't forget pajamas twice. The good news is that OYO is double-edged: it comes with perks. Paired with responsibility is choice. You have freedom to choose: Sleep in or not? A lazy day or a productive day? You decide.

I poke my head into Erik's Ottawa bedroom on one of these OYO packing days, checking on his progress. I see a list and stacks of clothing. Adjacent to the bed, Erik paces. He's getting there.

"Erik, did you pack the aliens?"

He smiles his shy, handsome smile.

"I don't need to," he says. "They pack themselves."

He is speaking of something we half-jokingly refer to as an alien attack. I say half-jokingly because it is no laughing matter. It's an ongoing riddle, a neurological puzzle. Alien attacks are what we call those moments when we lose Erik to something beyond him. Is it autism? We are not sure. But what we do know is that he is out of reach, though right there with us. He is both close and distant, and that is the disconcerting, perplexing bit. Where is Erik? Indeed, *who* is Erik?

Alien attacks are a daily feature in our lives with autism. It is this I observed from the hot tub the night before high school, a throwback to elementary school Erik: lips move, eyes enlarge and hands slice the air. It's as though something or someone moves into Erik's body and pulls the strings. He is a good host for this entity, graciously providing a platform for the silent performance, for it is both muted and animated, a highly visual, rapid flutter of gestures, articulation and emphatic jabs in the air between him and us.

As quickly as it materializes, it dissolves, the curtain rises, and Erik is present. It's a fleeting vignette—an enigmatic act—and we are left wondering what it is and how we are to react. Address it, ignore it or roll with it?

Erik says he is not aware of the takeover. The aliens come and they go, flirting with us, teasing and testing us, flitting in and animating Erik in those brief seconds we turn our heads. When we turn to look for them, they disappear, fairy-like. Why? What? Really?

They do exist. We know because we have caught them on video, unexpectedly, like surveillance feedback. It happened during filming on Parliament Hill. As I was panning behind the parliamentary library, there they were—the aliens. They had swooped in, expertly animating my son the moment the focus had turned elsewhere. Erik's lips revved up; his eyes widened and a ripple swept through his body. I kept the camera on him as his hands slashed and soared, slicing invisible shafts of air. I paused and then moved on, feeling like an intruder, recording something I had not been invited to watch. I played the scene back to Erik, and he gasped.

"The aliens!" he whispered, transfixed, and he played the clip again and again. Though he has played host for years, he had never observed a performance.

"I never knew," he said quietly. "I don't feel a thing. It just happens. Maybe it's how I recharge?"

"I'm not sure," I replied. "But it's fascinating, isn't it? It's like another you that we have yet to discover. Maybe that's the autism part. And you could be right: maybe it's your recharge. I don't know."

We live with, are perplexed by and are unable to explain or exorcise the aliens. We ponder their function and their role. They fascinate us and frustrate us because we aren't able to make sense of their message and their meaning. But they provide us a glimpse into another Erik, the mysterious Erik that used to be so much more a part of our lives.

CHAPTER 48

Airports and Autism

GRADE 12, 2015. ERIK AT seventeen is tall, wiry and gentle. What is most striking about Erik as he emerges from boy to man is his sincerity and his strong and committed work ethic. If you want something done, ask Erik.

The Learning Enabled program is a good fit. I swap my advocate hat for a strategic planning hat and meet with school counsellors. We plot possible pathways for Erik beyond Grade 12. We are entering the murky transition-to-adult zone. I am crawling along on all fours in the dark, by instinct and by feel. Situation normal.

Throughout Grades 11 and 12, we slow the pace of learning by inserting support blocks into Erik's schedule. Because of this, Erik is short one credit and does not graduate with his peers. This is deliberate: he isn't ready for the end of public school. Neither am I.

We design two additional semesters, our version of Ontario's now-extinct Grade 13. "Life isn't a race to the finish line," we tell our three. "No one wants to get there first." Stretching the time-line means that Erik can relax through Grade 12; he has a bonus ten months to switch tracks to graduation and beyond. We have wiggle room.

A MARCH BREAK TREK TO Nicaragua serves up a reminder that this autism journey belongs to all of us. It's not so much about the principal performer but us, the supporting actors and our reaction to autism. As a cast, are we accepting of difference or not? It's that simple. Song brain chimes in with Alessia Cara: "You should know you're beautiful just the way you are . . . And you don't have to change a thing . . .

The world could change its heart." Are we enabling or disabling? Where does the disability lie? In the doer or in the receivers? Or both?

We are on board, sitting on the tarmac at Montreal's Pierre Elliott Trudeau airport, awaiting de-icing. Bright green trucks roar up, spray us a brilliant orange and then plaster us with neon green streamers. The frosting is beautiful but fleeting; it drips and blurs, and from the outside, our aircraft must look like a sundae in the sun, ruined but oddly good to go. Erik loves this juxtaposition: random décor eclipses high tech-metal. Preposterous enables precision. He captures it on his iPhone.

"Better than a car wash!" he gushes.

We are approaching thirty-four thousand feet, forty-five minutes after takeoff. Erik is taking pictures through his oval window; he leans to me and tilts his phone my way. "Look, I think I found Manhattan . . ." I look, and though the digital shadows somewhat resemble Long Island, the direction is wrong. We are headed south-west toward Central America, not south-east. At that moment, the captain announces the flight plan: we are headed down the east coastline to Cuba and then over the Caribbean to Central America.

"And folks," says the captain, "if you look out the left side of the aircraft, you may be able to see Long Island. We've just passed New York City."

Erik, of course, is right. I ask to see the picture again, and he zooms it and points out Central Park, the Brooklyn Bridge and even the Statue of Liberty from thirty-four thousand feet above the earth. Like fuzzy needles in a grey haystack, the dots make sense.

I digest this. I could never have deciphered the landscape; to Erik it is perfectly clear, and when he shows it to me and calmly points out landmarks, it is. It's like someone explaining an algebra solution, logical and tidy once puzzled out by a mathematician. Someone's opaque is someone's obvious.

Erik does not say, "I told you so." He simply smiles, clicks off his phone and slides it back into its soft case. Autism is matter of fact. Autism is humble.

I ruminate some more. I marvel how this day, in the airport and on board the flight, has been illuminating in terms of the autism spectrum and how it may present. First, the anxiety at security—there always is—made doubly troubling this time because Erik is randomly selected for a security swab. An agent asks him to lift his shirt and reveal his waistline; Erik flatly refuses and clams up, a mix of indignant and befuddled. He performs a peek-a-boo burst of shirt flicks, and whenever the agent gets the instrument close, Erik snaps his shirt down like a Venus flytrap. It would be humorous but for where we are and that Erik's behaviour appears bizarre and suspect. He is attracting attention.

I gently coax him to comply. I am about to pull out the autism card when Erik relents and scoots away, casting dark looks behind him and muttering, loudly, *"How inappropriate!"* He has been taught that private is private, and now he is asked to make private public. It makes no sense.

It takes Erik an hour to come back into himself. I tell him I often get pulled over and checked, and he feels better about it, but he remains agitated, ticked off. I am reminded how quickly things can flare up and that it takes deliberate debriefing to bring him back down.

A bout of anxiety, a fascination with de-icing and a Manhattan bird's-eye bull's eye. We have nailed the autism spectrum—angst, captivation and keen observation—all before 10 a.m. It has been another round of frustration to fascination. We never know when or where or exactly how, but we do know the what. And we also know that it is the response to the what that determines outcomes. Autism requires unflinching finesse.

Autism also requires self-talk. I remind myself to slip into Erik's skin. *Teresa, Erik's shoes.* This is like telling myself to floss. Both are nudges to do what I already know.

Back in Erik's bedroom, I spy his yearbook: pristine, unsigned, just the way he likes it—unblemished. Reflecting on my own high school yearbooks, I recall the excitement around the end of the school year, the signing rituals and the cementing of friendships. I feel sad that this is not part of Erik's high school experience. I project this sadness onto Erik. But then I stop myself. He doesn't mourn what he does not desire. This sadness is my own, not his. On one hand, I want life to be rich for him, full of connections. On the other, I need to respect his space and his pace. It is a constant tug and a forever disconcerting pall that hangs over me, over Erik, over all of us.

Autism forces continuous reflection and refocus. Autism asks you to dig very deep.

CHAPTER 49

Panache

THE SPRING OF **2016** SEES Erik back on Parliament Hill. He speaks to a crowd gathered to hear voices united for autism. He speaks for parents of children with autism when he says that their belief is like the Centennial Flame that burns on the Hill. It never goes out, just as our hope and our belief for our children burn brightly within each of us. Politicians, autism leaders, scientists, moms, dads, grandmas, grandpas and siblings wipe a tear as Erik speaks of his poppa's belief and of the four words that have become his guiding light. When autism speaks, we listen.

Thank you for having me here today.
Charlotte, I enjoyed your speech.

I am Erik Hedley.
I am seventeen.
And I have autism.

Someone asked me once what it is like to have autism.
I told them that I see things that most people miss.
I think seeing things in a *different* way is a good thing.
I do.

When I was asked to speak today, I thought, *I can do this as long as I have a chance to practise. And then I should be okay.* So we came here to Parliament Hill every week for the past month.

I stood right here with a fake microphone, and I practised.

My mom gave me some advice.

She said, "Erik, focus on the eternal flame. Pretend it is your audience."

And then my mom and I realized that the eternal flame really is my audience.

You are all eternal flames for your children with autism.

Your flame *always* burns and it never goes out.

This is your *hope* and your *belief* for your child.

Someone also asked me what I thought parents can give their children with autism.

I answered in one word: *belief.*

Without belief, what have you got? Not much.

If you believe in me, I believe in me.

If you think I can do it, then *I* think I can do it.

What you think of me is what *I* think of me.

Eleven years ago when I was diagnosed with autism, my poppa said to my mom, "Erik will surprise you."

Poppa was one of my first believers.

Those four words have been my guiding light.

"Erik will surprise you."

Give your child a *guiding light* and give them your *belief.*

Remember, you are their *eternal flame.*

Thank you.

FORMER *CANADA A.M.* HOST TURNED member of Parliament Seamus O'Regan speaks directly after the two autism self-advocates: Charlotte, a savvy ten-year-old whose rock star *"I have AUTISM!"* ignites the crowd and Erik, her calm, baritone counterpart. They are an unlikely pairing, this sparkly, outgoing girl and this gently candid young man. Mr. O'Regan's follow-up message is concise and precise: "These voices have spoken with style, panache and authenticity. Thank you for giving us insight into how you see the world."

Panache lingers. I like it. Autism is that, too: a certain flair and flamboyance that is not forced. Panache, like autism, just is.

WE ARE NOT WITHOUT OUR hiccups, our sticky, humorous and often perplexing moments. One unfolds during a practice session on the steps of Parliament, the night before the big day; the other blip, just as we are set to leave for the Hill the next morning. We write an email to Gramma the night before: An Arresting Speech.

A humorous moment on Parliament Hill this evening . . .

Erik and I trekked back to the Hill one last time today so that he could practise his autism speech.

We get there, it is a lovely evening, and people are camped out all over the lawn. Erik positions himself on the steps in front of the Peace Tower, hauls out his Rock Band microphone, stuffs the cord into his shorts pocket, pulls out his speech and launches in. "I am Erik Hedley. I am seventeen. And I have autism."

At that moment, I look up to see not one but three RCMP officers running toward us. Erik has his back turned, so he cannot see the approach. He takes a breath and is just about to launch into paragraph two when I signal for him to hold on. The police have reached us and have surrounded Erik. He looks up, clearly surprised.

"Good evening. How are you this evening?" one officer asks me.

"I'm fine," I reply. "And how are you this evening?" I ask. I have an idea where this is going, and I am trying not to smile.

"Oh, we're fine . . . but we need to ask what you're doing here."

"We're practising a speech."

"And what is that?" the officer asks, pointing toward the microphone.

"A microphone."

"And do you realize that it's against the law to use a microphone on the Hill?"

"Even if it's a Wii Rock Band microphone?"

"It's not live?"

"It's plugged into his shorts pocket," I say, gesturing toward Erik.

The female officer bursts out laughing. "Oh jeez, guys! I told you it wasn't live! It's a toy!"

She finds this pretty funny. The guys, meanwhile, look sheepish. I explain that Erik is practising for an autism rally on the Hill on Tuesday, and that he will be speaking alongside members of Parliament and advocates. That he has autism. They are feeling worse by the moment.

"We had to be sure you weren't staging a demonstration."

I raise my eyebrows. Erik?

"It's against the law to use a microphone on the Hill without a permit. You need a permit."

I assure him we are not demonstrators. I pull the cord from Erik's pocket; it dangles between us.

The quieter cop has a question for me: "You mean to say, you've been up here every weekend for a month, and no one has said anything to you?"

"That's right," I reply. "You are the vigilant ones." And after a beat: "You get the prize."

Big smiles all around.

"So how about a picture?" I ask. They are feeling a bit bad, but I insist.

We get a good group shot and they disperse. We carry on with the speech . . . twice more. Erik belts it out loud and proud into the toy microphone. The low-key officer stands behind Erik, off to one side, in cop pose, arms crossed as though on guard, listening intently, Parliament behind him. It is a poignant moment.

We thank him afterward, and he turns to Erik. "Good speech. I think you'll change some minds out there. Keep up the good work." And to me: "I've got a friend who has two kids with autism . . . it's a tough go. Keep up your work with your son."

A nice moment on Parliament Hill this evening . . .

ANOTHER AUTISM MOMENT PLAYS OUT the morning of the big day. We decide on the clothes the night before. In the morning, I pop into Erik's room to inspect. I stop short.

"Erik," I say, stepping forward, "what are these checkered bits poking out under your shirt?" I hadn't realized that the turquoise shirt was a two-piecer. "Wait a minute," I observe, tugging at the sleeve. "Are you wearing two shirts?"

He looks down at the ill-fitting shirt, at the bunched up, layered mess, and smiles a lopsided, embarrassed grin.

"I didn't think this looked right, and it feels *terrible*, all tight and pulling," he admits. "But you said, 'Wear the turquoise shirt' so I thought to myself, this must be right. But now I think, this can't be right. *Is* it right?" He is still unsure, talking himself into and out of his wardrobe malfunction.

"Do you really think I meant for you to wear *two* shirts, one over the other? What makes sense?" I seem to be asking this a lot lately.

"One shirt makes sense. Now it seems obvious. But when I looked in my closet, I wasn't sure. I saw more than one shirt on each hanger, and I wasn't sure what you meant. I was stuck. But now I know."

He smiles at me, and I turn to leave. Good. Lesson learned. A teachable moment. We are making great strides; we are learning from mistakes, and we will talk about this some more later on, to cement it. We learn from history. This is ongoing but doable.

I am about to close his bedroom door when he pipes up and interrupts my lofty thoughts.

"If you like this look," he giggles, "you would've really liked me ten minutes ago." A laugh takes hold of him as he pauses to remember. A big teary laugh-out-loud memory ripples through him.

He looks directly at me, composing himself: "There were *THREE* shirts on that hanger."

CHAPTER 50

Darkness and Light

GRADE 13, 2016. WE ARE now off-road, breaking trail beyond the familiarity of K-12. I feel wobbly, unsure of what to do next. This floating sensation is disconcerting, but it's good for me. This is what it feels like to be Erik most days. Untethered.

What we do have is time. We have built in a transition year so that Erik can slowly switch tracks from Grade 12 to something beyond. The truth is, we haven't figured out the something beyond. So we create an eclectic holding pattern and an opportunity for capacity-building and self-reflection. That's the idea.

I pull on my life coach hat and ask Erik how he sees himself: his talents, his ambition, his inclinations, his preferred activities and his comfort zones.

"How do you define yourself, Erik?"

He looks at me and frowns, like I need to back off. I have seen this face before: it's the dark, long-distance run grimace.

"Think about it and answer when you're ready," I suggest, knowing this could take days. I am learning to sow seeds and let Erik sit with them. Big question, big buffer.

He speaks in three days. "Here's what I think," he says out of the blue as he adds a baggie of carrots to his lunch kit one evening, " . . . a videographer, an actor, a writer and an artist."

That's what I get: his reply, straight up, out of context, boom.

"And I sure liked helping Gramma in the summer," he adds, voice softening. He says *Gramma* in a slow, breathy way. "I liked doing the cat's paw with her."

Cat's paw refers to taking my mom's arm and guiding her, helping her get from A to B. He says the weight of her curved fingers around his forearm feels like a cat's paw, clamped on, steadied, warm and grateful. He is considerate in his interactions with Gramma. Patient. Attentive.

I process his definition of himself. A week later, a plan emerges: high school co-op.

And so it begins. Erik returns to school and takes an art therapy class for alternative neurologies. The school counsellor and the art teacher design this course with Erik in mind. Afternoons are filled with co-op work placements: two days a week as a cameraman for Rogers TV and three days a week as an assistant aide in a long-term care facility. There is a huge amount of driving to ferry Erik to and from these placements, and Frank takes on much of it. He begins to call himself Uber Frankie.

"This feels pretty good," Erik announces two months into the new rhythm. There is no homework, just the expectation that he work hard. He can do that. I feel relief: we aren't asking Erik to walk a generic path. Everything unfolds in Erik-time. It has to.

I AM SITTING UP IN bed one morning on a Friday, Labour Day weekend, writing, in pajamas. Feeling cozy and productive, I am enjoying connecting to the world via my soft office. And then I hear it, faint at first, a mild tapping on the front door.

Go away! We don't want any. But it doesn't go away; it gets louder, more insistent. Persistent. I get up and creep into the hall. There I meet Erik, and we both peek out the upper hall window. We see nothing, but now the tapping-turned-sharp-knocking is a thumping. Something isn't right.

Erik and I exchange a look. "Rude!" I whisper to him. Something deep inside my subconscious senses something else: that I need to whisper, that we need to remain hidden. We wait. The thumping becomes rhythmic, thunderous, splintering and then explosive.

CRASH! It sounds like an explosion, like glass breaking, a splintering shattering. I snap to attention.

Running to the top of the stairs, I sail down, three steps at a time. Midway, I see it: the front door is open, sunlight floods through and creates a triangle on the slate tiles, and yet there is darkness, a shapeless shadow. It is coming in.

We all hear it: a bellow so loud that it raises the hair on my head. It stops us in our tracks. Even the shadow halts. *"HEEEEEEYYYYYYYY!"* It is masculine and menacing. It is me.

Adrenaline will do weird things. If you had asked me how I would have reacted to a home intruder, I am not sure what I would have said, that I would have curled up, hidden, caved. But I do none of these things, and what I do that morning when light becomes dark surprises even me. It is not planned. It is pure gut reaction. NO ONE will touch me or my children. No one. It frightens me to think of what I may have done, what I may have been able to do, if I had laid my hands on the man who attempted to invade our space. I felt murderous, and that scares me. But now, looking back in calm, I know what this was. It was a mother's instinct, and it was full-blown. I have reacted no differently with autism, and it, too, has been an invader of sorts. This to me is fascinating, this inclination to serve and protect at all cost. But let us continue. Autism plays a part, and it is unexpected.

My throat hurts. The "HEY" has exploded from me so forcefully that I physically ache. But I am not done. I am at the bottom of the stairs, Erik behind me. Heather meets us at the door. She is shaking, near tears. We stare at the scene. The door is largely fine; it's the frame that is smashed and unrecognizable. This is our first lesson: it is easy to break in. It is hard to get in.

I step through the broken wood and run outside. Looking back, my reaction is raw and wrong, but it is natural, what I feel. I want to hunt down the bastard who dared break down the door and then run away. He is bounding down the driveway, and spying him, I bellow, voice irate, as though he is a kid who has pinged a hockey puck at the garage and then attempts to sneak away. I am reacting like an angry mother: "Hey, you FUCKER [well beyond the words of an angry mother], you can't just bust our door and run away! YOU. FUCKER."

I am shouting like a crazed woman. Heather and Erik back away into the house. Which is scarier, Mom or the villain? We're not sure. But I can't stop. I run after him, hurling "FUCKER" at him over and over. Talk about projections.

"Mom?" It's Heather. "Maybe you should . . . um . . . come inside?"

She's right. This is potentially not good. Dangerous, in fact. What if he's armed? What if he comes back? We are vulnerable. Broken.

I go back inside, and I finally see it for what it is: a break-in. Up to this point, my brain has been scanning, trying to convince me what it could be. It runs through everything it knows and it even suggests that the UPS guy has gone berserk and has heaved a package through the window, and I believe that for a moment. Adrenaline will do that, too. But now I know what this is: a crime.

It takes me time to react rationally. I text and text Frank, who is out for lunch. No reply. It is then, after more delay, that I call the police. It takes that long for me to register "not good." Even then, I don't call until I change into real clothes and apply lipstick. *Lipstick.* To report a crime. Lipstick to birth a baby. If nothing else, I am consistent.

Five police cars roar up within minutes. "Five?" I ask them. "We, uh, were just heading out for Thai food . . ."

I apologize for delaying their lunch. I also contaminate the crime scene by walking down the driveway to greet them (the police dog goes back to sleep, unamused). I admit to having touched the doorknob (I did this to check our security after I had stuffed a chair under the handle on the inside).

"What took you so long to call us?" asks one of the officers.

"I texted my husband first."

"Your *husband*? In the future, call us first, not him." He looks at me like I am a child, and I feel like one. I become his projection.

"But I text him every day; I never call you. It's what I know. It was a reaction." Everything makes sense from my shoes.

As I slowly return to earth, I discover that although I had come face to face with the criminal, I cannot describe him all that well.

"Womanly . . . full-figured . . . ," I begin, "Not at all like the image on the security sign . . . you know, slim, stealthy, dressed in black." I gesture to our little sign. It had been hidden by the shrubs; I move it out before the police arrive.

"Plump, mushroomy hair . . . ," I recall, and with an ironic laugh I add, "I thought it was a woman at first. It was not what I expected." I pause, recalling more. "And the funny thing is, I think he thought I was a man, the way my voice exploded, masculine . . . and the *words* . . ."

I look down and then back up. Our collective eyes meet (there are five vehicles, many eyes). We all know the script by now. I filled out a police report fifteen minutes before this conversation and there is a lot of caps lock on a certain word. The officer who collected the report bit his lip. "You said, 'Tell it how it happened.' So I did. Should I scratch that out?" He told me not to. I imagine them reading it out over Thai food. But I digress. The autism part . . .

I am stumbling over the description when a voice, deep and sure, cuts in. "Well, actually, I know," it begins. It is my details guy. He has my back.

Erik rattles off an in-depth description that makes the officers stop talking and notice. I mentioned to them, earlier, at the end of the driveway, that my son has autism and that is the reason why this is doubly delicate. I am not sure how Erik has been affected, I tell them. None of us imagined it like this. Erik becomes the calm one, the voice, the relayer of precise details. We stand there, stunned, amazed. But should we be? My recollections are blinded by emotion. Erik's are not. His inability or disinclination to identify emotion has allowed him to observe coolly and with accuracy.

Out of darkness comes light: when autism speaks, it is often time to pay attention.

I AM TRIGGERED FOR WEEKS, months, afterward. We all are. Bizarrely, I am afraid to leave the house. I feel I need to protect it, not hide within it, and I do this by wheeling a few bags of bark mulch in a wheelbarrow out front and leaving it on the driveway, as though the gardener is near. We do not have a gardener; the wheelbarrow, the rake and the soiled gloves, all are decoys. But I do this compulsively for weeks. I can't stop myself. To this I think of "bad rash." I can't stop that, either, asking for what is needed until it is done right. What appears to be irrational, over the top, is, in the mind of the doer, the only way forward. It is pure reaction.

Erik thanks me again and again for shouting. "Thank you for raging back!"

Frank pieces the door frame back together like a fine bit of dental surgery. He also researches and installs new strike plates— longer, stronger. Three-inch screws replace the builder's half-inch variety. We move forward, fortified.

Scott finds a seven-second YouTube vine of a polar bear raging against a grizzly bear: his mother, on guard for thee.

Heather taps my extreme emotion and lets it rip on stage during a dramatic vignette. I see me in her rage. You never know what's good and what's bad.

CHAPTER 51

Erik-Vision

"I HAVE A PROJECT I'D like to move forward, a vision, and I think I know who might be able to make this work."

The voice belongs to Kathy Thompson, manager for volunteer services at the long-term care facility where Erik hopes to become a co-op student. She might have said "no thank you" to having Erik join the staff, but she does not. Instead, she invites him on board, leans back in her office chair and listens as Erik talks about his YouTube work with Heather.

"She actually *played* one of our YouTube videos in her office!" Erik blurts as soon as we reach the parking lot.

He doesn't miss the irony of the random title Kathy pulled up: a popular skit about aging in reverse, born old and wrapping up, no pun intended, in diapers. Erik is flabbergasted that she would click on this title out of the hundreds of videos we have created. "What are the chances?" he sputters. "In an old age home?" He bursts out laughing again, hoping we haven't offended her.

"I don't think so . . ." I steer the conversation to something Kathy proposed at the end of the interview. "She wants us to help her with a video project. Did you catch that part?" He did, but he is vague on details. He is still erupting in giggles, teary-eyed: Kathy saw Heather's character in *diapers*! This bit of pure randomness grips him. He can think of nothing else.

"She wants you to help create a documentary video about aging and person-centred care . . . you know, seeing people for who they are and not a list of medications and health concerns. Her idea is for you to deliver the message, Erik, to illuminate aging through your eyes. No stereotypes. No prejudice."

I let this settle. "Her thought is that if you can reshape and overcome the projections around your own label, and you do this all the time with autism, then maybe you can help people reframe and see worth and value in the elderly. If you can see autism and aging differently, maybe we all can. You'd lead the way."

He sits a little taller. He wipes away the tears, interested.

Kathy, Erik and I meet twice more and share ideas; we are excited and wonder whether this is something new, these dots we are laying down between aging and autism and perception. We are turning autism on its head, taking what some people consider a deficit—the disinclination (inability?) to judge and showing how this can be positive.

"This video is being shot in *Erik-vision*," I announce one day between filming clips.

Erik likes the imagery. "Like night-vision glasses," he says. "I can see through darkness."

"These people are survivors," he declares, facing the lens. "Whole, not broken. I don't see seniors. I see stories."

Perhaps it takes a young man who sees without filters—stereotypes, assumptions and preconceptions—to see things for what they might also be.

We get partway through scripting and filming and have to scrub the project because of scheduling glitches. We are disappointed, none so much as Erik. But he sees himself a little differently now: one who sees in the dark.

CONTRARY TO WHAT I READ online, Erik is empathetic.

This truth is delivered to me via a ham casserole just after the New Year, 2017. I spin it into a narrative and email my mom in near disbelief, fingers flying. This is nothing huge, I write, but it *is* big. I press SEND on an encouraging vignette:

Erik chats with me in the kitchen as I am making dinner.

He says, "As I sat there eating my nacho chips, I watched you cutting up the ham for the casserole. And I thought, *I bet she wishes she was sitting here eating nachos and not cutting up ham. I bet she doesn't really want to be doing that at all . . ."*

And then he abandons his nachos, stands up and walks around the kitchen island.

"Can I do anything to help? Because one of my New Year's resolutions is to think about things from your perspective."

I blink. We have been working on perspective-taking for fourteen years, and although I have seen glimmers of it in the past couple of years, never anything approaching this. Imagine, a self-initiated resolution to step into his mother's shoes . . . from an eighteen-year-old boy . . . with autism. I blink again.

"I would love some help, Erik." And then, "Do you know that your resolution has made my day? My year? According to the textbooks, you're not supposed to be able to do this—to see things from my perspective. To empathize. But you do, you can . . . you want to . . . All amazing." And I hug him. He looks proud, but also practical.

"What can I do?"

So I get him an apron and we chop, reading the recipe together, chatting side by side. The vibe is relaxed, connected. Proud.

Heather comes in for a snack, and I excitedly tell her the news. "Erik has stepped into my shoes!" I relay her brother's New Year's resolution. Her face softens. She looks at him, and like her mother, she finds herself in his arms, hugging him. For all of her frustrations with her brother, he is the sweetest, most authentic person she knows. "Erik, you've just made my day," she says. There is emotion in her voice. He smiles. He has heard this twice within ten minutes. It's not that hard to please a woman after all.

We continue to chop, fry, sauté and blend. He crushes potato chips for the casserole topping. He looks at me, brightly, pleased with himself. "It's more fun with me here, isn't it?" I agree that it is. The people factor is something we've talked about for years. It's a social world . . . most activities are better with people. He is serving my lines back to me, and I smile. Our casserole project has been fun. A combined effort is always better than a solitary march.

This has been another Erik life lesson. Just when you think Erik isn't with you, he is. As I garnish the casserole with paprika, I glance at him, hovering, watchful. Erik is an interesting study into what is possible in life. He has a sparkling positivity that is rare with autism. Rare, period.

We pop the casserole in the oven. I tell him, "That's it . . . Thank you . . . you can take your apron off now." He doesn't seem to want to. He looks at me, and with big Erik eyes feeds me another favourite, a maxim we've used for years with the kids. It fits.

"It's never about the place; it's always about the people."

CHAPTER 52

Cloud Nine

WE SIT IN THE DARKENED room and wait. A screen brightens. A red velvet curtain gently sways. Music, dramatic and sweeping, fills the theatre. The curtain parts, and across the screen swoops a superhero, arms outstretched in flight. He wears a jetpack and he soars over a city, Toronto, in animation, but the superhero is real. This slender hero is recognizable. Erik!

It is spring 2017. York University, Toronto. Erik is the virtual commentator for this TEDx event, Spectrum Innovations. We watch from the audience as on-screen Erik greets us from Cloud Nine.

"Well, hello there!" [Erik looks up, catches his breath.] "It's me . . . Erik! You're probably wondering what I'm doing up here," [gestures around him] "and . . . I can't wait to tell you! I'm hovering in the sky just above York University." [Erik gestures and peeks down, and we see a bird's-eye view of the university.]

"And yes, look! You've probably noticed I'm on Cloud Nine!" [He gestures to his cloud.] "And why am I so happy? Well, because I'm watching a live stream of the Spectrum TEDx from York University!" [Erik holds up his iPhone, revealing the screen and the word *TEDx*.] "Isn't technology great? . . . I can see you down there!" [Erik waves down.]

"Anyway, yes, I'm on Cloud Nine because I'm very, very happy! As a Canadian living with autism, I am watching these amazing Canadian speakers who are making a difference for people like me." [Erik gestures to his chest.]

"Today's speakers are visionaries and they are social innovators." [Key words float on the screen.] "They see a social problem," [he swipes the air, pretends to grab "a problem" and holds out his hand] "they think about it," [ponder pose] "and they come up with a creative solution" [show light bulb] "that not only makes life better for someone like me," [he gestures to himself] "but for thousands of people like me!" [He gestures wide.]

"And that's why I'm on Cloud Nine. I'm watching social innovation in motion and I'm excited about it." [Key words are on the screen.]

"So, thank you" [shouts down] "to our TEDx speakers for sharing your innovations with us today. But even more, thank you for never stopping and for making your ideas work for all of us."

I AM TRANSPORTED TO OTHER darkened theatres, to other stages, to a collection of skins: Jungle Boy, emerald, sleek and elf-like; Erik the Greek wrapped in a bedsheet; Erik the gnarly surfer dude; Erik as on-the-scene reporter on Parliament Hill; YouTube's zany, blue-haired, mustachioed Carlos; and now here, cross-legged, hovering over Toronto on Cloud Nine. Portals to potential, each.

Earlier this year, we are contacted by York University's TEDx organizers, doctors Weiss and Lai. They are looking for a fast-paced overview video to outline the upcoming TEDx, Spectrum Innovations. *Cloud Nine!* It comes to me over morning coffee. We'll have Erik report virtually from Cloud Nine!

Together, Erik and I film the script. To have him appear to fly over Toronto, we spread a green screen over our front hall floor. Erik straps on a jetpack (his school backpack) and stretches out on the green fabric, arms pitched forward like Superman, pretending to fly. Climbing a stepladder, I capture our superhero from above. This is tricky because Erik feels ridiculous fake-flying. Our superhero has the giggles. Clips complete, we turn the footage over to Heather, who translates five hours of filming into a five-minute production. We are ready.

Wearing matching Hedley T-shirts, Erik and Heather introduce the Cloud Nine video on the York University stage. Frank and I observe from the audience, giddy and dazed. Who would have thought? I recall the dreary reports early on, the sticky, weighty words and how this journey may have played out. Although Erik has not produced this video, he has brought it to life, fed it panache. But first, we fed him the belief that he could do this. The script begins in the mind.

JUNE 2017. OTTAWA. HIGH SCHOOL graduation.

It is a sultry June day in Ottawa, Erik's last at his high school. Fourteen years a student, his public school education is wrapping up within hours. This day, Grade 12 graduation, has always hovered, hypothetical. Distant becomes present and then, one day, present is past. Tomorrow will be that day. Today Erik will walk out of his high school for the last time. It's an emotional day—for Erik, for me, for all of us. Change is hard. Are we ready for this?

We shuffle into the auditorium, the hushed, velvety room Erik and I peeked into at the end of Grade 8. Five years ago. Is it possible? Erik's arms were skinny then; he could barely pull open the door. So much has changed, and yet?

The auditorium fills with colour, sound and anticipation; I wonder how Erik is doing, somewhere in the bowels of the school, pulling on a silky blue graduation gown and being arranged in alphabetical order. Is he talking to anyone? Is he quiet? Excited? Stressed? Alone? I wonder about Erik; I worry about Erik. Will I ever stop?

We hear it. Bagpipes. The graduates are being piped in. Tradition. We rise. I feel prickly tears. Emotion rises. This has been a long journey, side by side, elbow to elbow. We've made it. This is my graduation, too. I feel it. Deeply. This is our fluffy-haired boy. This is me.

We see Erik and wave. Heather is clicking pictures with her phone; Frank mans the video camera, and I cover each stride with the good camera. As the graduates file into the section cordoned off for them, we see Erik light up when he spots us. A shy wave. An unfiltered smile. He is not holding back. He never does.

And then something astonishing happens. The line cuts in front of him. He starts down a new row, toward us. He walks to the end of the row. I am also at the end of my row. His seat is directly across the aisle from me. In a theatre of seven hundred seats, we are within arm's reach. We are astounded.

"How ironic!" Erik half-whispers to me. "After all this time, in this huge auditorium, we're still side by side!"

He can't believe it. Neither can I. His smile is of the "who woulda thought?" variety, very bright. Pure randomness! It fits. We fit, and here we are, after all, side by side, as always. Don't wish it away.

CHAPTER 53

Weebles Wobble, but They Don't Fall Down

WE ARE AT THE END of the public school tether. What now? I don't know. I say this a lot, because in-the-dark travel is like that. There are no clearly lit paths. We are groping for a handhold. The trail is obscured at the transition from adolescence to adulthood. I stop on the path and ponder. Really, should it be any different here than any of the other switchbacks? I think not. This will be a slow ascent. As always.

Do we do more of the same, create a loop in the path to buy more time and allow Erik to catch up to chronological Erik? I don't know. I decide to consult the source. Borrowing a line, I ask Erik, "What do *you* think?"

"Hmmmm." Processing time is required. I am patient. In a few days, he speaks: "I've liked co-op and volunteering, but I think I've had enough of doing that. I want to try something new, but I don't know what. Do you?"

I get a half answer, but to me, it is significant. He is willing to step out of himself and try something new. He wants to move forward. This is good; it wasn't always this way.

I know in all honesty that college is not an independent option right now. High school has been possible via a specialized program and with Mom-as-tutor, but now we need to see what Erik can do independently.

Receptive and expressive language delays pose a hurdle. Sitting in a lecture hall and taking notes and following along will be overwhelming, a showstopper. Reading textbooks and processing information will be difficult, as will a full-time program—in fact, next to impossible.

"Aha!" I say to Frank one morning, visualizing what it is, exactly, that is holding our son back. "A battery and a sponge!"

He sits forward, attentive.

"You see, it's like this . . . ," I begin, seeing it clearly, at last. "The battery doesn't stay charged long. It needs to rest and refresh. Like Erik. For every social hour, he needs to retreat to a quiet refuge and recharge."

Frank nods.

"And the sponge doesn't absorb well. By the time Erik reaches the end of a sentence or paragraph, he forgets what came before it. The sponge is already saturated. It cannot absorb more. Battery and sponge. Erik."

"Yes, I see," Frank muses. He likes this. "One won't hold enough. One doesn't absorb enough."

Never quite enough. That is the hurdle.

EDUCATION ASIDE, ERIK DOESN'T KNOW what he wants to be—such a difficult and demanding concept.

I read a testimonial for North Island College on Vancouver Island, written by a young man from Taiwan seeking a sheltered and small-scale start to his post-secondary education. I am reminded of Erik. And Erik reminds me of this young man. Ideas begin to coagulate, far-fetched and far-flung, but reasonable. Sensible. Everything is always impossible before it works. I investigate and come up with a scenario.

What if we allow Erik a slow start to college via the Employment Transition Program—no strain but a lot of common sense gain? What if we pull in nature-nurture and have this college immersed in west coast wow, in Douglas fir and rugged mountain peaks? What if the town is small and manageable, allowing Erik to attempt public transit without fear of getting lost; learn to drive beside the ocean, where life is slow and steady? What if we live along the shore, where community is big and expectation is small? In this place, eccentricity is originality; different is valued and deviance is a virtue. Different is encouraged, not feared. What if?

I IMAGINE ERIK AS ONE of those small foam capsules, the toys you place in water and watch swell and grow. What if we give him new water? Will he stretch and grow? I ponder this visual: absorption and unfurling, quickly at first and then more slowly and deliberately. Perhaps there are two processes at work as the foam enlarges: stretching and expansion.

To stretch is to move outside of borders and comfort zones and to learn new things—like driving. Stretching delivers new ways of being and of knowing. I want this for Erik.

To expand is to broaden the base you already have, to build on experiences, like mathematics nine, ten, eleven, twelve—a layer a year. Both forms of growth demand wilful open-mindedness and the desire to update. Erik wants this for himself. As do I.

Take him to the water and feed his soul.

There is one certainty: we will move forward; we have to. I am reminded of a 1970s toy jingle: "Weebles wobble but they don't fall down." Shaped like raindrops, Weebles are a league of stout plastic people, easy to grasp but impossible to knock over. They rock but they never fall. They are weighted; they have a solid foundation. I want this for Erik, for all of us . . . a foundation so strong that it can be rocked but will not falter.

WE ARE MADLY BUSY.

Uber Frankie delivers Erik where he needs to be: Rogers TV and St. Patrick's long-term care facility. The van gets a workout.

I am writing daily, mostly for Heather's weekly YouTube skits. This collaboration has ramped up and expanded. There are international sponsors, clothing companies attached to these weekly movies we make. Our stories are a conduit for kiddie fashion. It is a new world to us, this soft sell advertising, but I do not have much time to contemplate it; I write, pumping out a script a week.

We begin to fly to Orlando and Los Angeles for frenzied fan meet-and-greet events. I am often up late, bent over my iPad writing skits about jealousy and revenge and goodwill and good fun. There are endless pranking videos; kids like calamity and dirty laundry. I love the creativity, but the pace and the ongoing filming and the advocacy—the spinning plates leave me reeling.

I explain the west coast idea to our family doctor: "Hmmm, yes . . . well, you never know . . . maybe if you step out of your family for a bit . . . ," she suggests, half-jokingly, "your blood pressure will come down."

I am feeling restless. I recognize this agitation: I felt the same way half a lifetime ago at twenty-five, just before I became Christmas Cake. In 1988, I hoisted myself up and out to Tokyo, seeking new experiences and adventure. My plan is to do something similar for Erik, nearly thirty years later, only now, the place I ran from is the place I will return to—Comox on Vancouver Island. Our New Tokyo.

Everything is always impossible before it works.

Weebles wobble, but they don't fall down.

CHAPTER 54

When We Know Better, We Do Better

"YOU CAN'T DO THAT. YOU'RE married. And he has autism."

Two of three statements are fact. One is projection.

That is the response to the west coast plan. To me, it is obvious; to others, audacious. I am seeking a quiet place for Erik to unfurl and gear up to adulthood. In truth, I am buying time for my son, elongating the runway and allowing him to grow into himself. This year is less about achieving grades (there are none in this transition program); it's about trying life on. Our year beside the ocean will be a Pacific loop in the path. Loops are us.

My hometown on Vancouver Island fed me joy, creativity, salt air and ocean delights for much of my young life. Why not Erik? Why not swap a hurried city, a daunting transit system and a cement-based college for craggy peaks and sea swells and sandy drives along the coast? Why not immerse my son in a forest-based campus and tap into a no-stress college transition program. Why not learn to drive along those beachy lanes? Why not stop and inhale, as required? Why not just do it?

Each "you can't do that" belongs to someone else, not to me. It is someone else's hesitation, someone else's way of moving through the world. Not mine. I tap into instinct. It tells me to create an optimal transition environment. Where is Erik best? Take him there.

I realize I can be married, have a son with autism and relocate. Like everything before it, it is a family project.

I NEED TO SEND DOCUMENTATION to North Island College on Vancouver Island to prove that Erik is a candidate for the

Employment Transition Program. I dig up the diagnosis and the reports, and something is unearthed in me. Unhinged. I feel the need to download, from me to me. Writing is cathartic. Fingers awoken, iPad warm, I tap:

Today I returned to the past and it wasn't pleasant. I felt the sickening clench. I felt defeated before I had begun. I was pushing the string, trying to create opportunities where perhaps they don't exist. I am blazing a trail . . . no wait, not blazing. Pickaxing. Is that a verb?

Today I was working with college intake advisors, trying to piece together a first-year transition program for Erik. Alongside the Employment Transition Program courses, I also want Erik to sample "real college courses" and get a feel for the college milieu. Can he handle courses like this? Is the subject area—healthcare assistant—one he's interested in? Are we hitting the mark? You never know till you try, so I asked if Erik could try.

"He can't do that. He isn't able to sample courses. He has to be full time or not at all."

"No sampling? No gradual access? Really?"

"That's right."

I slumped. We were already on plan C, and we hadn't even packed our bags. We would have to think some more, come at this from yet another angle. Situation normal.

Before we could proceed, we would need to haul out old boxes and expose the foundation. I would have to dig and find the papers that got it all rolling a dozen years ago. I'd have to reawaken Erik's diagnosis and all of the other damning reports along the way. It's called Erik's historical assessment information. To me, it is dismal and limiting. There are lots of very low percentiles and words like *severe* and *below the norm* and *requires significant support*.

Rereading the reports, the paralyzing emotions crept back and took hold. This surprised me. I thought the alarm would be less. I thought time would smooth the prickliness of the pages and the ugliness of the words. But no, the feeling was the same, and so was the physiological response: I became aware of my heart, my hands and my breath. The heat was back. Background became foreground. I felt despair all over again. I felt the sadness, the hopelessness and the anger at the experts for having exposed the most unflattering facets of my child. Damn you. I remember thinking then, and I felt it again today. Damn you for shining the light.

For a moment I forgot that that was then and this is now. I thought that the numbers could continue to reach out and choke Erik, to stop him from moving forward. To create another pool of non-believers. But then I looked at the date on the report. 2005. That was twelve years ago.

And then I exhaled. It had been a snapshot in time and was possibly accurate at the time, but it no longer packed a punch today. It could not touch us. We had moved on. We had believed and persevered past the fifth percentiles and had worked to override the numbing numbers.

"You look tired."

Heather found me in the storage room, surrounded by the archeological dig.

"How do you feel, exactly?" she asked.

"Sickened, again," I said to her, "but also triumphant."

"Triumphant?"

"Yes, because we didn't buy in back then. Those numbers represented Erik at that time, possibly on that day. Possibly not. For example, he scored below the first percentile for writing. That surprised me because I felt he was better than that. So I asked. Apparently on the assessment day, he wrote very little. He sat there. The assumption was that he could not write.

I asked him about it a few days after I had seen the report. "What did you have to write about?"

"Our favourite sports team. I don't watch sports. So I had nothing to write about," he said, matter-of-factly.

Heather nodded.

"He was honest," I sighed. "His response was pure autism. Instead of explaining or faking it, he responded the only way he knew how. Accurately. Authentically. I don't watch sports. I don't have a favourite team. I don't have anything to write about. And that did him in. It delivered a stamp: Erik can't write."

Below the first percentile. That half a number had been attached to Erik and had defined his ability to communicate via the written word. Everyone read the number and accepted it.

I remember it surprised me that Erik would let this happen. But really, it was an illumination point: Erik doesn't fake it. The results were about a flawed test, not about Erik's ability to write. Good throw. Good catch.

"So that's why I feel triumphant. Because we didn't embrace the words, the projections. We looked at growth over time and we counted on it. We moved beyond stamp and stuck and static."

I snapped the lid on the tote and I felt relief. The dismal prognosis could not touch us now.

When we know better, we do better.

I click off my iPad. Exhausted.

CHAPTER 55

Autism Transplanted

AUGUST **2017**. THE HEDLEY FIVE minus Scott drive five thousand kilometres west to Vancouver Island. Frank and Heather fly back to Ottawa to launch Heather's final year of high school. Erik and I settle into a rustic beach lodge and become west coasters.

I have always dreamed of living here, at this funky little stretch of shoreline called Kye Bay. It has an artsy, retro feel to it, and where there is art, there is alternate thinking, and often, acceptance. Difference is not feared because sameness is rare. These beach-dwellers cultivate their own pulse. In life, you either find your people, or you seek them. In choosing to live here, we are doing both.

Home is a faded 1920s oceanfront cedar lodge, facelifted and tucked up alongside a time-worn string of cottages, soft peppermint, with doors painted tangerine and lime and fuchsia and violet. Beyond, scattered on a beachfront boardwalk, rest candy-coloured Muskoka chairs, coated to coordinate with the decorative doors. Vines twist and support wonky strings of outdoor lights. There is charm in the peely-paint disarray. It is reminiscent of something you might find on a Greek island. The perfection, Erik and I decide, is in the imperfection. Like autism, I muse. Neither is cookie-cutter. The beauty is in the dough outside the perfect cut-outs.

"It's like a little Marigold Hotel," I whisper to Erik. We both love the British film, its motley characters and how it is that people colour the palette. "When you think if it," I say to him, "we are all characters, and this," I gesture around at the waves and the minty wood and the twinkly lights, "is the set. We are the performers."

I think of my father, the storyteller, and I imagine our lives here as movies. Like a wall of televisions in an electronics store, the screens are lit up simultaneously: mine, Erik's, our neighbours', a wall of flickering light, of stories, of scripts. As main characters, we are the authors of our tales. The thought makes Erik and me giddy with possibility.

"It makes me think of that line in the movie *Dead Poets Society*," I suggest, "when the teacher, played by Robin Williams, has the boys gather around the trophy case and he points out former students and what they've accomplished. He adds that it is up to each one of us to make our lives extraordinary."

Erik nods.

"So here we are in this exceptional backdrop," I continue. "We must make it good; we must create great."

WHAT I WANT ERIK TO know is how community feels. What is it like to greet people each day? To get to know your neighbours? To watch out for them? To learn more about them? To help out? To celebrate? To problem-solve together? To express joy? How does it feel to share hopes and dreams and fears and successes? To say goodbye to old friends and to welcome new ones? How does all of this feel?

I want Erik to know. To live it is to know it. The people part is an education beyond the college classroom. "*This* is his education!" I whisper to the ocean one day. Erik is learning what it is to connect. If autism is the inability to form reciprocal relationships, a daily dose of social is a potent curriculum. To connect and to feel is to be human. He is becoming.

We are an assorted cast of characters. In choosing this transient year by the sea, we are all individuals in life transition. For Erik, it's a surprise and a comfort to realize that he is not the only one shifting gears. He is surrounded by people in metamorphosis: changing jobs, changing relationships, changing homes, changing minds, changing direction. It's good to know there are like-minded travellers on the trail. We have plenty.

Here by the ocean, relationships stretch us because *unlike* us is the norm. There is something to admire in everyone. My mother tells me this, and now I know it to be true.

Here beside the sea, eclectic is electric. Diversity recharges us. Erik is learning about shamanism; about herring runs and sea lion slaughter; about tracking transient orcas and local killer whales; about cultivating and cooking shellfish; about bracketing each day with meditation; about photographing stars with high-powered lenses; about brewing medicinal marijuana tea; about identifying ovoids in Indigenous art; about reading tides; about little boys who have had three open-heart surgeries by age four; about jewelry-making; about the gifts from the sea; about taking the time to seek sunrise and sunset; about playing Frisbee at low tide by the light of a full moon; about kite-flying; about military fighter jets and what it looks like to punch through the sound barrier; about sea birds and yoga and drumming and playing the ukulele by the sea. We do not learn such things in our Ottawa neighbourhood.

"No way!" says Erik when I read him the list. Our world is expanding well beyond anything either of us has ever known. In trying on new, we lead a life of possibility. We are taking owner-ship. We create great, and we don't give up.

For a person carrying a diagnosis, it is important to do your own writing, to define yourself. Don't accept anything less than what you feel. Do not settle. "Autism is authentic," I say to Erik, "so allow your stories to reveal that authenticity. Besides, we haven't come this far to go mediocre. Let's make your life extraordinary."

IS THIS A GOOD IDEA?

I ask this late at night. My reserves are low; my passion pales. I become my biggest detractor. I never make decisions at night. At night, I rehash.

Uprooting autism is risky, experimental. Plucking Erik out of his well-worn Ottawa comfort zone, we have transplanted him 5,000 kilometres from all that he knows. Now we watch and wait and wonder. Our plan is perfect on paper. But perhaps autism cannot be so easily fooled. Perhaps it is much bigger than a shift to an ideal backdrop.

Three months in, there are cracks in the foundation.

Alongside Erik's transition program—courses covering workplace themes such as expectations, safety, communication and relationships—we plan beyond for a possible career as a care aide in a seniors' facility, much like what Erik sampled in his Ottawa high school co-op. We are laying a foundation for college, ticking off the program prerequisites: WHMIS (Workplace Hazardous Materials Information System), First Aid and Food Safe.

It is here we stumble, crash, right out of the opening gate. In aviation terms, I redline my son and inadvertently push him to his limits and beyond.

We take the prerequisite courses together, me in tow as a second set of ears and eyes and note-taking fingers. I am Erik's education assistant. But Erik is drinking from a firehose. It is all too much, too fast, too in-depth. He is drowning in facts. Without me slowing things down and re-teaching, he cannot complete these weekend courses. That much is clear to both of us. I tell him that the delivery and pace is what regular college would be like, but more so, full time. He would have to be able to do this largely on his own. His eyes widen.

"Good to know," comes a small voice.

He feels defeated, and in observing his body, his face, I intervene. "Erik, to me, this is not failure. It's illumination. Now we know. And it's not a no; it's a not right now. Perhaps in a few years with more life experience and maturity, you'll be ready and able to take this on. Just not right now. You know that song by Phil Collins, 'You Can't Hurry Love'? It's like that. You can't hurry anything. And readiness is one of those things. You're ready when you're ready. Or not. And if that's the case, we switch tracks."

"Like Dad says . . . You can only be who you are? It's hard to be someone you're not?"

"Yes, like that. We can revisit this. In the meantime, we need to meet you where you are. We need to find a program that fits and a delivery that works for you. No firehoses. No full-time, full-speed. Part-time, hands-on maybe. We'll know when it's right."

And to myself, another illumination point: you cannot mandate readiness. It comes to you. Readiness knows when it is ready.

And another: you cannot manufacture ability. You can enhance it, but beyond that, potential is singular and varied. *Was tutoring Erik throughout public school a good idea after all?* Perhaps I filled him with a false sense of competence. Maybe I pumped too much air into the bouncy castle. In the moment, we were trying to meet demands, diffuse anxiety, tread water. How much air? It's hard to know.

CHAPTER 56

Redline

OUR OLD GHOSTS ARE BACK. Like uninvited house guests, they will not leave. To me, they are disturbing, but to Erik, they are blessed, just-in-time collaborators. They are rocking and whispering and hand flicking and finger gazing. They are sniffling and hair twirling and endless pacing. They are prolonged silence and sometimes bizarrely animated conversations with the air around him. Erik looks like he is on nonstop Bluetooth.

I thought these behaviours had been outgrown; turns out they were submerged, tucked away for a decade, consigned to privacy. But now they are on display, in the lodge as though I am invisible, and out in the courtyard, alongside the seashore. I am flabbergasted. Many years ago, I asked these ghosts to leave. But they dodged the door and hid in a closet.

Remove familiar Ottawa, and they are back. Now it is my turn to slump. I thought we had replaced these regulators with something age appropriate, *acceptable*, but here they are, smack out front, like when Erik was seven, home from school and on the run.

Reframe, I remind myself. They are here for a reason, these in-your-face-regulators. Erik is doing what he needs to do. But I feel like the years between then and now have collapsed, imploded, been for naught. I feel like we are unravelling, defaulting to genetic.

Nature—one. Nurture—zero.

It surprises me that Erik doesn't seem to care, that he lets me see all of this. Private is public, indoors and out.

"What's going on with Erik?" a few neighbours ask. They want to know about autism. So do I.

"Well," I begin, "looks like I pushed him too hard, too fast, too soon. But the messy stuff is good," I say. "It's the stuff of redlines, of taking a person with autism to the edge of themselves . . . to test the borders, to expand them. I think of the Kenny Loggins lyric, you know, from *Top Gun*: 'You never say hello to you, till you take it to the redline overload.'"

The image of saying hello to oneself is *good*. It's self-awareness. If you don't know, there is no speed except idle. "So redlining is a good thing," I explain to the other renters. "At least, I think it is . . . It's just that most of the time I feel like I'm pulling Erik along through the water . . . too fast like an unwilling waterskier."

We chuckle at the image of Erik, windswept, clutching the rope, sputtering, trying to stay upright; and me, hunched, throttle full forward, speeding the boat along. It isn't funny, but it is. We are laughing at me and my inclination to go all in. I remind myself that for Erik, high speed is terrifying.

Our default has to be his speed, not mine.

MESSY NOVEMBER DELIVERS POSITIVE CHANGE. Up go the traffic lights, once more, after the accident. One of the things we do in the aftermath of redline is redesign Erik's bedroom. It is spartan; that's about to change.

I think of my own apartments abroad and what comforted me when home was distant. I created a wall of faces, a familiar and friendly frame for my new life. From Bristol board backdrops, my family and friends greeted me daily. I loved those walls, sometimes plastering my kitchen, sometimes my bedroom. The photos were my foundation and my self-regulation. How could I have forgotten to do this for Erik on his first foray from home?

When the wall of faces unveiling comes, Erik gasps. "This . . . this *defines* me!"

He stares at the images for a long time. "This tells me who I am. It's always about the people," he half-whispers to himself. "You always tell us that." He is cocooned by these walls. These faces are just-in-time responders. He is beginning to thaw.

On the floor sits a pile of discards, pictures we ordered that won't fit, that he has decided not to include. Some of them surprise me because they are Ottawa moments with notable people, faces I expect he may want to display. I ask him why not. I figure he may opt to swap out a few unknowns for well-knowns.

"No," he says. "I don't know those people. They're famous, but I don't know them. I put up people that mean something to me."

In this, I am offered another glimmer of autism illumination: autism is not boastful nor is it showy. Erik chose plain over fame. It is never about a display for others; it is about self, after all, and this brand of "autos" is impressive. *Ego is private; authenticity is public.* We neurotypicals are the inverse: ego on display, authenticity tucked away. Which is right? Which needs rejigging?

WE LEARN FROM LURCHING. WE learn from leaning. We do not toss our failures, our hot potatoes.

I report our triumphs and trials daily, weekly, to family and friends. I take stock of our life by the ocean, and I list the adventures by car, by kayak, by bike, on foot—the challenges, the options, the stumbling blocks and the current battle plan. We wobble; we lean; we inch forward; we learn. But overall, what I am trying to figure out, is this: *What does growth look like in Erik? How can I support subtle growth? Is this runway long enough? Is it supporting takeoff? When will Erik be ready to lift the wheels and take off? To merge with a slightly neurotypical post-secondary path? Or, will he, ever . . . ?*

In placing Erik in this Employment Transition Program, he is tasting independence. He is on a college campus but this program is not a college program. It is safe, measured, informative and without homework or expectations other than "this information will make you better on the worksite." But the reality is this program will not get Erik a job. It is a section of runway.

I STARE AT THE TWO words, and in their wake, at the blinking cursor. Growth hurts. I resume typing. It's an email to my friend Sarah.

I had a long phone conversation with Frank tonight, painting the autism picture in vivid and true colours. I could tell Frank was a bit rattled. We're seeing full-blown autism reactions in Erik such as I haven't seen in a decade, proving to me that perhaps you can't simply pull out the tree and disturb the tap-root and hair roots, transplant it into amazingly rich soil and expect it to grow and blossom. The roots have been disturbed. Erik is wilting.

Frank wasn't really understanding how and why. I said to him, "I think it's not so much about reacting to the new environment as it is a reaction to the absence of the old environment . . . And it seems to be cumulative, over time."

Or maybe it's both . . . Maybe it is missing the old and still adjusting to the new. Either way, displacing autism was not recommended to me . . . And I'm seeing that it isn't as simple as I thought it might be. The tree reacted brightly, at first, but now it's drooping.

To live is to adjust. Your mom told you that, Sarah, and I keep telling myself this. While disturbing and perplexing to see Erik like this, it's also a little fascinating and intriguing. Maybe we need to put him back. Not sure . . . We press on and stretch through the minor growing pains.

But in the meantime, I still love it here. No regrets. Only moving forward.

We are tilting. Tilting is stretching, and stretching is painful. It's a productive kind of pain—pain with gain, like workout ache. "Pain is part of growth," I tell Erik. "No pain, little gain. So good news, we must be growing. Yes, we are growing."

Still, I didn't expect this withdrawal and regression. We were doing so well for so long and now this. It feels like defeat. Like

I have ruined Erik by ripping him out of his comfort zone and hauling him out here to the west coast. Perhaps I didn't think it through well enough. I thought I had.

CHAPTER 57

Let Him Lead

IT IS **5:30** A.M. MY neighbour, Jane, is up early, walking her dog. Or rather, her dog is walking her. It's still dark, but I know she is out there, in our ocean community courtyard. She wears a headband with an LED light, and it bobs and bounces against the night sky, the endless Douglas firs. I call her the mysterious miner. I jump to my feet and open the patio door.

"Good morning!" I whisper loudly enough so that she can hear me, but not loud enough to waken the others. I ask her if she is looking for something—her path is so erratic—and she says, "No, I'm just letting her take the lead." *Her* is the dog, Denali, an enormous Alaskan malamute. "I let her lead the way because she knows where she wants to go, needs to go. Likely rabbits," she adds with a laugh.

I tell Jane that I've been awake since 1:30 a.m. because my brain is trying to download, but that it's not convenient because I'm still in bed. My brain doesn't listen and continues to deliver, and it's good stuff. Epiphanies and metaphors are being churned out, slipping away in the dark bedroom. This annoys me, so I click on the light and read, switch channels. I try to sleep again, but my brain will not be taken there. It keeps stirring. So I click on the light again and get up at 4 a.m. I fire up my iPad, and I allow the flow of words. My fingers race to catch up. I tell her all of this. Looking at Denali now, I get it.

"I'm letting my brain lead."

I tell her that Erik has been silent, in another funk of some sort. She doesn't huff or judge. She says, simply, "That's okay. It's what he needs to do."

It strikes me that just as I write at awkward hours, she is allowing them both to take the lead—the dog and the young man with autism. Maybe I need to listen and do the same. Stop trying to pull and manage everything. *Let it be for a change, Teresa.* Let him breathe. Let him lead. It's good advice, and I need to hear it. I will write it on a sticky note and flash it when Erik is silent, withdrawn. "Let him lead. It's what he needs to do."

Perhaps we slide back before moving forward. Regression before expansion. Maybe the rocking and the whispering and the pacing are helping to pave this transition, to make it possible. I didn't forbid the childhood regressions so maybe I shouldn't react to the autism arsenal. It's what he needs. Let him lead.

I SIT BENT OVER MY iPad, taking stock, writing to my friend Karen. As you can see and feel, we are a family in transition . . . And to me that's okay . . . I tell Erik, to stretch is to grow. If it's too easy, we're too dull and complacent. I like trying options and turning over rocks . . . exploring possibilities . . . A little daunting and also exciting . . . I just have to check on my waterskiers!

And to Frank on the phone, later in the day: "I see it like this. It's all about pathways and the way they look for each of us.

"Heather," I begin, "knows that she wants to study acting. It comes down to 'Which film school?' Her path, so far, is quite straight, direct. She's a girl with a plan.

"Scott's path has curves. He is sorting out what he wants to do . . . An online poker career? Economics? He is working out the what; his path meanders, like a wildly snaking river in a valley. It's a little hard to follow, but from the air, you see it clearly. It's a wiggly path. An oxbow river. But it is moving forward.

"Now Erik, his path is different again. It's not a straight line nor a wiggly line because Erik doesn't know the *what*. With Erik, not only do we not know what to study, we don't know *how*, the ideal delivery, or *where*, the school. Or whether school is an option. Erik's path is a maze. Seen from above, the entry and exit points are clear, but we're not there yet. We are not privy to a bird's-eye view.

"With Erik, we're face on, trying pathways, hitting walls daily and weekly. It may seem like we're not making progress, but these walls aren't walls at all: they are illumination points, options that either aren't viable or maybe not right now. Each bump is a nudge in a direction that might be more Erik. Like our friend Maryanne reminds us, 'When you get a no, a better yes is coming.'

"So we work through the maze, and as we do, we are trying on life and lengthening the cognitive runway. We are building in readiness and we are learning more about Erik. And Erik is learning about Erik, becoming more self-aware. With each trial and error, we are elevated slightly higher, delivered a different perspective, able to see more of the maze. Until eventually, we'll be given a bird's-eye snapshot and we'll see the whole picture, beginning, explorations and a way through. That will be Erik's path."

Frank sums up: "the arrow, the oxbow and the maze." We smile through the phone. A man of few words, he has described our three to a T: the explorer, the experimenter and the enigma.

IT TAKES FOUR MONTHS TO figure out the obvious.

We came here seeking the ideal transition program, nature-nurture, a community living experience and a smaller fish pond. But what I missed in my projection is that we have slowed down to Island Time. As well as place, we are seeking *pace*, one in sync with Erik's distinct metronome. We are looking for an autism pacemaker.

I first spied the expression "Island Time" on a silky tourist brochure. There were pictures of tourists oohing and ahhing in old-growth forests; paddling over glassy ocean ecosystems; admiring Maui-like sunsets. Tucked in the imagery, three words: imagine yourself here. Slow down to Island Time. And this is where we find ourselves, stretched, not thin but more appropriately, over a less demanding backdrop—one that values stopping to check the tide—and a climate temperate enough to do so year-round.

We find our groove. I call it part-time downtime. Erik goes to school and volunteers part time, takes public transit and is learning to drive. To balance the busyness, we factor in plenty of solitude and downtime. Part-time downtime. We strike a balance.

It is also a place where we are inspired to create. The ocean has that effect. I can't stop making trees from the exquisite pieces of driftwood we collect on our beach walks. Lining up our gnarled driftwood in descending order, we take turns drilling a thumb-sized hole in the centre of each piece, and feeding the twisted, bleached limbs, one by one, onto a metal rod. Et voila! A tree is born! I call our driftwood creations *story trees* because the branches are eclectic; they have former lives. There are sticks thrown for dogs; curious, twisty walking sticks; wormy Swiss cheese wood; smooth, bone-white limbs; wood charred in beach fires and bits of boats and signage washed in to shore. These little histories are stacked and skewered to become story trees, highlighted by hundreds of twinkly lights. I joke to friends that we have produced either a tree house or a light house; I'm not sure which.

On the huge slab of wood that is our kitchen table rest gifts from the sea: bowls of bleached clam and oyster shells; wedges of speckled rock, sliced and polished; glass cylinders filled with maroon and sage seaweed, dried and suspended in air, illuminated by tiny lights; massive spikey mauve sea urchins; perfect, smooth white sand dollars; scrubbed, plump moon shells; fragile tangerine-pink crab backs, brittle to the touch; and shiny black bald eagle feathers, capped with a slash of white. We love it all, this ocean treasure.

Amid the backdrop of driftwood and shells and ocean flora, the waves pound, the wind howls, the rain hammers and the sea birds soar; in front of it, Erik and I live and we fumble and we adjust.

CHAPTER 58

Word Quotient

It is early February. A winter storm rages outside. Lashing wind and rain pepper the windows and the corrugated tin roof. There is no snow; this is the wild, mild west coast.

The storm no longer rages inside. September and October were idyllic, new, a bubble. November and December were testy, dark, dysregulated. The temptation was to surrender to the anxiety, to fold the plan and return to home base. But we did not. We held course, changed tack, tweaked the strategy and rode out the squall.

Quietly and without notice, autism retreated as stealthily as it had reappeared. The rocking, I realize, has completely abated. It's gone. Like a baby whose cries fade to grey, you get used to it, and then there is silence and calm. And that is what happened. Erik's body reacted to being transplanted and pulled and stretched; autism took charge and regulated him until the pace became Erik-friendly. And then silently, autism abated.

I realize that which I feared—the return of the rocking and the flapping and the constant eerie whispering—was a helper, not a hindrance. It was part of Erik's default toolkit. I did not teach him this. Autism gifted him these resources. Instead of being fearful, I ought to have been grateful. Autism took Erik by the wrist and said, "Here, I'll help you over this hurdle, Erik." And then it happened. He made it over.

In this I feel Grinch-like again. But this is not the plotting Grinch nor the cunning Grinch. This is the epiphany Grinch, perched on the mountain peak, heart expanding, mind flooding with realization. When you think you know, you stop thinking. And like the Grinch, now I know.

Here we are, on the other side of the storm. I didn't guide Erik here. Autism did. Erik did.

WHEN THE KIDS WERE LITTLE, one of the games they loved to play was something we called *Protect You from the Storm*. I suppose it was a scenario, not a game. We'd be tucked together on the bedroom sofa, often after bath time, warm and fragrant. I would be reading to my ducklings—three under age four—and we'd be snuggled together, connected by words, drawings, blankets and perfumed warmth. Every now and then, we'd pause, and arms wrapped around the trio, I would pull them close and whisper, "Protect you from the storm." As though huddled on a ship's deck, we would heave as one, a school of fish, toward the edge of our perch, and then at the last moment, Mommy's arms would pull them back, reposition and whisper, "Protect you from the storm." We loved this sensation, this sense of synergy and togetherness. Of peril and of protection.

For me, it was defining. I was the protector, the watchman, the rescuer. As the kids grew up, the game diminished and eventually dried up. The storms arrived, but each child began to venture out and meet the waves. Except Erik. I felt protective, vigilant and responsible for years beyond Scott and Heather.

That is also part of the autism portfolio, the portrait of the armoured parent. It is the role of the soldier to plan, to strategize, to outmanoeuvre, to reposition and to never, ever, give up. The lessons learned from falling and from bruising are instructive because they hurt and they leave marks. We work for scars. We behold the blemishes and we reflect and we remember; we are proud of our scar tissue because it signals grit, fortitude, perseverance. These are the hard-earned autism stories, and from them we make a plan and move forward.

I am letting go of Erik, resisting the urge to pull him away from the edge. I am allowing him to face the waves. He is learning to protect himself from life's storms.

I remind him that in uncertain times, we are like jiggling apps on a smartphone, vibrating within our environment, facing challenges, responding and then quietly settling back into place.

Jiggling apps are good and they are normal, because change is constant. The uncertainty does not last. Eventually, we settle into the new context and that becomes our new normal. We update. We evolve.

ERIK IS QUIET AT THE dinner table a lot. He is quiet period. But not always. Some days he is animated, asking me endless questions about relatives and what they are doing and marvelling at the many connections in his life. And then the tap turns, and he is silent. The words are all used up.

To me the inconsistency is hard, and I want to control that, too—even it out. I ask him to talk to me, tell me anything, and one night, he snaps back. This is uncharacteristic and from a distance, slightly humorous.

"What do you want me to do?" he barks. "*State the obvious? Talk about the weather? Well I won't do that. I did that yesterday. I talked to you yesterday.*"

I absorb this. It is not a communication failure; it is a neurological mismatch, but mostly, it's a misguided expectation—mine. Erik is happy with the twenty-eight words he has spoken. I want more, always more. I give him too many, a truckload, and he gives me too few, a trickle. I want him to talk and he wants me to stop. It's all about expectation and need. It's not a failure. It's a failure to meet expectation.

So I change mine. I reframe. I pretend I want this. *It could be worse. He could be a chatterbox and I could be trying to shut him off, stop the noise. But I have silence instead, and that is golden, is it not? He is offering me gold. Use it. Mine it. Write. Contemplate. Do yoga. Do whatever. He is giving you a gift and you are baulking, giving it back.* So I take it and I don't expect him to speak, but still, it bothers me.

Who will live with this? Like this? What kind of mate will be attracted to few words? No words? Not talking means not connecting. And not connecting means little relationship building. How will this ever work and with whom? But then I steer my brain clear, and I do not fret for the future because I cannot control that either. I content myself with the gift at hand, the silence, and I do my thing.

But the reality is that after a while my words are brimming and longing to spill out. I have a quota to fill. So I step outside and walk to the water. A few of our community mates are out front, walking their dogs, mucking about on the beach. We linger, talk, compare notes, laugh. I am chatty, my words eager to play, to rally, to spin, to collide. To do anything but to be met with silence.

One of the guys asks where Erik is, and I tell him about the word quota situation. In storytelling and explaining, I am an autism translator. I help him to understand. I help me to understand.

"Oh, I get it," he says. "Now I know why you're so chatty. You're not talking in there so you're talking out here . . . with everyone!"

I laugh. I hadn't thought much about the overflow until that moment. "You're right. You're all my outdoor roommates. I guess sooner or later, it spills out . . . It has to. And you're it."

My neighbours help me to see my son. Let him lead.

ONE DAY IN THE SPRING, Erik and I are out for a walk on the beach, not together as I had hoped, and as one may expect, but separate, the way it usually is. To backtrack, this solitary stroll routine surprised my sister because during her September visit, Erik was on, animated, full of questions, overflowing with words. He walked with us, kept up with us. I was so proud.

"But he's not normally like this," I told my sister. "He doesn't walk with me when you're not here. We walk separately, alone."

She was surprised.

"I've figured out that I'm the recharging station. Home base. He doesn't talk around me because he is comfortable. He is charging his batteries, warming up for the outside world, and while that happens, he is silent, filling up. So he walks alone. He is quiet." She nods. She is beginning to understand autism.

And on this day, six months after her visit, Erik and I walk separately along the beach, in opposite directions because I don't want to appear to be pursuing him. He turns around, and slowly, we approach one another. I am happy to see him and am about to speak as we draw closer, but then I notice his face. It's pinched, closed, somewhere else. And as he passes me, just a few metres between us, he doesn't look; he digs in and walks on by.

I feel chilled by this. We appear like strangers even though we are mother and son, linked by autism and by blood. I expect something, a hint, but I get nothing, zero response. My mind flashes the scene at the end of the movie *Life of Pi*, where after surviving weeks at sea, adrift, wary and yet connected, the Bengal tiger stalks away from the boy without looking back: wild after all. In that moment, I feel it, too: wild after all. I thought we had come so far, and we have. But we also have this frost, and when it happens, I am left frozen, speechless, just like the boy in the movie. Live without expectation. I am learning.

Inside the lodge, Erik cements my epiphany, serves it back to me as only Erik can: directly, no mincing, no mercy. "You know that I'm not like you, so don't expect me to talk to you much. I'm just sayin'."

CHAPTER 59

Two Dogs

OUR DARK DAYS COME IN many forms. What surprises me most about them is how abruptly things change. One moment we are having a good day; the next, not. I wonder whether this is hormonal. Erik has been steady for so long. Now he is mercurial, the way he was when autism surfaced at age three.

On one of these changeable days, I ask him to put out the recyclables. He does. There is a complex system here: some things go in the green tote just outside our door; others go in individual garbage bins in a common area. He tells me he did the right thing and deposited empties where they needed to go. I soon discover not and this surprises me—angers me, in fact. We've been here five months; has he been inventing his own system the entire time? Why didn't he just ask? I react and he is not pleased. He storms out.

Shortly after—*ping!*—I receive a text message, short and sweet, a one-liner: You need to be more like Sarah Holliday.

I am not sure whether to laugh or to take this to heart—or both. I have spoken highly of my friend Sarah, and Erik has decided he would like to swap me for her. In his moment of anger, this is his solution: a mother exchange. In fact, I don't blame him. It's a brilliant bit of self-advocacy and solution-seeking. Zap your monster mother. Replace her with a serene selection. In that moment, it makes sense.

"Use your words," we encourage our children. And now, Erik has spoken.

I AM AT ERIK'S COLLEGE and I cross paths with Marla, the free-spirited fortune teller. We immediately break into big smiles and hug. Marla isn't really a fortune teller, but if you didn't know, you would think she was. Her own son playfully calls her a cartoon character; and if she were one, she would be drawn in animated strokes, round, vibrant, small but large in presence.

On this day, Marla is meandering back to her post behind the campus cafe window. She is Marla the latte lady, the mocha matron, the dispenser of delicious drinks and wise words. Erik loves her eccentricity, her creased sensibility and the way she makes him feel, in a glance. Worthy. Welcome. Wonderful. He visits her twice a week, and they check in, exchange updates. She is one of his campus tethers. He to her is gentlemanly sweetness.

Marla smiles, a crinkly one, and lights up. "Erik's mom! I love your boy!" And then more quietly, "I love that boy like he was my own." I know she means it because in some ways they are much alike, Erik and Marla. They dare to be different. Erik is. Marla dares. She goes on to say how well Erik is doing on campus.

One of Erik's teachers kick-starts class with a walk around campus, a nature immersion, and it is to this march-past Marla refers in her next breath: "I see him once a week . . . part of the parade, you know, and we look for one another. I see him looking for me, trying to catch my eye, and when he does, he beams. I feel so good inside. And I am also smiling because he is smiling. We light one another up, me and Erik."

I tell her that when life ramps up, I reflect on something she told me in 2016 as I checked out the campus. "Don't push him too hard, Mamma. He's doing his best."

As I remind her of this, her head cocks slightly, and a smile forms. "Erik reminds me of my dog," she says with a laugh. "And you," waving her hand at me, "my neighbour's dog." She chuckles. We both do. I've been called many things but never the neighbour's dog.

She continues. "My dog is slow-moving, quiet, loving. Erik," she indicates, punctuating the air with her right index finger. "My neighbour's dog," she gestures with a second jab, "well, she's all over the place. Zero to eighty."

"Me?"

"Yes, that's you. Pure energy. Now, the neighbour's dog, you, and my dog, Erik, are out for a walk. My neighbour's dog bounds ahead, races here and there, sniffs, comes back, barks, runs ahead again, exuberant. My dog, well, he sticks pretty close to me. He sniffs, he checks everything out, slowly . . . he may lift his leg and pee, stop, sniff again. He doesn't get too far too fast, but eventually, he finishes the walk. They both do, quickly and slowly. That's you and Erik," she tells me, but I have already figured this out. "And the two dogs love one another and get along well," she assures me. "But they have their own timelines, their own agendas."

I think about this later, this dog analogy, and I tell Erik. He laughs at first and then abruptly, he asks me what Marla was wearing. "Fortune teller clothes," I tell him, and we both know I am only half-joking, for Marla, like Erik, sees things for what they are. I understand Erik a little bit more, his timeline and his trajectory. I am the greyhound; he is the hush puppy. We walk different paths, but we'll both reach a common destination, in our own time. In our own way.

I AM WORKING THROUGH MY to-do list, and at 9 p.m., I am done. Drained. As I used to say to our three when I was tired and overwhelmed, "The Mommy Store is closed." But on this particular night, I have miles to go before I sleep—more emails and texts to write before bed. There always are.

"I'm *soooo tired*," I say, turning toward Erik, muffling a yawn. And then, half to myself and half to him, "I'm way too tired to write these emails." And then defiantly, "I don't want to!"

His reaction is so Erik and so delightful, simple and pure.

"You don't have to."

With that, he clicks off the light and climbs the stairs to bed.

I sit in the dark, smiling, thinking so many thoughts. *He's right. He's wise. He's authentic. He's learning to discern. He is teaching me to honour me just as he listens to his body and honours himself. He sometimes doesn't follow social convention, but he doesn't cave to it, either.* And then I laugh into the still room. He's becoming his father!

I sit in the shadows, ruminating, and I hear myself say out loud, "You. Don't. Have. To."

IT'S HARD TO LIVE HOLDING your breath. But if you have a child with autism, you do, out of necessity. You don't notice that you're holding it until you have a chance to fully exhale. And then you hear it, the rush of air, and you realize you must have been braced. That happened yesterday. Yesterday is a portrait of many yesterdays and a string of exhalations.

I drop Erik off at Driver's Education, the classroom portion. We have prepared for this, the six-hour stint in the classroom and how to cope and what to expect and when the breaks would be and what to do in those breaks to self-regulate. And once back in the classroom, to understand that this day would be long and weighty and tiring for everyone. And to understand the bigger purpose for being here: to learn to be a safe, knowledgeable driver. And, and, and . . . We have talked and prepared until we are both wound tightly, ready and already tired.

I drop him off, babble at the instructor and try to be informative and informal without being vigilant, wondering whether the memo has squirted through from head office and whether Erik's file has been tagged, as promised: autism. Neither of us say anything. Erik has asked that I not bring it up, but we both hope the instructor knows.

I spend the morning deep in activity, making ham soup and programming bicycle odometers, but what I am really doing is checking my watch, wondering, imagining. I text, cheerfully, over the lunch hour: E, how's it going so far? Dave seems friendly, like Pete, the cop. Dave was also a police officer and taught driver training to new officers. So you're learning from someone well qualified! Hope you're enjoying it . . . See you just after three!

Twelve minutes later, *ping*: It's going well so far! Very informative. I'm recognizing the road rules. Dave talks about them with pictures projected up on the board. I'm glad I'm here! The last line delivers relief. It is then I hear the exhalation.

Erik is a product I can neither predict nor promise. I tell instructors what may or may not happen, but I never know. With Erik, I cannot make assurances, and certainly, there are no guarantees. I can only prepare him and the environment in the best way I know, and then sit back and wait and hope, ready to re-muster if need be, to move on to plan B, C, and down the line. Breath held. So when success happens, it is a celebration and an illumination: a tell-all portrait of me, mouth pursed, poised, living with breath held. And that is an exhausting way to be.

I do not rejoice long in the exhalation because there is a decompression stage, and I am still learning to follow Erik's lead on this.

I pick him up from driver training, and like young Erik returning from a frenetic day at elementary school, Erik sags once he reaches his seat in the van. He chooses the second row because he doesn't want to talk much. He did that already today. Although I am bursting for details, he is not ready to give them. He is turtling, retreating into himself.

I glance at the rear-view mirror and see him close his eyes. He is immediately asleep, and in this, I register the energy it must have taken to negotiate the day: to fit in, to go with the flow and to absorb six hours of driver training. Of fluorescent lights. Of small talk. It would be like flight simulator training for many of us—taxing beyond belief.

We arrive home; he wakes up and stumbles from the van. Once in the boot room, I gesture toward the new odometers I have installed on our bikes. "Erik, you wouldn't believe what a big deal it was to figure these out and mount them . . ." But I am talking to air. Erik has brushed by me and has disappeared upstairs.

Two hours later, he re-emerges, but makes a beeline for the rear door and the ocean. He's gone for another chunk of time and ducks upstairs as soon as he gets back in. He is not speaking, but he is not angry, just immersed in the art and science of decompression and self-regulation.

Let him lead, I tell myself, but just as he is bursting for quiet, I am bursting to talk, to know, to hear. *We are opposites*, I muse, but I have learned not to judge. I simply observe.

Another hour passes. He saunters downstairs all smiles. Before I can speak, he does, seamlessly and as though no time has passed between returning home and now. We have warped to readiness: "Show me the odometers!" he enthuses, and I do. We marvel and exclaim, and I pretend I am not affected by the four hours of silence. Of course, I am. But I am also in receiving mode, and what I've learned is this: with autism, there is an absorption quotient, and the energy required to be, to take in, to learn, is enormous. Erik has had enough words for today. He's full. I respect that.

CHAPTER 60

A Jungle Safari

SUNDAY EVENING. I AM TIRED, and I glance at my watch. Only 8:15 p.m. Too early to go to bed, but I could justify it if I read until past nine. Then it would seem reasonable.

I start to click off the lamps, the fairy lights, the driftwood trees, and I head upstairs. Erik does not. He heads for the boot room, and I hear him pulling on his coat, his boots.

"Going outside?" I call down, pausing on the staircase.

"Yes," he says, "to the beach . . ." And then he adds, "Out to the sand desert. That's what I call it. I love it when there's a really low tide at night. I walk way out and I pretend I'm in the desert, in a sand desert and that I'm somewhere else, not here. I like that the ocean can be both . . . crashing waves but also a sand desert. I like that it changes."

He has given me a truckload of words, and this surprises me— and not. He loves the ocean; he likes to talk about his loves.

"What a good idea! Taking advantage of being here . . . of this fantastic evening, the beach, of us right here on the beach. Maybe I shouldn't go to bed. Maybe I should go outside instead . . ."

I stand in my thoughts, and I hear the door open. He is heading out. Is he going to walk out without acknowledging me? I expect that he might because sometimes he does this, impatient that I've broken his flow, his trajectory, with more words. But he surprises me, as he often does, and he says two words that make me smile: "*Carpe diem.*"

And the door closes.

Don't go to bed early, surrender to the day. Seize it. Expand it. Enlarge it. Storm the beach at night; there is a sand desert to explore. I am grateful for the reminder. Who's teaching whom?

I pull on my bottle-green gumboots, and I cinch them up around my calves. I will go wading in the tidal pools, poking, prodding, on the lookout for hidden communities, curious to see what happens when I flip a rock. Who scurries? Who defends? There is potential for discovery.

I step onto the sand, negotiate the band of rocks that separates the high tide line and the rest of the beach, and then I tiptoe through the slick stripe of seaweed, a reminder that the ocean is both a desert and a jungle. I've made it out onto the hard, wet, rippled sand. And oh joy! I am standing at the edge of Erik's sand desert!

I scan the huge expanse for Erik. I don't see him, but then again, the tide is way, way out. That could be him over to the far left, the stick figure pacing the shoreline. Or maybe not. There are groups and singles in the last light of this day, and it is golden and pink out here, tinged with mauve. The glow wraps me and pulls me into it.

I step into transient ponds and streams. I take stock: an eagle pair soar; a lone heron is poised statue-like in a tidal stream, anticipating dinner. Sandpipers dot the water's edge; their stamping feet have something to do with dinner preparation. Everyone is busy here, on task, and there is quiet splendour in their purposeful routine.

I am aware of a shadow on my boots, and I look up to discover Erik. He is beside me, bent low to the ground, capturing a crab's perspective. He shows me his picture. It's exquisite, alternative. We walk a bit, side by side, silent. The evening summons silence and observation. After a while, it is Erik who speaks: "I never get tired of this."

"Me, neither," I reply, bending down to pick up a shell. I am filling a bag. "I don't think you ever get tired of the things you love. And besides, there's always something new to see out here, even if it's just the changing light."

"I know," he says. "I was thinking about when we first moved in, seven months ago. This was all new, but it still feels new in a way because the ocean is like that. It leaves us gifts."

"You're right," I begin. "And like anything in life, you just need to be open to what it has to offer . . . to explore . . ."

"And not go to bed?" he interjects, eyes cheeky.

"Yes, touché . . ." We smile at one another, acknowledging his point. "And not close your eyes to new," I add.

"Maybe this awakening is part of your growth, Erik . . . our growth this year. It's the part that we didn't plan for because you can't anticipate it. You don't know it till it happens to you . . . the unexpected bit, the subtle growth . . . in the way we see and approach the world. This is another sort of growth, alongside your college transition courses, the workplace experience, the social stuff you've learned living here in this beach community . . . This seeking new, heading out into the desert at night. This is also a layer."

He nods. "So this is what growth feels like?"

"Yes, it's like a refreshed outlook, a novel way of seeing and of being. A brand-new default . . . an approach to living. Kim Barthel calls it a conscious evolution. You're right . . . this is what it feels like.

We walk on, wrapped in the glow.

"BUT IT HASN'T ALL BEEN good . . . the year," he says to me. "Some parts were not good. Actually, kind of awful, like when we tried to do too much too quickly in November and I got all stressed. Or like the noisy neighbour in February. That was terrible." He pauses. "Do we talk about the bad stuff?"

"Yes, we do. Because the lasting lessons in life are usually the hard ones, the ones that hurt most. They affect us more deeply than the good ones because you have to do something about what bothers you. You feel these lessons instead of just realizing them. Kim says that the hard stuff sticks like Velcro; the easy slides off like Teflon."

He thinks and brightens. "Like how our magazine article series started with a stressful school year?"

"Yes! Exactly! I once read that you shouldn't toss pain like a hot potato, eager to get rid of it. You should let it cool and hold it in your hand like a rock of realization," I explain, curling my fingers around an imaginary stone. "And you may be surprised. Maybe that rock becomes the foundation for something bigger. It did for us. More times than we can count."

Erik is silent, absorbing.

"In Finland, they have a word for this, for transforming challenges into opportunities. They call it *sisu*. They use sisu to mean mental toughness, not giving up in the face of challenge, big or small. Poppa used to call it 'stick-to-it-ness.' You know, perseverance, grit, tenacity. Just keep going."

"Hmmm," he says, his processing sound. And then, brightening, "Like the song?" He hums a familiar tune from a Christmas animation, "Put One Foot in Front of the Other."

"Yes! Like that!"

We walk, leisurely sloshing through the incoming tide, deep in thought. Growth, I decide, is multifaceted. Acknowledge everything. That can look messy and bleak because it's where the heavy emotion lies. But sometimes, it's where the light comes back in. Where you least expect it.

THERE ARE TWO QUESTIONS I hear as this college year winds down: "What will you possibly *do* with all of this *stuff?*" and "What will you do next?"

I am a magician, expected to pull out a wand and make our gear disappear. And in the next swish, cast a light on future plans. But no, I am not that. I don't have a magic formula. I do have a sense of what I feel is the right thing to do at the right time. But instinct can't offer direction until it feels a pull, and then it tells us what to do next.

We are forever gauging the length of the puppet strings; the longer the better. My aim is to become invisible, parked somewhere high up in the rafters of life where I can hang out and offer support, like a prompter in a play.

Frank puts it another way: "It's like a duck on the water. The duck appears to be floating calmly, but there is a tremendous amount of paddling under the surface to keep it afloat." That's us, the parent paddlers. With autism, nothing is incidental. It is all taught and re-taught, and the teacher is often the parents and the siblings. Growth is honest: it is earned.

As for Erik, he is always conducting internal scans, checking for exactly what we are scouting for: the capacity to be on his own without prompts from others—Dad, Gramma, Heather, Scott . . . workplace supervisors, driving instructors. How much can he do without repeated instructions? Without drop-down menus? Can he initiate action on his own and create a plan moving forward? Everything is a process, characterized by nuances and nudges and never-ending now whats?

Navigation by heart and instinct is like painting: a good paint job is done in thin layers. You let one layer dry completely before you apply the next. If not, the paint bubbles and peels. With Erik, we are learning how to prime and to paint when the time is right. Capacity-building is a layered process that unfolds both over time and without a timeline.

I think back to my Ottawa life. A fellow advocate, Tara, leans in at a parliamentary cocktail reception and tells me that she sees our journey as a safari through the jungle: me leading Erik through tall, thick bamboo-like stalks, sickle in hand, slashing a path. Erik is close behind, wary but trusting. We fear not what we might encounter because we know we must keep moving forward. Our conviction keeps us safe. Instinct is our compass. The visual is rich and it transports us far from the ornate banquet hall where colleagues enjoy stellar snacks heaped on glittery trays. We are deep in the musky jungle, imagining.

I thank Tara for this, for helping us to define our journey. I hold this visual close to me, inspired by it and also daunted by it. It is the autism parent portrait, and in that, it is a challenge—or perhaps an invitation—to keep swinging the blade, to keep moving forward.

As for Erik, my safari sidekick and willing waterskier, I am proud. He stumbles and retreats, but he always returns, batteries charged, ready for more. I default to what Erik reminds me: "You put one foot in front of the other."

CHAPTER 61

The Contest

WHEN I WAS LITTLE, I loved to enter contests. I was sure I would win. I waited to win, and when I did not, I assumed there had been a backup with Canada Post. The results would come. When they did not, I assumed there had been a further glitch and that I would hear, eventually. Because I had won. And when I did not hear, I would enter another contest because the former had been flawed.

I kept entering contests. I kept trying, but I never received the results I felt certain would come. Something deep inside of me— an absolute certainty, a greater affirmation—spoke and said, *Just keep going, Teresa. It will happen. Eventually. Somehow.* And so I believed. It was part of my fabric. To believe, steadfastly, earnestly is to be me. Ignorance is bliss. Perseverance is also bliss.

What kind of thinking is this? Optimistic? Some sort of blind denial? And what kind of person is that? Gullible? Trusting? Over-achieving? Foolish? Determined? Undaunted?

It is me. It is the skin, the persona, that grows around each autism parent. If it was not there to begin with, it develops. It grows and it gels without being summoned. It is parenthood forti-fied, on supplements. It forms, reinforces, protects and propels. It cocoons, comforts, cushions and connects us with our child.

I am grown up and my contests are different. They are about possibility and about leading Erik toward goals and toward adult-hood. I believe we will win this contest too, although we rarely get the results I imagine. We get different results. Outcomes delayed not by Canada Post, but by a complexity evasive and pervasive.

As for the wins, I have stopped waiting for dazzling triumphs. *Move out of your head and into the space in front of you.* That's what I tell myself. *Savour the tiny scratch-and-wins en route. Those may be all you get, all Erik gets, and it's going to have to be enough.*

MY MOTHER AND I HAVE the same habit. We skip to the end of novels and we read the last page. Of course we do. Why would we not? It's there for the knowing. I thought everyone did this until I started to ask. Turns out most don't. "You do *what*?!" I've stopped asking. But it surprises me that if you could know, you wouldn't peek. I do, and then I can relax, knowing.

The need to know is back. I want to know, to be reassured, that everything will be all right with Erik. I want to know the end of this autism story, how it will turn out. But I cannot know; this is life and you can't just flip to the end. Besides, not knowing keeps us on our game. We never become complacent.

There is no crystal ball, no guarantee. Even if you go at autism full force and from every conceivable angle, there are no assurances that you will get the result that you want. In fact, you probably won't; what you want is expectation. It's life in the mind.

What you will get is a mined and primed version of what you already had. If you had done nothing, growth would have been less. A spirited reaction to *pervasive* has delivered a potentiated and self-aware version of our little blond boy. But that's all I get to know right now, and I am going to have to be satisfied with that.

I see it this way, this life with autism: we live in an autism advent calendar. Each day we open a door and we learn something. Some days are hard. There is awe behind this door, torment behind that one. Some days we get to see something mundane in an entirely new way.

REFRAME IS OUR LIFE REFRAIN. Change up what you expect and you will appreciate what you receive. I don't miss the irony in this because it is exactly what Frank and I have always said to our three in the context of gratitude: "You get what you get and be glad to get it."

I ask Erik his feelings about the coming year, and he looks pensive and then impatient. "I just enjoy each day. Today is a gift; that's why it's called the present, you know?" And then he disappears.

Somewhere on the journey, Erik and I have become Buddha's hands. Who is teaching whom? We are inextricable, another set of entwined Christmas lights. Maybe it's exactly the way Buddha imagined life with autism would be: inseparable. In contemplating this fusion, there is ever more confusion. I am back to where I started fourteen years ago, with similar thoughts. *Can you separate Erik from autism?* Now, however, there is a glimmer of clarity.

I'M HAVING MY HAIR CUT; and peeking from under wet bangs, I chat with my hairdresser, Debbie. "I enjoyed that book you told me about . . . you know, *Gift from the Sea.* She nods. "Something Anne Morrow Lindbergh said about relationships, about how they evolve, reminded me of Erik and autism." Debbie is used to this by now, to me linking most things to autism. "Maybe Erik and autism are also intermittent, ebbing and flowing like the tide. Maybe it's like a dance; the halves move together, always present, but like high and low tides, sometimes one is in, sometimes the other is out. Maybe."

Sometimes Erik is wholly like us and so observably neurotypical. I am often told, "You'd never know," but on those occasions, Erik is very focussed and conscious of his projection. Observe him when no one is watching, and you will see a different Erik, one who paces and talks to himself, gesturing, eyes glassy, as though receiving a private delivery from beyond. Or perhaps the tour guide is present, reminding him of who he also is. He is both.

I had thought that one half—Erik or autism—arrives when the other is lost, that autism sweeps in in times of stress as Erik's default first responder, igniting the pacing and flapping and rocking. Erik surfaces when all is calm; autism is permitted to recede. Perhaps this is accurate, perhaps not. I often see both, paired, not consecutive but simultaneous. It depends on who's around. Like two halves of a relationship, Erik and autism evolve: each half grows out of its existing form and into new, updated versions.

MY FRIEND KAREN HAS ANOTHER question. "One more question to poke the bear. When you said there was slower progress than you wanted in the fall, and some regression in behaviours, could that be Erik relaxing into his true self? Why is it seen as a possible reaction to change and stress and not a truer representation of himself? Assuming he gets comfort from retreating."

I respond, "I often wonder the same thing. Which is the real Erik? The polished one we've helped to create or the rocking, whispering one I witnessed in November? Or both? The only thing that suggests to me that the polished version is preferred, to us both, is that he is cheerful, relaxed, creative and talkative. The reactive form is anxious and agitated, like he's closing in on himself, a silent withdrawal. He's pinched and inaccessible. It strikes me that one is a coping version . . . treading water. The other is an open, blossoming version."

I return to the egg analogy. Can we separate one from the other, like plucking the egg yolk from the white? Perhaps you can isolate the two halves, but then it would not be an egg anymore. It would be two parts, and each appears to have function, together.

I don't want to cleave my son. Besides, who would the dissection be for? Me and us because *different* is challenging? Or Erik because he will fit in better this way? Be happier? But that is also for us because it allows him a space in our context. I struggle with this. Maybe we need to adjust the environment and then he will be okay as he is.

Perhaps we need to teach both types of fine-tuning to the Eriks of the world: teach them how to sculpt environment *and* self to create the best fit. This is what we do with our children, autism or not: we teach them how to be the best versions of themselves, how to contribute and how to cope.

Perhaps, too, we need to prime the environment to receive an individual with autism. We need to be handing out catcher's mitts. It is one thing to recognize autism—the awareness piece—and to accept autism. It is something else to appreciate autism and to amend the reaction to "different." Appreciation offers worth.

CHAPTER 62

Still and Awe

WE MOVE FORWARD IN THIS transition to adulthood with more questions than answers. The questions I had at the outset continue to swirl.

I have four questions and one resolution, I tap onto my keyboard. I am writing to Karen but as much to myself.

Here is what I want to know. Still.
1. What does growth look like in Erik?
2. What will takeoff to adulthood look like?
3. What surprises me about this journey? What do I learn as I open the autism advent calendar?
4. What does winning/success look like to me? To Erik?
5. Continue is the power. Is this possible?

SOMETIMES WHAT I SEEK IS hidden in plain sight. The other night I heard it, and growth sounded like this, "I want to keep trying on new. I don't want to lead a plain life."

I observe Erik paddle-board across a choppy lake. I applaud, and he says, simply, "I want to challenge myself to try new things." This is a one-eighty from the skinny boy dressed in green silk who hid in his jungle bedroom and begged that I not sign him up for anything. Jungle Boy has emerged and is asking to try on new. Growth in Erik is an updated willingness to do more and to be more.

TAKEOFF TO ADULTHOOD IS NOT what I imagine, which is an elongated version of my own path: a formal education, a series of career-related jobs, relationships; perhaps a continued mix of education and experience. Mine is a typical trajectory. Erik's path has never been typical so why would it necessarily merge now? Everything has taken longer—repeated swimming levels; exams written and rewritten; grades duplicated; driver's tests repeated and repeated—so I expect this process will be more of the same. Why would it not be?

I was told early on that when it comes to autism, multiply by ten. Sensory sensations will be felt tenfold; social learning may take ten times longer to grasp; expect a ten-times timeline for integration and application; factor in lots of downtime, up to ten times a neurotypical debriefing. Why would transition to adulthood be any different? Erik's load is weighty; perhaps Erik's runway needs to be ten times the length to facilitate liftoff.

I expect that formal classroom education will not serve Erik well or at all. He is experiential. He needs to be shown in the moment. He needs concrete instruction. He becomes overwhelmed with too many words too quickly. Reading is also taxing because the words and their meanings fade and disperse.

"Words evaporate like they didn't even happen." Actions are visuals. Visuals adhere.

Erik may need to learn about life in life, not abstractly and not in anticipation of doing. The learning will be in the doing. He will need to try out job sites in order to really know what he wants because he can't imagine what he doesn't know and has never felt.

The transition to adulthood will not come abruptly with a job offer. It is not a takeoff. It is a taking off: gradual, imperceptible, deliberate, cautious and methodical. It is an "-ing" process. The runway is very long. The aircraft lifts and the wheels begin to retract when we are not watching, a slow and continuous tuck. The wheels take a very long time to stow for flight, if ever. But that's okay; the plane will fly. It will be a different sort of flight.

WHAT DO I LEARN AS I open the autism advent calendar?

I am surprised by how many people it takes to power Erik. Still. He is not an independent operator.

In 2017, for the Canada 150 celebrations, Ottawa hosted a set of mammoth mechanical street creatures from France named, aptly, La Machine. A massive spider, Kumo, and a fire-breathing dragon, Long Ma, traipsed throughout the streets of the capital, on occasion coming together to do battle. Each creature required a team of behind-the-scenes function engineers—raising arms, creating convincing eye rolls, swinging the torso—in order to make it appear lifelike.

As a family, we are a team of function engineers, setting Erik up for success, keeping him on track, supplying him with options, drop-down menus and choices because he seems unable to generate them himself. We are Erik's tour guides. This surprises me. I had hoped that the scaffolding could be removed. True, it is less, but Erik remains a collaborative effort. Will he become an independent operator?

I thought the lessons we've been hammering out for so many years would have been aced. There are still daily reminders. Remnants. Stragglers. Have you put on enough deodorant? Here are your lunch options. Will he go hungry in his own home? My mother asks me why I annotate what I am about to do. "Because we'd likely bump into each other if don't keep up the commentary. Erik has a hard time anticipating my moves." My words are like a convex mirror; without them, we collide.

The aliens remain. The *other* Erik appears when no one is watching. We spy it often. Erik paints a few boards at the cottage, he steps back, does a happy trot on the spot, paints, paces, all the while engaged in a joyous lightning conversation.

"It's like his emission system," I muse to Frank one morning at breakfast. "Like a factory smokestack. The excess product has to come out somewhere." Frank nods and thinks about it some more.

"Like a car exhaust. You can't have performance without some form of surplus and release."

We are both surprised that these alien attacks have persisted. Perhaps we ought not to be. You cannot eliminate a functional part of the system, extinguish the exhaust or replace it with something more palatable (to the onlooker). It doesn't work that way. As a family, we are learning this.

I continue to make phone calls on Erik's behalf. I encourage him to use his debit card and spend money. He is positive and friendly but without lasting friendships, happily solitary or content to hang out at home with family. I am still my son's part-time prompter: letting him know which lane to swim in; offering structure to his day; suggesting hobbies; setting up a social schedule for us both. I sometimes wonder whether we are trying to make changes to a document that is set to protected view. We are often unable to overwrite what is. It feels like something has reached the edit and save keys before us.

BUT THERE IS A FLIP side to still, and that is awe.

As I lay awake at night fourteen years ago, and as I tried to imagine what our lives would look like now, I never in my best-case-scenario mind imagined that I would look to my son in admiration and for inspiration. I never imagined he would be Buddha's upper hand, held up, facing out and offering me sage guidance. But he does. Daily.

Erik reminds me that I don't always have to go with the existing flow. I have choices beyond stereotypes. "You don't have to act according to stereotypes for different ages and stages." He reminds me what I used to remind him. "You don't have to." Erik shows me what authenticity looks like. He has no ego to stoke and maintain, no agenda, no pretense. He is the same at home and in public. This is refreshing.

I am struck by something I read about *self* in Glennon Doyle's *Love Warrior:* we each have two—an authentic self and a representative self. We send our representative out in the world to project what we would like people to believe about us. We are often quite different at home, doors closed. Home is where we park our authentic self. Maintaining two halves is draining. As we age, we are more authentic, more direct, less perfect and more true to ourselves. We park the ego at the door and retire the representative.

This revelation inspires a message to Sarah. I think maybe those with autism are already doing what this author aspires to do. Autism is pure authenticity. There is no representative.

Sarah responds, Yes! . . . It is not perfection and admiration that bring happiness, rather to be real and loved. I think "loved" means connected. So perhaps neurotypicals struggle with real and those with autism struggle with connection.

We both seek what the other has—already *is*.

ERIK'S COLLEGE WORKPLACE SUPERVISOR TELLS me a story of authenticity that made his day. Mine, too. When fabric and wood samples were out of place in the furniture store where Erik volunteered, he would rush to make everything right, often prefaced by a sharp intake of breath—the joy of discovery—and capped by a second rush of air: "Hoh!" the delight in restoring order.

It changed the way people saw disorder, the supervisor writes to me in an email. While most complained, Erik framed the chaos as opportunity, not drudgery. The harder Erik worked, the happier he became. He was our bright light. We figured, if Erik can elevate the mundane, then so, too, can we. Funny, we all tried, but we couldn't sustain the reframe. It's hard work to be Erik.

I read this to Erik and he beams. He is surprised. He has no idea of his effect and his potential to create change. I ask him more about the messy store samples and his reaction to the jumble. "Do you remember what you said to make your coworkers smile?"

He thinks a moment and then replies, "Yes, I think so . . . I said, 'This is *gold!*'"

That Erik and others like him live without so much—the ability to discern, to judge, to actively compete—allows them to live *with* so much. It is possible to exist without expectation of praise, reward or recognition. To do for the sake of doing, of cleaning, of serving, of putting things right. To do the right thing. Erik does, and that is altruism in its purest form. I discover folded piles of laundry, swept floors, unstacked and restacked dishes and tidied up spaces. I know the doer.

Erik cheers for everyone. He does not consider that triumph for one may diminish the success of another. I am left to wonder where the disability lies.

So much is projected onto the Eriks of the world. In coming to terms with autism, in puzzling and classifying, our words create projections: *this* is who you are. Autism is more gracious than that. *Erik doesn't project. He lets me be me.* It's the way you make people feel, we tell our children. Unlike many, Erik allows me to choose my own words. Around Erik, I feel good.

While the *stills* make me slump and wonder whether we will ever get there, the *awes* invite me to sit taller, to see the big picture and to understand what counts. For every slump there is a sliver of insight. There is clarity. Erik and other Eriks do that. They feed us perspective because they flip convention. They slow us down and offer mindfulness straight from the source. We are being offered platinum. In the words of the Honourable Mike Lake: "We just need to take time to notice."

In the thick of diagnosis, I never dreamed that I would try to be like Erik. *What would Erik do?* I ask myself. And then I often do that.

CHAPTER 63

Winning

WHAT IS MY IDEA OF success for Erik? I scroll back through my text messages and find the one Karen wrote to me about winning, success and what we are trying to achieve.

> K: You said you are the girl who wins, or likes to win, or thinks she has won. What is winning in your eyes for Erik?

> T: As for goals and outcomes and winning when it comes to Erik, I think bottom line, self-awareness is the ultimate goal. Because if you know how you present and how what you say and do affects others, then you can do something about it. Or not. It's always a choice, isn't it? And it's no different with autism. Some want to remain unique. Some want to blend in. So I think it's an individual and/or family choice as to how to move forward. Winning is personal.

Self-awareness is winning because it's illumination. It is what we have tried to do with Erik all along: feed Erik to Erik in small, digestible pieces until he was ready for the word, which capped the well of words. But there is more self to explore. There always will be.

Winning for me for Erik is to max out on *self*. It is for Erik to understand himself well enough to hone his talents; to discover what feeds his soul; to figure out how to match his inclinations to a career; to begin to imagine how he might live independently— or supported—and what will allow him to live functionally and happily (i.e., What are his accommodations for life?). Winning is giving legs to self-awareness. Winning is activating self.

Winning is to discern, to know when to pull on the bulletproof vest and allow only select, defining words to hit their mark; or as my sister Lori says, to know when to slam the fire door on the words that don't feel right. Wearing the vest is about allowing in the words Erik chooses. Winning is the ability to choose your own words and to define yourself outside of labels and predictions and projections.

Winning is having the confidence and the capacity to dream, plan and do. It is the ability to create a vision and to attempt to live it, or as the saying goes, "fake it till you make it." The ultimate win in my mind is for Erik to form rich, layered connections with others. He does connect, but rarely in a deep and lasting way. I want Erik to recognize that life is better connected.

What does *connected* mean? To connect is to open up, to become vulnerable in front of another and to share hopes, fleeting thoughts, ambitions, fears, big ideas, little details . . . all without judgment and all with appreciation and a listening ear. There is an in-sync joy in discovering overlap in things that puzzle, intrigue, frustrate, amuse, inspire, frighten, excite and perplex. You, too? What flows is a sharing and a blurring of feeling. This is what I want for Erik—for each of my three.

The ocean community moved Erik closer to connection. Like the tide, there was an ebb and flow of people. With each arrival and departure, there was an effect, a gift, like shells scattered across the sand, and there was learning and there was emotion. Erik noticed. As we pulled out of Kye Bay for the last time, Erik spoke up from the back seat: "This is a little hard for me. I feel emotional." In hearing his words, I was delivered a solid win.

There is one more win. A big one, and Erik is already there: to affect others positively.

It's the way you make people feel that attracts people to you. They will like you for how you enable them, not for your accomplishments. It is not about you; it is up to you. What is your effect? In the end, the win I envision for Erik is the win he already possesses: the gift of affect. "He was our bright light." He is ours, too.

"ERIK, WHAT DO YOU THINK? What is winning for you from your shoes?"

He sits cross-legged on a cot at the cottage, pauses to think while my fingers sit poised on the keyboard. After a moment, he lights up and speaks: "Achieving what I said I was going to achieve."

I am pleased; we have always stressed the importance of finish what you start and don't promise unless you're sure you can deliver. Erik has been listening.

"Like when I say I'm going to do a project, I do it, like 'The Walking Tour of Parliament,' the TEDx Talk, the Parliament speech. I don't change my mind. Also, driving lessons . . . I keep trying the roundabout even though it scares me. I don't back down." He thinks some more.

"It's also achieving goals like being more outgoing with people and connecting with them.

"Connecting means finding a common interest. I don't want to be someone standing at the side of the party." He pauses. A slow smile spreads across his face. "I prefer to be the yellow light." He is referring to the colour-coded traffic light communication system used during the breaks at the TEDx talk. "Green is too social; red is too antisocial; yellow means that I'm somewhere in the middle. I have boundaries and I need my space, but I want to talk."

My fingers rest as his gaze turns to the window, to the lake. He is formulating his next win as I process his first: "Achieving what I said I was going to achieve." I smile. Poppa would be pleased. Stick-to-it-ness was high on his win list. Mine, too.

"Winning is also trying on new." Again, he breaks into a grin. "Remember the scene from the movie *Mamma Mia! Here We Go Again?*" he says. "At the beginning right after graduation? The main character turns to her friends and says, 'Life is short . . . the world is wide . . . I wanna make some memories!'" He continues, beaming, "I want to keep exploring; keep meeting new people; keep doing things in a new way . . . like how we would play Frisbee at low tide by the light of a full moon . . . and like how we stargaze on the deck under a blanket here at the cottage. I like new. I want to keep creating new."

CHAPTER 64

Ocean Epiphanies

How do we keep moving forward with energy and faith, feeding the flame, stepping back and assessing growth, watching and waiting for a taking-off that is unfamiliar? How do we do that? How long do we keep it going, this regulated inflow of air to the bouncy castle . . . this growing Erik?

Erik surprises me each day. Willing but not always able. Modest but at times muddled. Friendly but without friendships. It is a dance: one step forward and several back. Helpful but needing help. Gauging Erik is like playing the stock market. Is this as high as he goes? Do we pull out now, decrease the flow to the bouncy castle, or wait a little longer? Invest more? How long do we hold on, lengthening the runway and building capacity before we make some sort of decision? Will time intervene? Will serendipity take charge? Will Erik? It's delicate. Like an actor prepped and ready to go on stage, or a test-taker ready to sit and write, when is ideal? Or is it like that?

"It's like he's always stretching but is not quite the right fit," I suggest to Frank. "He's always getting better but it's not quite enough . . . for college, for independent living." When will there be enough? Is "ready" different from what we imagine? Ready for what? I'm not certain of anything, but one thing is clear. We must keep trying. We must keep moving forward.

What is Erik telling us?

He is saying, "I don't want to lead a plain life. I want to try on new." This is good. We have always told him, "Never feel swayed by an invisible scriptwriter: parental expectations, stereotypes for age and stage, diagnostic criteria or projection." If we perceive ourselves as stuck and bound by invisible ties, we will be.

What is Erik showing us?

He is showing us that nature nurtures his being, that environment enables his development and that place and pace matter.

In investing a year beside the ocean, we have honoured Erik's love of water. I am astonished to discover the connection between water and human creativity explored in detail in a book called *Blue Mind*, recommended to me by an artist friend. The water-nurture construct is new but familiar because I live it. Humans are drawn to water, whether it is the ocean, lakes, rivers, ponds, water features, spas, fountains, swimming pools, aquariums, the bath or the shower. We are mesmerized by, need and crave water, and through it, the calming, healing and focussed feelings water evokes. Being near water diminishes anxiety, amplifies creativity and enhances our overall well-being.

The more I read about it, the more I understand. Eureka! Yes! This is why I felt the need to bring Erik to the west coast—so he could tap into the vast Pacific Ocean and have it pacify and inspire him as it has done for me. In returning to this remarkable ocean playground, we have honoured our blue minds. We are living a regulated life.

Heading outdoors feeds our senses the diet they were designed to absorb. According to *Blue Mind*, in bombarding ourselves with human-created stimuli, we are using "the wrong key to a lock installed by evolution." No wonder Erik gravitates to all things natural. It feels better. It is also what my intuition tells me. *Take him where he longs to be. Feed him water.*

It is beside the Pacific Ocean, wrapped in a colourful wool blanket and meditating, that we meet distinguished and modest Canadian author and photographic artist Sandra Semchuk. We chat for a while and speak of the healing and affirmative effect of the ocean, of autism and of Erik.

"I've seen your son out there, along the shore," she says to me. "The ocean tells him who he is, and he is vast."

I watch a Canada Council video on YouTube, "Portrait of Sandra Semchuk," and I am stunned at the last line, because it is a question that belongs to each parent of a child with autism: "How do we come to know, across species and as well, across cultures . . . how do we come to know someone else . . . *without projections?*"

"GOTTA GO!"

Scott grabs some nuts, carrots and milk and disappears downstairs. He has an office set up in the cool, dark basement, and it is the envy of us all during these sizzling Ottawa summers. Like Erik, Scott is experimenting, tapping into heart and inclination and exploring professional online poker.

"Expected value," he explains between mouthfuls of carrots. "It's all about EV. The more games I play, that's volume, V, times my profits . . . that's the return on investment, ROI . . . equals my expected value, EV. That's what I'm aiming for . . . doing well, more often."

I blink and he runs. I slowly comprehend. EV is why he is always dashing downstairs. I am reminded of hockey great Wayne Gretzky: If you don't shoot, you'll never score. And the more you score, the more you are apt to reach your EV . . . or something like that.

Expected value. It dawns on me that this is our battle plan moving forward with Erik: explore as many options as possible (volume) and have Erik learn as he goes (return on investment), and odds are something will stick, work, click. He may discover a niche and reach his expected value.

It is clear that Erik needs to attach learning to life experience; he needs to learn in a work setting, not removed from one. Learning must be concrete, not abstract. My thought, returning to the west coast, is to have Erik try varied work placements.

When I ask Erik how he sees things moving forward, he says to me, "I really liked volunteering at Berwick (seniors' home) and helping with the maintenance team. I like working outside. I felt a lot of satisfaction helping to keep the place neat and presentable. I find cleaning up and organizing very satisfying."

What lingers is *outside, satisfying* and *organizing.* Just as preschool Erik tidied toy bins, Big Erik finds pleasure in cleaning up, in creating order. He also loves to be outside. What were you doing before you were programmed to do and to be? This is what is referred to as our spark.

Perhaps Erik is telling us.

In sampling and trying on new, I am reminded of dress shopping. A store clerk once suggested that when trying on dresses, choose three: one you like, one you don't like and one somewhere in between. What pleases may surprise you; you may exit the change room with a different ranking. Perhaps in trying an assortment of work placements, Erik will be pleasantly surprised.

"Sometimes what you get turns out to be what you need," Erik commented in the context of co-op education. Perhaps expected value will kick in. As Scott reminds me, if you increase your volume, odds are, you'll eventually hit your mark.

What are the odds?

In stretching and growing Erik and in exploring multiple options, I am reminded of Malcolm Gladwell: "Whenever we find a late bloomer, we can't help but wonder how many others like him or her we have thwarted because we prematurely judged their talents." With Erik, I fear turning off the tap too soon. So we keep the flow going.

The words begin their download, more quickly now.

"Don't quit before the miracle." These are not my words, but they belong to me, to us. Retired professional hockey player Theo Fleury signs his book this way. It is the ultimate "What's not allowed?" We never give up.

I think of my friend Maryanne in New Zealand: "When you get a no, a better yes is coming."

And then it dawns on me. I cannot flip to the final page. There is no happy ending in this autism journey because there is no end. There is a continuous becoming. Erik, updated. When nothing is certain, anything is possible.

What is the power?

I return to the words spoken on a rainy evening in Japan, 1988. In sharing "Continue is the power" with a psychologist from Erik's college, I am delivered a slightly different, elevated version.

I visit Dr. Wendy Harris a month after sharing the Japanese calligraphy with her. She greets me with a relaxed smile. Her grin heightens as she swings her computer monitor around so that I can see the screen. She points to a yellow sticky note in the bottom right corner: Continue is your power, it says.

"This," she indicates, touching the yellow note, "has changed the way I've approached counselling. It has changed everything for me." She pauses to look out the window, gathering her thoughts. "Students love it; they feel like they've discovered a gift inside themselves. Treasure they didn't know existed."

Like finding money in an old wallet.

Where is the power?

I ask Wendy about the new wording—from Continue is the power to "your" power. Her forehead creases. "I thought that's what you said. I guess that was my interpretation of your message: the ability to continue is something you possess, not something you harness. It's already in your grasp."

For thirty years, I had thought of the phrase as an external tool one could borrow and apply. Not as something each of us already has, something to tap, like extracting sap from a sugar maple. "I like your version better," I say to Wendy.

We can make that.

And in that moment, I am seven, back in Grade 2. I am gazing into the little round mirror in front of my classmates; and now, for the first time, I understand the secret. I see my power. Erik's, too.

To continue is your power.

AFTERWORD
An Autism Pyramid

THE HEDLEYS HAVE BEEN ON an extraordinary adventure—one that has been far more extra than ordinary. I feel grateful for the opportunity to read what is essentially their family's personal travel diary.

If I had read this book before I began working as a psychologist in the autism field, I might have made fewer mistakes. I would have spent more time listening and learning about the unique qualities of each child, because until we really know what makes a person tick and what makes a person stop ticking, how can we come up with a plan? I also would have shamelessly "borrowed" Teresa's practical yet wonderfully playful ideas and passed them along to other families and professionals. I intend to now.

Needless to say, it's hard to match Teresa's skills in teaching, creative writing and metaphor. However, as I read *What's Not Allowed?*, I came up with an analogy that describes how the Hedley family helped maximize Erik's success and shone the spotlight on his talents, skills and abilities.

I found myself visualizing Erik at the top of a human pyramid, the kind that cheerleading teams make on the football field during the halftime show. For these pyramids to work, you need a strong base of support with the bigger and sturdier people on the bottom row, providing a solid foundation. You also need teamwork, coordination and balance. If you do it right, the star cheerleader ends up on top, arms outstretched with a smile as wide as the base of the pyramid.

Isn't this what we need in autism? A strong support base, integrated and coordinated teams, and a balanced approach to services that doesn't leave families feeling exhausted or marginalized. Parents and siblings are typically the rock-solid, sometimes even immovable, ones on the bottom row—constant and unwavering in their determination. But who are the other cheerleaders?

While autism awareness has grown, there is still a need for meaningful inclusion in communities, classrooms and workplaces. The environments in which autistic people live, learn and work determine whether they will thrive or struggle to simply survive —an autism oasis or an autism desert. An autism oasis has allies, those that enable success and cheer loudly from the sidelines. For parents of children with autism, cheerleading is often called advocacy, and as Teresa can attest, sometimes this is welcomed, sometimes not.

I invite you to think about how you can become an autism cheerleader. Come down from the stands, join someone's pyramid, raise a person with autism to the top and let their light shine.

– *Dr. Katelyn Lowe, registered psychologist, Calgary, AB*

ABOUT THE AUTHOR

Teresa Hedley is a mother of three young adults, one of whom, Erik, has autism. She is also an educator, a curriculum designer and an author. As a teacher-trainer, Teresa taught English in Canada, Japan, Greece, Spain and Germany. Later, as an armed forces family, the Hedleys lived coast to coast in Canada. Aiming to build resilience in families living with autism, Teresa and Erik co-wrote a twenty-article series for *Autism Matters* magazine, "I Have Autism and I Need Your Help." Additionally, Teresa worked directly with families and school boards in Ottawa as an autism consultant and advocate. In collaboration with the Family Education Centre, she co-designed an interactive online parenting program, Pathways to Potential: Parenting Children and Youth with Autism. *What's Not Allowed? A Family Journey with Autism* will be followed by the *What's Not Allowed? Companion Toolkit* filled with practical strategies, insight and inspiration for the autism journey. Teresa and her family live and play on Vancouver Island.

ACKNOWLEDGMENTS

IT TAKES A COMMUNITY TO grow a family. It also takes a community to write a book. Together, we become Buddha's hands: a learning circle.

Imagine, now, a banquet hall. We are gathered to thank and to toast a few who represent a great many. Picture a goblet. Imagine your favourite beverage. Let's begin.

To . . .

Kim Barthel—for encouraging our conscious evolution. We are your disciples.

Kathleen Rooney—for inspiring me to write.

Pat O'Connor—for introducing me to publisher Heather Down.

Heather Down—for saying "yes" and for patiently guiding me.

Colonel Telah Morrison—for seeing the value in our messages.

Dr. Katelyn Lowe—for capping our journey with insight and originality.

Sarah Holliday—for her uplifting and illuminating brand of Sarah sunshine.

Karen Kloske—for poking the bear and for asking the hard questions.

Leah Pan—for sending Erik a steady stream of "What's not allowed?" photos.

Tracey Shaver—for teaching me "When we know better, we do better."

Mrs. Power and Mrs. Reis—for being mischievous and positive . . . and for making school fun!

Miss Waters (Noble)—for being one of Erik's early believers.

Frank—for being the brake pedal to my gas pedal.

Scott and Heather—for showing Erik that life is better from me to we.

Audrey—for her big three: You don't ask, you don't get. We can make that. Where there's a will, there's a way. Mother really does know best!

Tom—for his appreciation of words, his belief and his quirky sense of humour. If you can't come to your ol' faaatha, who can you come to?

Lori—for teaching me to think deeply and differently.

Leslie—for leading the creative and colourful way.

Emmeline and Harold—for sharing their guiding lights: It's not what happens to you, it's what you do about it that matters most. You never know what's good and what's bad.

Aunt Adrienne and Aunt Harriet—for personifying positive reframe.

Great Aunt Mima and Great Aunt Kaye—for teaching us that attitude —and a good laugh!—trumps all.

Friends and family members—for continuing to see Erik beyond a label.

Claude-Paul Boivin—for his passionate three: What? So what? Now what?

Brenda Joy—for buying the first book online. What joy!

Denyse and Scott Becker—for cheerleading in the wings . . . and for buying the second book!

Esther Rhee Carnat—for being Erik's Cinderella.

Marjorie Favretto—for setting Erik to poetry.

Maureen Bennie—for filling me with knowledge via her Autism Awareness Centre.

Nanci Burns—for encouraging me to keep the plates spinning.

Dr. Jonathan Weiss—for the reminder "We all deserve to thrive."

Dr. Jonathan Lai—for embracing neurodiversity.

Dr. Yolanda Korneluk—for making Erik glow.

Hon. Mike Lake—for inviting us to notice the treasure in autism.

Peter Mansbridge—for asking, "What do *you* think?"

Hon. Marc Garneau—for finding time for autism in the pandemic swirl.

Elisabeth Ruel—for graciously facilitating communication with the Hon. Marc Garneau.

Dawn Hunter and Patricia MacDonald—for their keen copy editor eyes.

Our endorsers—for strengthening the messages in this book.

Erik and all of the Eriks of the world—for showing us that it is possible to live humbly, graciously and authentically.

Thank you, all.

–Teresa and the Hedley family

CONNECT

Facebook: @WintertilePress

Instagram: @WintertilePress

Twitter: @Wintertickle

If you enjoyed this book, you may also enjoy other titles by Wintertickle Press including:

Not Cancelled: Canadian Kindness in the Face of COVID-19 by Heather Down & Catherine Kenwell

Stories: Finding Your Wings by Heidi Allen

A Medic's Mind by Matthew Heneghan

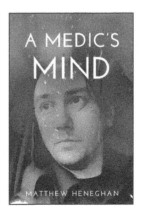